FRANCE 1914–18

France 1914–18

Public Opinion and the War Effort

P. J. FLOOD, BA, PhD

Head of History
Truro School

MACMILLAN

First published 1990

Published by
THE MACMILLAN PRESS LTD
Houndmills, Basingstoke, Hampshire RG21 2XS
and London
Companies and representatives
throughout the world

Typeset by Footnote Graphics,
Warminster, Wilts

Printed in the People's Republic of China

British Library Cataloguing in Publication Data
Flood, P. J.
France 1914–18: public opinion and the war effort.
1. France. Social conditions, 1914–1918
I. Title
944.081'4
ISBN 0-333-49640-X

For Edward and Anna

Contents

List of Tables and Figures in the Appendix

List of Abbreviations

The following abbreviations have been used in the Notes and Appendix:

AD   *Archives Départementales de l'Isère*, Grenoble

AN   *Archives Nationales*, Paris

SHA   *Service Historique de l'Armée*, Vincennes, Paris

Perrin Correspondence   Letters to and from the front, 1914–18, of Henri and Louise Perrin, Vienne, Isère

Oral testimony   Refers to interviews with various male and female veterans of the 1914–18 war, residents of the Isère

Acknowledgements

My thanks to Dr Roger Price of the University of East Anglia, who supervised the research for this study in its original form as a doctoral dissertation, and to Professor Douglas Johnson of the University of London and Dr Robert Short of the University of East Anglia, who both offered constructive criticism and advice when the dissertation was examined. The staff of the *Archives Départementales de l'Isère* at Grenoble were always accommodating and helpful during my researches and M. Michel Perrin of Vienne in the Isère was most generous in allowing me to see the private correspondence of his grandparents.

On a more personal note I would like to thank my mother for her assistance in enabling me to submit this study for a doctorate, and finally of course I wish to thank my wife, who not only assisted me in my research, but showed great patience and forbearance while I was writing this book during long summer holidays.

Preface

The First World War has a very special place in the history of the
Third French Republic. In France today there are still those for
whom 'La Guerre' was not the 1939–45 war but that of 'Quatorze–dix-
huit'. Historians have contrasted vividly the mood of 1914 with that
of 1939. The war itself is seen as the Third Republic's 'finest hour'.
All the bitter social and political divisions which had plagued the
early Third Republic were shelved in August 1914 as the nation
experienced an extraordinary *ralliement* in the face of the enemy.
With part of their country invaded and occupied for four years, the
French population underwent sacrifices and hardships and their
morale began to weaken in the 'crisis' year of 1917. Nonetheless
the people of France, military and civilian, did hold out. The Third
Republic survived unscathed, but the memory of the war experience and the great sacrifices made for *La Patrie* lived on, enshrined
in the *monuments de guerre* even in the smallest village *communes*.

It was to understand why the French people 'held out' that the
research for this study was undertaken. To do this it was necessary
to determine the nature and extent of the hardships and sacrifices
made by the civilian population for the war effort. It was assumed
that in order to bring to life the war experiences of the French
people the necessary detailed and close examination of communities and individual case histories could best be achieved through a
local study.

The ideal administrative framework for a local study in French
history is the *département*. For the researcher, the *préfecture* in the
chef-lieu is the focal point for administration and the *départemental*
archives house police, legal, educational, economic and military
records as well as all forms of correspondence with the *préfet*'s
office. The *département* chosen for this study was the Isère in South-
East France. Three main considerations governed this choice.

First, the *départemental* archives possess particularly good
sources for researchers into the First World War. The Isère is
among the few *départements* which have preserved *instituteurs*'
reports of attitudes in and organisation of local village *communes*
throughout the war, an invaluable source for the study of local
opinion. The archives also possess abundant, although uncategor-
ised, correspondence from *maires*, *adjoints* and individual local

farmers and townspeople to the *préfet*'s office. There are also the *Archives des Bénéfices de Guerre*, providing a wealth of information on the fate of small and medium-sized business enterprises during the war.

Second, the geography of the Isère is such that a variety of local areas can be studied. For example, the mountain ranges of the Oisans and Vercors, with remote populations living at high altitude and having little contact with the outside world, can be contrasted with the small textile towns like Voiron and Vienne and with the *Chef-lieu*, Grenoble, a thriving and growing industrial centre. Thus socially and culturally backward areas were juxtaposed with fast-developing industrial centres and market towns to provide a good example of French provincial life.

Finally, the political divisions and variations within the Isère during the Third Republic make the *département* a particularly interesting one to study in the context of the 1914–18 war. Clericalist and reactionary *communes* existed side by side with Socialist ones. Vienne, the second largest town, had a strong tradition of revolutionary and anti-militarist activity stretching back into the early nineteenth century.

The main reservation about local studies of course is that they tend not to be representative and hence the conclusions that can be drawn from them are necessarily limited. This is a particular problem in a country as diverse culturally, geographically, politically and economically as France. However, to a large extent the topic under study here, the First World War, removes this problem. The war was just as much a fact of life for the peasants of Brittany as it was for the prostitutes of Marseille or the dockyard workers of Bordeaux. Obviously one's reactions and attitudes to the war might vary according to whether one lived in a town or a village. However, in a society in which all able-bodied military-aged males, with few exceptions, were mobilised irrespective of class or region, it was personal circumstances which governed one's war experience rather than whether one lived in the Pyrenees, the Alps or in Paris. In this sense the only meaningful difference of region was that between communities in the war zone in the occupied North-East and those outside the war zone. With this in mind, the conclusions that will emerge from this study will be fairly wide-ranging, although account must always be taken of various local peculiarities and nuances.

PJF

Introduction: The *Département* of the Isère in 1914

The Isère is situated in the South-East of France in the region of the Dauphiné. It is the eighth largest *département*, with a surface area of more than 823 hectares. It is flanked on one side by the Alps and to the North-West by the Lyon–St Etienne conurbation. In the North-East lies Savoie and in the South is the Vercors mountain range. Nearly half the *département* is situated at an altitude of over 1000 metres, with peaks reaching 4100 metres at La Barre des Ecrins and 3983 metres at La Meije. The topographical division of the *département*, mountain ranges to the East and plains to the West, is matched by the respective spheres of influence of the Grenoble and Lyon regions.

For administrative purposes the *département* in the early Third Republic was divided into 564 *communes* grouped in forty-five *cantons* under four *arrondissements*: St Marcellin, La Tour du Pin, Vienne and Grenoble. The first three were each under the jurisdiction of a *sous-préfet* who in turn was subordinate to the *préfet* at Grenoble. The *arrondissement* of Grenoble had the largest number of *communes*, 213, including the mountain *cantons* of Bourg d'Oisans and Corps.

According to the census of 1911 the population of the Isère was 555 911, an increase of some 17 000 over the 1906 figure. Nearly half of this population lived in small towns or large villages by 1911. There were only four towns with a population of more than 5000: the three textile towns of Voiron, Vienne and Bourgoin, and Grenoble, whose population had more than doubled from 31 340 in 1851 to 77 438 in 1911. There were 46 769 males and 31 918 females classed as industrial workers.[1] The major industries on the eve of the war were: chemical, distilling, shoe making, food processing, glove making, electrical, mining, paper making, metallurgical, tourism and textiles. By far the biggest industrial employer was the textile industry. Silk weaving was predominant in Vienne and Voiron (where 25 per cent of the total population worked in silk-weaving establishments of some kind). The region's chief export was gloves and by 1911, in Grenoble, glove making remained the biggest employer.

In the years before 1914 Grenoble had also seen the development of metallurgical industries. The engineering firm of Bouchayer et Viallet, for example, employed 850 workers in its Grenoble factory on the eve of the First World War. The majority of metallurgical enterprises, however, remained small family concerns employing between fifteen and thirty workers. Another developing industry was paper making. There were two main paper-making regions: the Bas Dauphiné and the foothills of the Chaîne de Belledonne. To the south of Grenoble, around La Mure, were anthracite and coal mines which by 1912 already employed some 2000 face workers.

The Isère was well served by the great *routes nationales*, for example the *'Rue d'Italie'* from Lyon to Chambéry, the RN 85 from Grenoble to Gap, the RN 7 from Lyon to Vienne and the RN 90 from Grenoble to Chambéry. By the eve of the war there were railway lines from Lyon through Voiron to Grenoble, from Grenoble to Chambéry, Grenoble to Serres and Grenoble to La Mure. In 1895 railways had begun to reach the mountain regions of the Oisans with the opening of the Jarrie–Vizille–Bourg d'Oisans line.[2]

Less than one-fifth of the total population of the Isère were classed as agricultural proprietors and some 6 per cent as agricultural wage earners, so around a quarter of the population worked directly on the land. The Isère was largely an area of small freeholders, and the average size of holding in 1892 was four hectares, the smaller holdings being concentrated in the alpine regions.[3] In the 'dead' season of the winter much of this agricultural labour worked on a temporary basis in local textile or paper-making factories. In the Grenoble region particularly, farmers' wives supplemented their income by glove making.

The people of the mountains were used to a hard life in adverse climatic conditions and the women of the Oisans were accustomed to coping for long periods in the absence of their menfolk, for this was the region *par excellence* of *colportage*.[4] Paradoxically, a strong sense of individualism co-existed with co-operation and *entr'aide* in times of need. Indeed Grenoble itself is said to be the birthplace of mutual aid societies. In 1850 a *phalanstère* was established at Vienne and a *restaurant populaire* in Grenoble, followed by the development of consumer co-operatives in both towns. By 1900 there were 472 mutual aid societies in the Isère with a total of 41 738 members.[5] Perhaps the most succinct impression of the characteristics of the *Dauphinois* was given by the *Préfet* of the Isère in 1882: 'although superficially calm and lacking in emotion, the *Dauphinois* can be moved to passionate and even violent extremes and they lack deference to authority for authority's sake; indeed they are at times inclined to be a little *frondeur*'.[6]

Certainly the inhabitants of the Isère did not lack interest in politics, both local and national. In the legislative elections of April and May 1914 there was an average 75 per cent turnout of the electorate for the eight electoral *circonscriptions* of the *département*. In the municipal elections of 1912 the average turnout for the 564 *communes* was 71 per cent but in some *communes*, particularly in the mountain areas, there were figures of over 85 per cent.[7]

Obviously, in municipal elections, local issues and the reputation and standing of the various candidates tended to predominate, but even here echoes of the great political controversy of the early Third Republic, the Church–State issue, could be found. Although the separation of Church and State was generally accepted as being inevitable, a large body of Catholic opinion continued to object passionately to the principle of separation. Traditions died hard and relations between the forces of the clergy and laity were particularly strained in some local areas. Anti-clerical activity of course was very much a tradition of the Radicals, provoking what was often a rearguard action by the local clergy, and hostilities between the local *curé* and the *instituteur public* were often conducted through the respective media of church sermons and school lessons.

The results of the elections of 1912 suggest that nearly 90 per cent of *communes* elected municipal councils that were solidly Republican in character. Only sixty-nine of the 564 *communes* returned reactionary, pro-clerical or anti-Republican councils. The three broad groupings of the Centre and Left of Centre (Radicals, Radical Socialists and Left Republicans) gained 69 per cent of the municipalities between them. There were eight Unified Socialist councils elected, six of them in the *Arrondissement* of Grenoble.[8]

This tendency towards the Left of Centre was confirmed in the legislative elections of spring 1914. Five of the eight deputies of the Isère were Socialists and the other three were Radicals. In fact in the three legislative elections of 1906, 1910 and 1914 the extreme Left had been steadily gaining ground, their share of the total vote rising from 7 per cent to 20.5 per cent. This advance was largely at the expense of the moderate Left and Left of Centre parties, for the percentage of votes for the 'established order' remained constant at around 20 per cent.[9]

A major issue of the elections of 1914 was the question of the extension of military conscription to three years and whether the law passed in favour of this in 1913 should be retained. In the spring of 1913 Radicals and Socialists in the Isère had joined to combat the law and the *Conseil Général* had voted by a large majority against it.[10] In the legislative elections of the following year all of the candidates in the Isère felt sufficiently strongly about this issue to accord it pride of place in their manifestoes.

If the voting figures are anything to go by, there seems not to have been a corresponding interest in this question amongst the electorate. Sentiments of *revanchisme* and the desire to avenge the defeat of 1870 had died down since the 1890s and ceased to be an electoral issue until 1913–14. Certainly the newspapers of the Centre and particularly the Right tried to maintain a *revanchiste* tone and a number of rifle and gymnastic societies were formed locally during the 1880s to prepare young men for future conflict with Germany. However these did not attract a great deal of support. The Isère had not been a theatre of war in 1870 and had not been invaded by the Prussians. The number of surviving *Dauphinois* veterans of the Franco–Prussian War was obviously declining, and memories of 'Prussian atrocities' during that war were fading.

It was not really until the international horizon darkened after 1911 and the possibility of a war with Germany increased that the question of a war of revenge was raised again by journalists, academics and writers. It is hard to escape the conclusion that the majority of *Dauphinois* remained largely unconcerned, and the election results of 1914 suggest that most of the inhabitants of the Isère either did not believe that a war with Germany was likely or did not feel the desire for revenge sufficiently strongly to vote in favour of strengthening the defences of the country.

1
Into the Unknown

Local press reportage of events in July 1914 makes interesting, if rather poignant, reading. There is a certain irony in the fact that heightening diplomatic tension had to compete for headline coverage with the major news story in France that summer: the trial of Madame Caillaux. The assassination of Archduke Francis Ferdinand, briefly reported at the end of June, was soon forgotten in the orgy of journalistic invective that accompanied the trial. Indeed, if one adopts a journalist's eye view, there was little to disturb the sense of complacency that pervaded the press during that month. If the Sarajevo crisis seemed but one more of a long line of international 'incidents' of recent years, so too did the murder trial of the wife of a recent prime minister of France, a veritable *crime passionnel*, appear as the latest manifestation of the type of political scandal that characterised the Third Republic. There was, as it were, an all-pervading sense of *déjà vu*.

It was not until the last week of July, when, with the mobilisation of Russia, Austria and Serbia, it became apparent that the crisis might not remain localised, that a note of uncertainty crept into the headlines. From 28 July events moved so rapidly that journalists had some difficulty in keeping up with them, the result being that their reports and comments were confused, hastily written and often contradictory.

It cannot be said that the local press adopted a bellicose tone on the eve of the war. Without exception, whatever their political bias, newspapers faced with the difficult task of reporting developments, forewarning the public and appealing for calm placed much emphasis on the reasons for hope of a peaceful solution to the crisis. As the editor of the biggest selling daily paper wrote: 'if it is necessary to be prepared for all eventualities, it is also very premature to fear a European war'.[1]

The reactionary clerical press was the most realistic about the possible outcome. On 28 July *La Croix de l'Isère* noted that the international situation had never been so serious and that 'one must take seriously the possibility of conflagration in Europe'.[2]

Two days later there was more gloom and more uncertainty: 'where are we heading? Nobody really knows. Things are happening so quickly ... it seems that the situation worsens.'[3] Three successive editions of *Le Petit Dauphinois* best illustrate the helplessness, uncertainty, confusion and grasping at straws that were the inevitable consequences of working in the dark. On 30 July it noted that: 'The general opinion is that the situation will improve. Germany will back down. The fact that France is not even proceeding to partial mobilisation indicates that our government has trust in a rapid and peaceful solution.' The next day there was a note of caution: 'Will France mobilise? We have to admit that the situation is serious. We must be prepared.' By 1 August a new note had appeared which was to have considerable significance in the following days: 'The Fatherland is in danger. France is threatened, but let us keep calm. Mobilisation does not mean war. Our alliances are defensive ... the war can be one of the most terrible ever. The population has unanimously accepted the necessity of armed conflict and each is ready to do his duty.'[4]

If editors and journalists were confused and contradictory in their reportage of events at the end of July (and these people were in the best position to know) how well informed, how well prepared were their readers for the possibility of war? Grenoble, as a *chef-lieu*, was well served with six daily newspapers including one evening edition. By comparison Toulouse, with a population twice that of Grenoble, had four. Alençon, the *Chef-lieu* of the Norman *Département* of the Orne, had only two bi-weekly editions. *Le Petit Dauphinois* had by far the largest readership in the Isère. On the eve of the war it had an estimated sales figure of 35 000 copies, followed by *La Dépêche Dauphinoise* and *La République de l'Isère* with 15 000 copies each. The largely urban readership of the Socialist *Le Droit du Peuple* numbered some 12 000 while the clerical *La Croix de l'Isère* had 7500 daily readers and 20 000 for its weekly edition.[5] In addition there were the big Lyon dailies, although these had more influence and wider readership in Vienne than in Grenoble. The extent to which newspapers were read outside the big urban centres can only be surmised and it is difficult to assess the number of readers there were per newspaper sold.

It was in the purely agricultural *communes* and the tiny remote villages and scattered homesteads of the Southern Alps that newspapers were most rarely found. Even if one could procure a copy it would most likely be two or three days old. Many isolated hamlets did not receive newspapers at all. 'On the isolated farms and in the remote settlements', remarked an *instituteur*, 'people live like hermits, completely ignorant of events in the outside world.'[6] To the east of the *département*, high up in the mountain regions of the Oisans, it was customary for farmers to take a hut or chalet for the summer months in order to make cheese and pasture their cattle. Here, close to the permanent snowline, one lived 'on the edge of the world, ignorant of all news, untroubled by rumour and hearsay'.[7]

In order to keep pace with the sheer speed of events in the last days of July 1914 it was necessary to read the newspapers daily and to have enough leisure to inform oneself about international politics and the rapidly changing diplomatic situation. However July and August coincided with the busy season on the farms, and in the valleys and plains of the Isère energies were devoted to gathering the harvest. Helped by superb weather in the summer of 1914, every able-bodied villager worked in the fields from morning to night, returning home only to eat supper and to sleep. There was no time for the café or to read the newspapers properly, and little opportunity (or indeed inclination) to talk politics.

THE MOBILISATION

At four-thirty in the afternoon of Saturday 1 August two police cars from St Marcellin arrived in the church square of the village of Vatilieu carrying the order of general mobilisation. Immediately the bell-ringer was sent for to sound the *tocsin*. The village *instituteur* described the effect that this had on the workers in the fields:

> It seemed that suddenly the old feudal *tocsin* had returned to haunt us. Nobody spoke for a long while. Some were out of breath, others dumb with shock. Many still carried their pitch-forks in their hands. 'What can it mean? What's going to happen to us?' asked the women. Wives, children, husbands – all were overcome by anguish and emotion. The wives clung to the arms of their husbands. The children, seeing their mothers weeping, started to cry too. All around us was alarm and consternation. What a disturbing scene.[8]

Supper was taken somewhat earlier than usual and in the evening, while women and children prepared the effects of those who were

soon to depart, many of the men went to the main café to discuss
the implications of the mobilisation. The harvest had only just
begun and there was much concern about how it should be
completed. Quantities of wine were drunk that evening, thus
spirits were raised a little: 'if we must go, we will go'. There was
some talk, especially amongst the older men, of the evil designs of
the Kaiser: 'yes, we will fight alright, against this aggressor who
wants to destroy the wealth and beauty of our countryside'. Within
a few hours, 'alarm' and 'consternation' had given way to 'stead-
fastness' and 'resolution'.

The inhabitants of the tiny village of Malleval in the Vercors, on
hearing the sound of the *tocsin*, immediately feared fire, the traditional enemy of peasant households. The sight of the mobilisation
order outside the *mairie* caused 'a kind of bewilderment amongst
us all, everyone thrown into confusion by this terrible news so unexpected'. After the initial feelings of shock and astonishment some,
'although overcome by the news, instinctively returned to their
work', but the majority left their tools and implements at the *mairie*
and hastened home in search of their *livret militaire*. In the evening
when small groups gathered in the street discussing the mobilisation
there were no noisy demonstrations, neither enthusiasm nor re-
crimination, 'rather a kind of stupor, a profound astonishment'.[9]

Not all of the rural population of the Isère had been in such
blissful ignorance of the unfolding international drama. The
Austro–Serb conflict and French and British diplomatic manoeuvres were known and commented on in the residences of
tourists, in villages situated along railway lines and near small
industrial towns. During that fateful last week in July there were
several indications that something untoward was happening.
Soldiers on leave were ordered to rejoin their corps, and battalions
on manoeuvres suddenly quit their camps and returned to Grenoble.

These comings and goings combined with fragments of imper-
fectly assimilated news of the worsening crisis to produce a feeling
of uneasiness. By 30 July there was a growing conviction that '*ça va
mal*'. One could, however, take refuge in an ostrich-like optimism,
and there was indeed some reason for hope. There had been no
major war in Europe for forty-four years. If war was declared it
would be fought a long way away, perhaps in Serbia. 'The
governments will arrange all that, that's their affair ... France is
not threatened.'[10] At Cognin, on the river Isère, the villagers were
sure that there would be no general war because no nation would

take responsibility for such butchery.[11] Many just wanted to get on with their work and not be troubled by crises and politics, believing that newspapers exaggerated the crisis to increase their sales: 'all this talk of war, it's just newspaper sensationalism. Let me work. I have no time to bother my head with politics while I am so busy cutting the hay and gathering the lavender.'[12]

Even on the morning of 1 August only a simple alert was suspected, a partial attempt at mobilisation just to prove that France was ready. When the *facteur* of St Cassien returned from the nearby town of Voiron with the news that general mobilisation was about to be declared, the villagers saw little reason to be diverted from their daily routines: 'this talk of serious developments has not bothered this peaceful rural population, and the groups of workers proceeded as usual to the harvest or to the vine'.[13] By late afternoon, however, all the villages in the *département* were in receipt, by telegraph or telephone, of the despatch from the Minister of War: 'Order of General Mobilisation: the first day of mobilisation is Sunday 2 August 1914.'

The scenes described at Vatilieu and Malleval were common everywhere. Suddenly the Place de la Mairie was full of farmers: 'On all the faces one can see signs of anxiety. Each questions his neighbour about the day of his departure. All are taken aback by this terrible shock.'[14] Perhaps the *maire* might give a little speech explaining the international crisis and the need for France to mobilise.[15] A more general reaction was that 'mobilisation does not mean a declaration of war, things will work out for the best'.[16] The *instituteurs'* notes, however, leave little room for doubt that by the evening most villagers were aware that war was about to begin: 'the men are pale-faced and worried, the women are weeping',[17] 'everyone understands the seriousness of the situation',[18] 'the women, already in control of themselves, reassure the men'.[19]

Naturally the mobilisation order was less of a shock and surprise in the towns, where café conversations, rumours circulating around factories and wider readership of newspapers had helped to prepare people for the worst. Indeed newspaper reports present a picture of a population avid for news as newsagents at Grenoble, Vienne, Voiron, Vizille, Beaurepaire and Rives sold out within minutes on 31 July and 1 August.[20] At Rives, for example:

Posters announcing the first day of mobilisation were put up in the various *quartiers* and soon attracted groups of readers, but

there were no recriminations. There was a general feeling of
calm and resolution, a great sentiment of patriotism. Among the
various remarks the expression most commonly heard was
'German provocation has lasted too long. We must put an end to
it. We will face them squarely.'[21]

At Tullins, the initial reaction was one of 'anguish'. There were
tears in the eyes of both men and women, but according to the
instituteur this did not last long:

> Mobilisation does not mean war, and our government is doing
> all it can to preserve peace. We are no longer in doubt that
> Germany wants war and that she is taking advantage of the
> situation to invade us and impose her will on the European
> population. If it does turn out to be war we will be equal to the
> task and all Frenchmen without exception will rise to defend the
> country, sustained in the knowledge that we are fighting for
> liberty.[22]

This sense of resolution was not shared by the citizens of La Tour
du Pin who were 'very frightened ... everybody believes the
worst, but we still hope for a peaceful solution'.[23] At Beaurepaire
nearly everybody regarded war as a certainty. Here all work
stopped in the small factories and workshops. 'A solemn crowd
filled the streets. There was no panic. People were discussing the
serious situation quite calmly. The women were as brave as the
men, furtively wiping tears from their eyes. It was like a funeral.
Our small town appeared to be in mourning.'[24]
It was the larger industrial centres and garrison towns, Grenoble
and Vienne, which came closest to experiencing the bellicose
demonstrations and scenes of 'patriotic enthusiasm' commonly
associated with traditional pictures of Frenchmen going off to the
war. Here, significantly, there was a sense of 'relief' rather than
shock on the news of the mobilisation. At the end of July there had
been a 'crisis atmosphere' in streets, shops and cafés. Newspapers
had been read and handed around and their headlines discussed
anxiously. The significance of large-scale troop movements into
barracks was fully appreciated. At Vienne, on 1 August, Sergeant
Paul Gourdant of the 99th Infantry recorded in his diary:

> We knew that the situation couldn't last long. Since 26 July in
> fact, people have been expecting the worst. We knew that the

Government was doing its best to avoid conflict and had taken all necessary precautions ... the population of the town was anxiously awaiting some definite news. There were big crowds in the banks and food shops ... the mobilisation order, when it came, did not really make a great impression. People had been expecting this.[25]

As an important textile centre with a turbulent strike history and a Socialist municipality, Vienne attracted much attention from the police and from the *sous-préfet*, who had forbidden a Socialist demonstration against war organised for 31 July at the *mairie*. In the event the working-class population of the town caused no trouble to the authorities and the extra police precautions proved unnecessary. The *Commissaire de Police* did note sullen expressions on the faces of some of the textile workers congregating outside factory gates,[26] and in the evening an occasional cry of '*à bas la guerre*' was heard in the huge crowd which had gathered in the main square. But in general the news of mobilisation was received by workers and the rest of the population alike with '*sang-froid*' and 'resolution'; indeed the workers appeared to accept the news with a 'remarkable patriotic calm'.[27]

The authorities had also expected a large-scale pacifist demonstration at Grenoble. Here too their fears proved groundless. In fact a demonstration had been planned by the *Union des Syndicats de l'Isère* to take place on 2 August, but at a meeting held on 31 July to organise the demonstration only seven representatives of the constituent *syndicats* turned up. It was decided to cancel the demonstration on the grounds that the authorities would forbid it and, significantly, on the pessimistic assumption that there would be little rank-and-file worker support. Judging by newspaper accounts of the reception of mobilisation at Grenoble, the cancellation of the demonstration was a wise move. Reports range from 'popular enthusiasm', 'a calm acceptance in the best patriotic spirit', to 'acceptance of the inevitable without bellicosity or rancour'. Even the staunchly Socialist *Le Droit du Peuple* had to admit that there was no discordant note, no hint of a demonstration in the town and that, on the contrary, there were several expressions of 'trust in the destiny of the country'.[28] The *Commissaire de Police* of Grenoble put the whole thing into some perspective: 'the official announcement, far from causing the trouble which we had expected, has produced rather a sense of relief'.[29] At last one knew where one stood. This was, at least, better than the uncertainty and wild rumours of recent days.

In the evening large groups of people congregated in the bigger public squares of Grenoble, discussing events, making plans. There were few doubts that mobilisation meant war. Cafés in the central square, Place Victor Hugo, hired orchestras to play patriotic tunes. There was some dancing and singing, but not, according to the *commissaire*, much more than usual for a Saturday night: 'on all the faces one could read signs of trust, hope, fortitude and above all, calmness'.[30]

THE DEPARTURE

The period of mobilisation officially lasted for fifteen days, with *mobilisés* departing in age groups. The youngest classes of the *armée active* were the first to go on 2 August and the older reservists and territorials were left to the last. Every day during that fortnight small groups of men left their villages for the nearest *chef-lieu* and then on to the main departure points, Grenoble and Vienne. How can one adequately describe the emotional scenes of farewell that took place in each home? Religious faith was, of course, a source of solace to many. Paul Gourdant, who was mobilised on 4 August, described the preparations for his departure thus:

> I made all my preparations for communion on the Sunday morning. This gave me courage, and I was certainly going to need it for it was terribly distressing to think that I was shortly going to leave my bed-ridden wife and my dear children and to leave all the cares and responsibilities of an important business in the hands of my ailing parents. God gave me the strength to put aside all my fears and anxieties and to think only of the defence of my country.[31]

For small businessmen, precious last hours before departure were taken up by the need to settle affairs. Henri Perrin, who owned a small ironmongery in Vienne, was mobilised on 2 August and thus had just one night to settle his debts, do the stocktaking and instruct his young wife on important aspects of the business. There was, perhaps mercifully, little time for reflection or to dwell on the sadness of the imminent parting. Late on the Saturday night

Henri, his wife Louise and their two small children prayed together for a short time before Henri, explaining that 'papa must go away for a while on business for the country', put the children to bed.[32]

Naturally the *mobilisé*'s point of view would vary according to personal circumstances. A young single man who had not hitherto travelled far from his locality might welcome a sense of adventure or a break from daily routine.[33] Indeed some young peasants refused to take the war seriously, regarding it as a form of holiday: 'at least we can have a holiday in the middle of summer, we who have never had one. We must take advantage of it.'[34] Some, however, resisted their mobilisation until the last minute.[35] The opportunity that the war gave to break away, if only temporarily, from rural life conflicted sharply with a sense of loyalty to families and the need to finish the harvest at the busiest time of the year. One *instituteur* noted cases of men going to hide in the forests, adding significantly that they were only persuaded to present themselves by the women of the village, who threatened to denounce them to the *gendarmes*.[36]

Clearly, personal reactions to mobilisation and departure for war were varied. It was at the departure points, railway stations and bus depots, that public bravado replaced misgivings about the future. The *instituteur* of Notre Dame de Commiers noted that from 2 August: 'a veritable pilgrimage accompanies our *mobilisés* each time a train stops at our little station. Everyone tries to put on a brave face, some with more success than others. We hear some notable expressions . . . "we will settle this business once and for all. We must defeat them or die."'[37] At Sechilienne: 'the men are showing plenty of courage. All want to defend the country. The women, a little downhearted at the beginning, have quickly understood the part they have to play. All are resigned to the need to do one's duty. We all place great hope in a rapid victory.'[38]

From the point of view of the authorities the military mobilisation was an unqualified success. During the whole fifteen-day period from the announcement of general mobilisation, in spite of successive departures of troops, there was little sign of disaffection and there is no record of any direct attempts at sabotage. Reporting to the Minister of the Interior on 18 August, the *préfet* could well afford this sense of satisfaction:

The mobilisation has been achieved with the utmost regularity in the *département*. The peasants in the remotest villages have

responded in the same patriotic spirit as the workers in the towns.
It is particularly pleasing to note the behaviour of the latter. If there
have been few signs of wild enthusiasm, there have been no
indications of anti-militarist or anti-war activity. Each has received
the call to duty with calmness and obedience.[39]

Tables 1 to 4 in the Appendix represent an attempt to quantify the
expressions, phrases and keywords most commonly found in all
available reports for the mobilisation period. They cover only some
10 per cent of all *communes* in the *département*, but since they
include the three largest towns, Grenoble, Vienne and Voiron, as
well as some of the most remote villages, they are sufficiently
representative to permit some observations and conclusions to be
drawn concerning the nature of public opinion in the *Dauphiné* in
August 1914. There was only one instance of 'protestations' at the
news of mobilisation. 'Resignation' and 'resolution' form by far the
largest category of reactions (around 42 per cent) and this mood
was most likely to occur in the evening, after the initial feeling of
shock and surprise had abated. The differences in reaction between towns and remote villages were considerably less than one
might have thought, although the population of towns, more *au
fait* with recent diplomatic developments, were rather more bellicose: patriotic songs, signs of enthusiasm and *revanchiste* sentiments were recorded in 31 per cent of the towns as opposed to only
5 per cent of the villages.
    This is not to say that, even in the towns, the mood was that of
the *esprit guerrier* on the outbreak of war. On the contrary, a feature
of the reports is the small number of references to *revanchiste*
sentiments and only in few *communes* were virulent anti-German
expressions noted. *Revanchisme* was certainly not absent in the
département but it was, by 1914, hardly a motivating force in public
attitudes to Germany. It was only after the initial feelings of shock,
astonishment or relief at the news of mobilisation, and during the
period of departure of troops, that desire to avenge the defeat of 1870
and recover the 'lost provinces' was manifested: an added reason, as
it were, for France, once provoked, to 'finish this business'.
    As Tables 3 and 4 show, there was a slight shift of mood during
the period of departure. Again, expressions of 'resignation' and
'resolution' predominate (more than 50 per cent of reactions) and
the increase in expressions of enthusiasm and *revanche* reflect a
general acceptance of the necessity of war. The most striking

feature of the expression of public opinion at the outbreak of war is that collective reactions both to mobilisation and to the departure of troops seem to have been governed by factors other than political. Only one out of eight reactionary municipalities experienced patriotic songs and demonstrations on 1 August, and the only sign of enthusiasm on receipt of the mobilisation order came in fact from a Socialist municipality. Clearly the dominant moods of resignation and resolution were common to municipalities of all political persuasions. Most surprising of all is the lack of feelings of *revanchisme* expressed in reactionary *communes*.

The Army General Staff had envisaged that up to 10 per cent of French conscripts might fail to respond to the mobilisation order. However on 20 August the Military Sub-Division of Grenoble, comprising 215 *communes*, registered only 459 *insoumis*, less than 1 per cent of the total mobilisable population, a remarkable figure.[40] The percentage was higher in small towns than in the villages. In the *canton* of Vizille, for example, the town of Vizille registered more than half of the total number of *insoumis*. Individual reactions to the outbreak of war appear to have been as little affected by political considerations as were collective ones. Only one of the twenty *insoumis* from Vizille was a member of the Socialist Party. Indeed it is hard to establish any kind of pattern at all regarding *insoumis*, other than the fact that they were overwhelmingly young. Of the 459 *insoumis*, 87 per cent belonged to the military classes 1906 to 1914, which would place them in the twenty- to twenty-eight-year-old age group in August 1914.[41] Of the twenty *Vizillois*, eight were married and five had children. Their various occupations were listed as weaver, gardener, carpenter, paper-box maker, mechanic, farmer, office clerk, grocer and bricklayer. Three were unemployed day labourers. They lived in diverse *quartiers* of the town and there is no indication that they met socially. The three day labourers might well have been 'vagabonds' but other than that there is little to suggest that these *insoumis* formed any kind of anti-social element living on the margins of society.[42]

The lack of any kind of pattern in collective or individual responses to the outbreak of war, particularly the absence of political debate, helps to explain the apparent docility with which so many young men accepted such a brutal disruption of their everyday lives. Few anti-war or anti-military feelings were expressed in the *département* during the crucial mobilisation period. The dominant picture is one of a population resignedly accepting its

fate. Assessing morale in the villages during the first week of
August, the Rector of the Academy of Grenoble made particular
note of the deep feelings of patriotism which the crisis had stirred
in the rural population, and of the stoic acceptance of the inevita-
bility of sacrifices. Everywhere the war was regarded as a necessity: 'the fervent desire of all our brave peasants is to finish this
business as quickly as possible. They are indignant that the
Fatherland has been attacked, but they know that France did not
want war. All they want is to be able to return to their villages in
the knowledge that our country can live in peace.'[43]

In the first weeks of August 1914 thousands of young *Dauphinois*
left their villages and small towns, not to reach Berlin by Christmas,
not to rid Europe of an oppressive Prussian military caste, but simply
to defend their country against an invader. In the main they did so not
out of an inherent hatred of the Germans and German civilisation, but
rather out of a desire to protect and preserve their peaceful way of life.
These were the first and second generations of peasants and townspeople who had been taught by the *instituteurs* of the early Third
Republic to 'love France but to hate wars'. The issue was simple
enough, if awesome in its implications. The French people and their
government had not wanted war, but France was under attack and
threatened with invasion. One had one's duty to do, and for the
overwhelming majority, that was all there was to it. Thus the mood in
villages and towns changed rapidly in the space of a few days from
shock, surprise and stupefaction to resignation, resolution and
acceptance of the need to 'finish this business'.

Of course one faced almost certain arrest and heavy penalties in
time of war if one failed to report for duty, and this only added to
the sense of helplessness and resignation. If the sheer speed of
events at the end of July and the beginning of August had caught
people mentally unawares and unprepared for the coming of war,
this undoubtedly made it easier for the military authorities to effect
the mobilisation as smoothly and rapidly as possible with the minimum of disruption and in the absence of organised opposition.

THE RITUAL OF THE *UNION SACRÉE*

On 4 August 1914, the day after Germany's declaration of war on
France, a message from President Poincaré was read out to a
packed Chamber of Deputies in Paris calling for an end to the
political, factional and class struggles which had riven the Third

Republic. All parties and classes must come together in the interests of National Defence against the enemy. The message was received with rapturous applause. Amid much back-slapping and hand-shaking between political enemies, the old revolutionary *communard* Edouard Vaillant is said to have embraced his bitter enemy Albert de Mun, to whom he had not spoken for years. At last, it seemed, a common cause could unite Nationalists and Socialists, Monarchists and Republicans, Catholics, Jews and Protestants. Soon the secretary of the CGT (*Confédération Générale du Travail*), Léon Jouhoux, sat on the *Comité de Secours National* beside the Archbishop of Paris, the *Préfet de Police* and leaders of *L'Action Française*, and on 26 August the Socialists Guesde, Sembart and Albert Thomas entered the 'bourgeois' government.

Thus, in an atmosphere of anxiety and near hysteria, was born the famous *Union Sacrée*. With hindsight the theatrical gestures and a rather emotional over-reaction by excitable deputies give its genesis a somewhat comical aspect. However, in the context of the history of the Third Republic, the *Union Sacrée* was an extraordinary interlude, *un sursis glorieux* in a period of social and political strife which culminated in the bitter divisions of the 1930s. No single formula or expression encapsulates better the image of sacrifices made by the population for the national effort during the war. Thus the *Union Sacrée* has attracted much attention from historians and political analysts. It has been seen as an expression of nationalism triumphant, 'a system of values and references which is that of the Right'.[44] It is also seen as a giant exercise in class collaboration which survived to become part of 'bourgeois mythology' in the inter-war years.[45] In this study attention will be focused on the uses to which the *Union Sacrée* was put during the war, on its multifaceted role in mobilising civilian effort and as a propaganda device guiding opinion and sustaining morale.

On the face of it the expression was well suited for journalistic use. In fact, surprisingly, it was not until the end of August and the beginning of September that the local newspapers began to talk of a *Union Sacrée*. However there was an air of political reconciliation and talk of *union des partis* days before the announcement of Poincaré's message. The assassination of Jean Jaurès on 31 July provided an early opportunity for political journalists to pay lip service to the mood of the country. The clerical *Croix de l'Isère* condemned the murder as 'a pointless act, solving nothing in this hour of danger and uncertainty'.[46] The moderately right-wing

République de l'Isère regarded it as a 'stupid and odious crime'.[47] In the reactionary press generally, the great Socialist was seen as a tragic symbol of the futility of working-class resistance to war.

It was the success of the mobilisation, the absence of anti-war demonstrations and the apparent upsurge of patriotic feeling in response to '*La Patrie en danger*' which brought forth a wave of self-congratulatory praise of the mood of the French people at the beginning of the war. The ardent Socialist Jean-Louis Chastenet, editor of *Le Droit du Peuple*, using rhetoric that would have done credit to Maurice Barrès, printed what was soon to become the standard formula of *L'Union Sacrée Politique*: 'There are no longer any political parties in France, no more of the problems which have torn our country apart. There is now one nation whose sons are standing, arms linked, ready to repel the invader, to shed their blood for humanity and civilisation.'[48] A few days later, in a letter to the *curés* of his diocese, the Bishop of Grenoble expressed almost identical sentiments: 'it is clear that the enemy has achieved in one day what our politicians have failed to do for decades. A real wave of patriotism has spread over the country and the whole nation is united behind its army. There are no more parties, only France, pacific and resolute, a fatherland united in calmness, vigilance and dignity.'[49]

Indeed in small industrial towns, where pre-war divisions between Socialists, Radicals and reactionaries had been intense, politics seemed to be forgotten in the mobilisation of Frenchmen of all political persuasions and religious beliefs. On 9 August the Rector of the Academy of Grenoble noted that in the *communes* of the industrial region of the valley of the Romanche 'party rivalries have been put aside', and at Vizille, with its largely working-class and Socialist population, 'it is particularly pleasing to see the spirit of co-operation brought about by the national crisis'.[50] Much the same sentiment was apparent in the reactionary municipality of Rives[51] and the fervently Radical Socialist town of Beaurepaire.[52] Even at Vienne there was a marked absence of political debate during the first weeks of the war after the bitter recriminations of recent years.[53] One very obvious reason for this was the fact that a great many of the politically active men were now in the army. Even so, as Louise Perrin wrote to her husband at the end of September:

Despite all the activity in the streets, the *Viennois* are calm. Nobody talks politics any more. There are signs of friendliness everywhere. Mothers are shaking hands in the street, enquiring after each other's sons mobilised at the front, even though these sons might have been arguing bitterly just a few weeks ago. I have never before experienced such an atmosphere of good will in our town. It is quite extraordinary.[54]

The *union des esprits* and the disappearance of political divisions was not confined to towns. It is a theme which occurs frequently in the *instituteurs'* notes on village life during the first weeks of the war. Here too there was much talk of 'common sacrifice' and the need to forget political differences as neighbours resumed friendly relations after years of animosity. Undoubtedly this was helped by a tacit agreement to avoid political controversy at a time when all hands were needed for agricultural work and, as has been seen, in many villages there was little enough time to talk politics during the busy summer months.

It is therefore rather difficult to assess the extent to which political reconciliation had any real significance in the villages. Often the *instituteur* would note simply that: 'the union of all in the common struggle has been felt since the first day. We all know what we must do for our country',[55] that 'petty quarrels, differences of opinion have been put aside'[56] or that 'in this hour of danger there are no longer any Socialists or anti-militarists'.[57] Much depended of course on the strength of political feeling which had existed in the locality before the war. In the village of Sechilienne the *maire* of the reactionary municipal council called a meeting of local farmers and *chefs de famille* on the first day of mobilisation in order to 'put behind us the quarrels and political discussions which have so divided us in the past'. After much friendly discussion 'the old and ardent Socialist Jules Finet embraced the *maire* and offered his services to the municipal administration for the duration of the war'.[58]

It must be borne in mind that the chief witnesses to events in the countryside at the beginning of the war, the *instituteurs publics*, were not always likely to be politically impartial. For example, in the following account by the *instituteur* of Viriville it is not difficult to see where the political sympathies of its author lay:

On 5 September a money collection was made in all the houses of the town. Eight teams of two collectors divided the various *quartiers* between them. The first pair were the *curé* of Viriville

and the President of the Radical Socialist Committee. It was the
latter who made this arrangement in order to show the population that there are no more political differences in our town and
that we are all working in harmony. The *curé* protested vehe-
mently saying that he would prefer to organise a collection of his
own at church. It took some time to persuade him to co-operate.
He did so only reluctantly.[59]

The fact that this *instituteur* made a particular point of showing the
reluctance of the *curé* to join in the demonstration of good will
between political rivals suggests the strength of the idea, or image,
of a political union at the beginning of the war. This really is the
essential point. As will be seen later, the renewal of political
antagonisms came about in villages as well as through the local
press not so much by a direct attack by one side upon another, but
rather when one side accused the other of being the first to break
the *Union Sacrée*.

The above example also reveals an interesting example of the
ritualisation of political unity in the locality. In the early months of
the war there were a number of what might be called 'public reconciliation ceremonies' in villages and small towns; a symbolisa-
tion of political collaboration in time of grave national crisis. What
better way to demonstrate this than by public signs of friendship
between those legendary antagonists of the Third Republic, the
village *curé* and the *instituteur*? In the village of St Etienne de St
Geoirs this took the form of a public hand-shaking at the *mairie*
followed by a short speech by both, emphasising their readiness to
combine the moral forces of the Church and of laic education in the
common cause. Finally, 'in front of nearly all the population of the
village, the *curé* gave me his *Croix de l'Isère* and I gave him my *Droit
du Peuple'*.[60]

More often, as at Viriville, the ceremony was combined with the
achievement of an *œuvre de guerre* to demonstrate that this was not
just an empty gesture. At Les Thébauds de Sechilienne, for
example, the *curé* and the *institutrice* jointly organised during
September a knitting campaign amongst the girls of the village in
order to send cardigans, balaclavas and so on to soldiers at the
front in time for the cold weather. A stall was set up outside the
church to put on show the finished articles. Prayers were offered
by the *curé* and the *institutrice* gave a short talk to the assembled
mothers and children thanking them for their contributions and

emphasising that their united effort, whatever their political and religious beliefs, was but a symbol of the efforts of the nation itself.[61]

In some cases both *instituteur* and *curé* might be mobilised at the front, and this fact could be used as a good example of the 'equality' of sacrifice in time of war, an essential component of the *Union Sacrée*. On 15 October *La Semaine Religieuse* reported that by an extraordinary coincidence the *instituteur* and *curé* of the small *commune* of La Veissière, both wounded, found themselves occupying beds in the same military hospital. Their pre-war political antagonism and mutual dislike, apparently legendary in the locality, was forgotten as they offered solace and consolation to each other. A real friendship thus emerged: '*Abbé* Chanson and *Instituteur* Vidolene will never forget each other, and after the war which will have changed so many things in this world, will live in peace in the *commune*'.[62]

These examples show that the idea of a union of political parties was not simply an invention of local journalists. However the public gestures of reconciliation, the ritualisation of new-found friendships amongst pre-war political enemies, do suggest a lack of spontaneity. They were largely the work of *maires*, *instituteurs* and *curés*, all of whom held, in varying degrees, positions of influence in the community. Each of these local pillars of the establishment received from on high, through their respective hierarchies, orders to stress unceasingly the importance and value of the union of all political and moral forces in the locality. A circular from the *préfet* on 5 August called on the patriotic devotion of all *maires* in the *département*: 'I count on you to group together secretaries, *instituteurs* and *institutrices* and *curés* in the name of the National Defence. You must let the population know that we are all, regardless of political differences, working together towards the same end.'[63] In his pastoral letter of 6 August the Bishop of Grenoble told his *curés*: 'We will invoke the union of all Frenchmen, whatever their political beliefs, for the national effort. You must emphasise in your sermons the theme of love and comradeship.'[64] In the same spirit the Minister of Education, in a circular to all *instituteurs*, stressed that they must show the need for good will to all sections of the community: 'explain to the children and to their mothers, their duties of solidarity, of collaboration, despite political rivalries'.[65]

In this way the national formula born in the Chamber of

Deputies in Paris was, from the outset, relayed to the populations
of towns and villages with the aim of implanting in people's minds
the image of a giant national effort galvanising the social, moral
and political forces that had so divided the nation. Just as the
inception of the *Union Sacrée* was given the characteristics of a ritual
by the deputies in Parliament, so it was formalised by the *maire*,
curé and *instituteur*. Therefore it was, right from the beginning, a
powerful propaganda device, a formula which could be invoked to
secure maximum effort from all sections of society in the service of
the country.

Why, though, this overwhelming emphasis on political reconciliation even in areas where political debate had never been lively,
and where, as has been seen, it was absent during the mobilisation
period? The chief reason lies in the serious predicament in which
the French Government found itself during the summer of 1914. It
saw itself threatened from within and without. Successive reitera-
tions by the leaders of the *CGT* of the likelihood of social revolution
in the event of war had spread fear amongst not only politicians,
but also certain intellectuals and all representatives of established
order. Hence the long list of suspects on *Carnet B* (the file of left-
wing subversives), the organisation of *Gardes Civiles* in every
commune, the elaborate military mobilisation plans calling for
speed. To this was added the threat from Germany, which was real
enough. The assassination of Jaurès on the eve of war only served
to add to these fears.

It was therefore to allay fears and to meet the immediate crisis of
August 1914 that the idea of a *Union Sacrée* was born. As a 'catch all'
propaganda slogan it had a two-fold purpose. It could serve as a
coherent expression, a symbol of the need for everyone in the
nation to pull together, to pull his weight in overcoming the crisis
and pushing back the Germans from the frontiers of France.
Simultaneously, by emphasising political reconciliation, it could be
used for the duration of the war as a constant form of reference, as
a form of social control, ensuring full collaboration in the national
effort. The reasoning was simple, if hardly innovatory: it is the
nation which unites, and politics which divides. Partisans of all
political persuasions were invited to submerge their differences in
the higher interests of the nation. Thus stood condemned as 'anti-
patriotic' the idea of politics and political activity during the war.
Thus also did *Union Sacrée* become synonymous with 'sacrifice'.

This is not to labour a rather obvious point. If it mattered little to the women, children and pensioners of certain remote village communities that Socialists and reactionaries put aside their differences and that *instituteurs* and *curés* were now on friendly terms, it certainly mattered to them a great deal that they themselves were going to be called upon to make considerable sacrifices in the name of the nation. The fact is that beyond the likelihood of having to bear unprecedentedly heavy casualties the civilian population did not know just what sort of sacrifice was expected of them at the beginning of the war. Hence the idea of political abnegation as a symbol, a means of identification with which to prepare people for the worst. In people's minds, political reconciliation could be linked with the difficulties and tasks that lay ahead. It is important to bear in mind here the 'truce' aspect of the *Union Sacrée*. It was conceived in an emergency for a war which, it was almost universally believed, would be over in a matter of months. Significantly, not one of the *instituteur*'s notes for the first months of the war makes reference to the possibility of prolonging political collaboration after the war. It was assumed that after a short war things would quickly return to normal and this meant, among other things, the renewal of political activity.

During the anxious first days of August 1914 people needed some form of reassurance, some tangible sign of security in an uncertain atmosphere, particularly in villages where the call to defend the Fatherland had been so sudden, dramatic and often unexpected. To whom could peasants turn for advice and guidance? Newspapers, even when the latest editions were available in outlying areas, were of little help as journalists' headlines, reflecting the general anxiety at the beginning of August, tended to add to the confusion. There was only the *maire*, the *instituteur* or the *curé*, who themselves were unlikely to be much better informed, as the *instituteur* of the small village of Sardieu makes clear:

About midday on Sunday 2 August I had a visit from the *maire*. He told me that all morning he had been besieged at the *mairie* by a constant stream of *mobilisés* anxious for news, asking advice: 'Did mobilisation mean war? Has France already been invaded? How long will the crisis last, who will finish the harvest, who will look after the wives and children?' and so on. He said that he had received instructions to alert the *Garde Civile*, and orders for requisition of horses, but little more than that. He planned to hold a public meeting outside the *mairie* that evening. By seven o'clock a crowd of some 300 villagers had assembled in the courtyard. We borrowed long tables from the school and draped *tricolores* on them. Here sat the members of the municipal council, the *curé* and myself. Here is the text of the *maire*'s speech: 'My dear fellow citizens, at this moment, this time of crisis for France, I am going to appeal to your sense of solidarity and fraternity. Let us forget our differences, all those things which have divided us. Let us put aside our resentments and grievances. We are all going to have to make sacrifices in the difficult times ahead. Some of you have already seen the departure of your sons, fathers and brothers. Some of us too, on the municipal council, will shortly be leaving to do our duty at the front. Let those who are not called help the families of those who are. Let those who stay work together so that the harvest can continue. Let us all unite in one same thought, one single idea, that of the love of our country. Mobilisation does not necessarily mean war. It is a cautious measure for the sake of security, but if the worst happens, we will be ready for our duties. Our soldiers will be united at the front and we will be united behind them.'[66]

This little sketch sums up beautifully the anxieties of the local population and the response of its local authorities on the very eve of the outbreak of war. It contains all the basic elements of the *Union Sacrée*, some two days before the expression was coined by Poincaré. There is the constant stream of anxious questions asked of the *maire* and his general inability to give definite answers. There is the posting of the *Garde Civile* and the ritual of the evening: the flag, the assembled notables all facing the large anxious crowd. Then the speech, its inconsistency reflecting the *maire*'s own lack of information, the general fear of war and the need for consolation, 'mobilisation does not necessarily mean war', and then, as if to accept the inevitable, the reference to the need for sacrifice, for solidarity and unity. Above all there is the linking of all this with the shelving of past differences on the municipal council.

SECURITY AND CENSORSHIP

If the symbol of unity in the face of danger was one way of mobilising opinion and effort, more tangible methods of control were also needed. Once Germany had put an end to any lingering doubts by declaring war on France on 3 August, the Government and military authorities moved rapidly to tighten administrative controls and ensure security in the provinces. Indeed, if the sheer speed of the military mobilisation, indiscriminately calling up males of military age, made any organised resistance difficult to achieve, the administrative measures decreed by the Government in the first week of August made it virtually impossible. Metropolitan France was divided into twenty-one military regions, each under the control of a military governor in the rank of general. The fourteenth region, Lyon, had responsibility for the Isère.[67] Already, on 2 August, a 'state of siege' for the duration of hostilities had been declared in eighty-six *départements*, Belfort and Algeria. This permitted the Military to assume 'all or part of the powers normally given to civil authorities for the purposes of public order and security'. In addition, drawing on a law of 1849, the Military was given 'exceptional powers'. It could make searches by day or night in citizens' houses, arrest any individual unable to produce proof of residence, forbid the carrying of any arms or ammunition, prohibit all publications and meetings 'judged likely to incite disorder' and exercise a permanent surveillance over all railways and roads. The military governor of each region could deploy civilian police as he wished and he could authorise the closure of cinemas, theatres, dance halls, casinos, hotels and cafés.[68]

This general militarisation of society was complemented by laws on press censorship. France, of course, had a long history of press censorship and from the end of July 1914 there appeared a bewildering succession of decrees aiming at nothing less than total control and surveillance of all publications. All telegraph messages were censored from 30 July and on 3 August a *Bureau de la Presse* was created at the War Ministry in Paris with powers of surveillance over all military information. On 5 August a law 'Repressing Indiscretions of the Press in Wartime' forbade publication of any war news other than that communicated and authorised by the Government or High Command. More specifically this referred to all operations of mobilisation and transportation of troops, numbers of dead, wounded or prisoners of war, changes of personnel of high rank, weapons and munitions deployed and movements of armies and fleets. To make doubly sure that the only war news communicated was 'official' news, all journalists were forbidden access to the front line area. Political news was also to be carefully controlled. There were to be no attacks on the Government or any political comments likely to be 'dangerous'. In sum 'all information concerning diplomatic or military operations susceptible of helping the enemy or of exercising a depressing influence on the morale of military and civilian populations' was to be rigidly suppressed. Any infraction of this was punishable by fines and in serious cases by imprisonment for between one and five years.[69]

The *Bureau de la Presse* acted as the centre for all press censorship during the war. It was divided into three sections dealing with daily newspapers, periodicals and telegrams. The *Bureau* was in constant liaison with the War Ministry through the intermediary of the *Section de la Presse*, which controlled all types of news gathering. Staff were chosen from people 'highly qualified' in military, journalistic and diplomatic affairs.[70] In practice these censors were usually retired senior army officers and civil servants, and within the guidelines laid down by the law of 5 August they could exercise wide powers of interpretation. Telegrams could be confiscated *sans avis* and whole sections of newspapers could be cut out or mutilated beyond recognition.

If press censorship at national level was, theoretically at least, in the hands of 'experts', locally it was exercised strictly by amateurs. In the provinces wartime censorship was in principle organised in every locality where newspapers were printed. In practice it functioned through *Commissions de Contrôle* under the double tutelage of the *préfet* and military governor. The censors themselves were chosen preferably from military officials, but failing this financiers, industrialists and various categories of senior civil servants could be used.[71] At the beginning of the war the *Commission* for the Isère consisted of the Commissioner of Mortgages, a president of the *Tribunal Civil*, a senior secretary at the *préfecture*, a military commissioner of the railways and two retired lawyers. Censorship at local level was thus exclusively in the hands of *notables*, usually old men representing socially and politically conservative views. It was they who determined what the public was actually to read during the war.

The Government was naturally concerned that newspaper proprietors and editors should co-operate in employing their resources for propaganda purposes in the interests of the National Defence. In the event it need not have worried. More serious was the counter-productive effect that a monotonous diet of sensational war news was to have on the public mind. If one aim of a rigidly controlled and censored press at a time of national crisis was to prepare, guide and direct public opinion in a positive fashion, it succeeded only in anaesthetising it, reducing in the process the credibility, status and morale of the newspaper industry and journalistic profession. In part this was an effect of the crisis into which provincial newspapers were plunged at the beginning of the war. With strict limitations on what they could actually report, with many of their personnel (journalists, compositors, editors) mobilised in the army and with a considerable shortage and rise in price of newsprint from the beginning of August, it is hardly surprising that the quality of the newspapers themselves deteriorated markedly. Indeed many of them had difficulty in finding anything to report at all. Often whole editions would be missed out, while others would appear with huge gaps as a complete paragraph or section of an article was returned from the censors too late to alter the format in time for the morning editions.

In the Isère the number of pages in the big local dailies was reduced from six to four at the outset. Sometimes only a single sheet would appear. Their format tended to become uniform, with war news dominating the first page and most of the second, a small section given over to local news, a leading article, a 'miscellaneous' section printing important decrees and measures affecting civilian life and one or two pages devoted to advertisements. Not surprisingly, with the official communiqué being the only source, there was little to choose between them in the way of war news. The only real difference was one of emphasis as newspapers, in competition for readership, attempted to outdo each other in sensationalism and patriotic fervour. Responding to the universal public thirst for news during the first months of the war, editors and journalists, denied first-hand information from the front, added their own embellishments and distortions to the already unreliable communiqués. Thus began the *bourrage de crâne* which was to cause much disillusionment with the press and was a source of much bitterness and misunderstanding between combatants and civilians later in the war.

Of the five local dailies the biggest-selling, *Le Petit Dauphinois*, acquired the most bellicose tone and entered the most completely into the spirit of wartime fervour and exaggerated patriotic optimism, with reports of excessive German losses, the tremendous reception given to the French 'liberators' of Alsace and the almost obligatory tales of German atrocities. Most of its attention was given to denigrating various aspects of German civilisation, with

articles on the decadence of German student life, outraged headlines on the bombardment of Rheims cathedral and a lengthy piece
explaining why Beethoven was in reality a Belgian.[72] From October
1914 the paper ran a daily *feuilleton* called '*Mémoires de la Comtesse
d'Eppinghoven*' purporting to be the diary of a courtesan in the Hohen-
zollern entourage, presenting the Kaiser in a ridiculous light as a
crippled, half-witted sexual adventurer ('*Guillaume II l'inconnu*').

For the clerical *Croix de l'Isère* the war was '*La Guerre purificatrice*'
visited on France for all her sins committed under the Third
Republic. Taking a strongly nationalistic tone, the paper often
printed verbatim articles which had recently appeared in the
Parisian *Action Française* and was the first to adopt *jusqu'au-boutiste*
rhetoric: 'As soon as the sound of the *tocsin* was heard we saw the
youth of France respond with a clear resolution to carry out its
duties until the end, until death, until victory'.[73] Peace was
therefore not possible until Germany was totally defeated.

Slightly more sober in its propaganda was *Le Droit du Peuple*. Its
proprietor, Jean-Louis Chastenet, presented the war as a great
disappointment and a great test for Socialists, but he stressed the
need to defend the country: 'The Fatherland, home of all great
revolutions, land of liberty, is in danger'.[74] However, in a more
aggressive tone two days later on 7 August the Socialist Deputy for
Grenoble, Paul Mistral, introduced the notion of a 'war of liberation', a crusade, like the war of 1792, not against the Austrian and
German people but against their emperors and governments. This
theme was to be reiterated constantly throughout the war, and
articles and speeches by leading French Socialists, particularly the
last writings of Jaurès on war and peace, appeared every few days.
Although *Le Droit* could steer clear of *revanchiste* tones, it was
unable to avoid adopting a chauvinistic note hitherto unthinkable
in a Socialist newspaper. On 12 August it began its own list of
German 'atrocities' and on the same day, in an article headed 'The
war for peace', Chastenet, reaffirming the French Socialists' need
to fight an economic and social war against German militarism,
glorified French culture and civilisation in a manner of which Paul
Deroulède would have been proud, adding that it was high time
that the German pride and arrogance which had intimidated and
threatened the French nation for forty-four years was deflated. The
theme of war against Prussian militarism could often become
dangerously blurred with that of a war against the German nation,
especially in the articles of Gustave Hervé, the violent anti-

militarist turned fire-eating patriot, who was a regular contributor to the paper from the end of August.

Whatever their political bias, therefore, the local dailies made a strong contribution to war propaganda from the beginning, and each in its own way had undergone a change of mood and emphasis: from anxiety, uncertainty and righteous indignation at the beginning to outright bellicosity by the end of August. It had been sufficient to invoke the spectre of 'the Fatherland in danger' for journalistic opinion to coincide with the mood in the villages and small towns during the early days of mobilisation. As the weeks went by and as the French army began to engage in a war of attrition, the newspapers, in giving their own reasons for fighting, added a second dimension to the mobilisation of civilian opinion. Whether one was fighting a 'purifying' war, a war against Prussian militarism or, more generally, a crusade of civilisation against barbarity, the implications were the same: within a matter of days 'official' opinion had changed the nature of the war from a defensive one to an aggressive one. This of course was facilitated by the victory of the Marne in September, reported locally as the ultimate 'defensive' victory. In an article on 2 October outlining the 'two conceptions of the war' Chastenet, while castigating reactionaries for wishing nothing less than the total destruction and dismemberment of Germany, stressed the Republicans' view that it was not enough simply to rid France of the invader; the war had to be won by a crushing and permanent defeat of the German army: 'we will not negotiate with the German Empire'.[75]

In addition to newspapers the big urban centres, Grenoble and Vienne, served their inhabitants with *Revues Hebdomadaires* of the glossy magazine type. From September and October 1914 one could purchase *La Guerre et l'Image* or *Vienne et la Guerre*. These generally offered a summary of the week's military events, usually taken straight from the local and national newspapers, and a leading article which, in terms of sensationalism and *bourrage de crâne*, tended to surpass those of the daily press.[76] The chief role of these small-circulation weeklies was to popularise the war effort, emphasising the common struggle of soldiers at the front and the local civilian population. Photographs and letters of local *mobilisés*, increasingly referred to as '*nos poilus*', who had distinguished themselves in battle, descriptions of trench life, drawings of French front-line trenches showing their 'superiority' over German ones, accounts of glorious deeds of the local regiments in battles, were juxtaposed with *vignettes* of life in the small market towns and local villages during the war.

About three of the eight pages of *Vienne et la Guerre* were devoted to drawings and crudely touched-up photographs of national and local *notables*, together with brief biographical sketches, beginning in the first issue with French and Allied generals and the *Préfet* and deputies of the Isère, and going on down through the various ranks and levels of social status to reach the local magistrates on 29 November and eventually the entire personnel of the *Gare de Vienne* by mid-January 1915. *La Guerre et l'Image*, as its name suggests, was even more pictorial, with drawings of French artillery and infantry in action and postcards, claimed to be authentic photographs, of German soldiers entering a French town, kicking dogs, looting shops and beating up old peasant women. Like the newspapers these *revues*, while describing the anguish and sufferings of civilians, essentially presented the civilian war effort as a 'back-up' to the military. A feature of *Vienne et la Guerre*, for example, was the weekly poem by André Rivoire, who would pick out certain themes: the silence of village life in wartime, the patriotic devotion of *maires* and *instituteurs* and, later on, the heroic achievements of those working in the war factories. Always these were linked with the sufferings and sacrifices of *nos poilus*. The moral, or underlying message, never varied: the sufferings of civilians are great, but they are as nothing compared with the sacrifices of our sons, brothers and fathers at the front.

Perhaps the real point about the daily and weekly publications in the early weeks of the war is not so much that they tended to try to outdo each other in their sensational and patriotic outpourings – that after all was only to be expected – but that they responded to a real need for some kind of news and a measure of reassurance amongst the civilian population. In August and September 1914 people at all levels of society, journalists and peasants, *maires* and *préfets*, pensioners, women and children, were entering the unknown and, given the restrictions placed on the relaying of 'concrete' war news by the Army High Command, the dominant expression and common thread was a search for mutual reassurance.

Optimism was of course the keynote and journalists were fortunate in that they could, with some realism, favourably compare the situation in 1914 with that of 1870. Unlike in the previous war, France now had powerful allies in British sea power and the

Russian army. Indeed an almost mystical faith was placed in the Russians, whose culture and civilisation were so little understood in the West, but who could, it seemed, mobilise an endless supply of peasant soldiers against the enemy in the East. On 19 October *Le Petit Dauphinois* published a letter from a former inhabitant of the village of St Pierre d'Allevard, now living in Moscow, entitled 'We can count on Russia'. According to this, eight million Russian soldiers were amassed on the German frontier, a modern army full of courage, all peasants fighting with a great love for their Tsar: 'let's have courage and hold out for as long as possible, our ally will do the rest'. The spectre of a vast Russian army pouring into Germany from the East was a great advantage to propagandists, especially at the end of August 1914 as the initial French advance into Alsace-Lorraine had been turned into the long retreat to Paris and the crisis of the Marne. From 22 August, without exception, the newspapers fell silent on French successes and heavy German losses and concentrated almost exclusively on the Russian advance.

After a month of monotonous optimism, a pattern began to emerge. All that the more perceptive and discerning readers could do was to read between the lines and interpret in their own way the slightest shift in tone of the official communiqués. The most sensational headline with the biggest and boldest type came to mean in reality that the military situation on the Western Front was not too serious. The more emphasis that was being placed on the achievement of France's allies, the more the likelihood that various French units had suffered serious reverses and heavy losses. Most worrying of all was the lack of war news of any kind. In fact this rarely occurred, but when the High Command deemed the military situation to be too serious to issue a communiqué (as for example at the height of the Marne crisis from 4 to 6 September), provincial newspapers with nothing to report would be reduced to a single sheet confined to an appraisal of the war situation in the most vague tones.

From the evidence supplied by *instituteurs*, police reports, newspaper accounts and private correspondence, it is hard to escape the conclusion that the peasants and townspeople of the Dauphiné were mentally unprepared for war in 1914. During the first few months of the war people's actions were governed by fear, uncertainty and irrational behaviour. There was an overwhelming sense of powerlessness and a feeling that 'nothing can be done, there is no alternative but to defend the Fatherland'. The sheer speed of events was largely responsible for this. Less than a week elapsed between the deepening of the international crisis at the end of July and Germany's declaration of war on 3 August. The departure *en masse* of able-bodied males undoubtedly facilitated the authorities' task of mobilising civilian opinion. The *bourrage de crâne* of the press fell on the receptive and credulous ears of a population shorn of its potentially most critical-minded members. This population was, moreover, anxious for news of any kind. The fact that people in towns and villages genuinely believed that France was fighting a war of defence is the key to an understanding of the mentality of the French people and the mood of 1914. Hence the success of the image of national consensus as a propaganda device. It is far easier for governments to call on the need for sacrifice when the country is seen to be fighting for its life. Thus the social revolution that the authorities had feared so much failed to materialise and the *Gardes Civiles*, informally disbanded in many *communes* from mid-September, were officially dissolved on 20 October.[77]

If the *Dauphinois* generally responded obediently to the need to defend the frontier, they did so with their eyes open. Clearly no one foresaw four and a half years of trench slaughter, and the illusion that the war would last only a few months was universally shared even after the Battle of the Marne, when it was thought that the war might last a few months longer than hitherto expected. No one thought in terms of years. However even in the villages there appear to have been few illusions about the horrors and potentially destructive nature of modern warfare. Indeed it was precisely because people felt that the war would be the most terrible yet known that they believed it would be short. It was beyond people's imaginations that the carnage and destruction wrought by modern mass armies could be sustained for more than a few months. It is therefore facile to state that the peasants of France meekly marched off to war without any idea of what they were letting themselves in for. The *instituteurs'* notes for August 1914 reveal an overwhelming sense of impending doom in the villages of the Dauphiné: 'we all have the feeling that a catastrophe is about to befall us, but thank God the war will be short and quick'.[78] 'Everybody is sad and, above all worried. Everybody knows that the war will be terrible and that many of our villagers will never return.'[79] Even at the beginning of the conflict one could feel that this was to be 'the war

to end all wars'. The last words of a group of *mobilisés* from St
Cassien, on leaving for the front, were: 'if we must go to war, at
least our children will never have to fight'.[80] It was not so much the
actual bitterness of the ensuing war that the *Dauphinois* failed to
comprehend, it was rather that they under-estimated its scale and
the capacity of society to sustain the total mobilisation of all
resources for a prolonged struggle lasting for years rather than
months.

2
Early Problems, 1914

GENERAL MOBILISATION AND ECONOMIC CHAOS

'The men have gone, the villages are deserted.' The image of a vast and sudden depopulation of country areas during the month of August was presented in the local press with an air of dramatic finality. 'So many men have left', wrote *La Croix de l'Isère* on 28 August, 'that an atmosphere of sadness and doom pervades the small towns and villages of the Dauphiné.'[1] The Rector of the Academy of Grenoble reported that 'all along the valley of the Isère the once familiar shouts and cries of farmers going to market, of animated "farm talk" in cafés and market squares has given way to an anxious silence maintained by women, children and old men'.[2] It was as if all the prevarications of the press during the last days of peace had given way to a full recognition of the inherent sadness of the situation. France would be deprived of all her able-bodied young men for the duration.

Of course the image needs to be qualified and there is no doubt that the newspapers exaggerated. After all, the idea of the deserted village deprived of its lusty menfolk fitted well with the theme of the giant sacrifice of peasants for *La Patrie* which the press were to adopt from the beginning. In fact the demographic impact of military mobilisation on the local community in August 1914 was more keenly felt in towns, where the age and sex structure of the population was more heavily weighted towards young able-bodied males. Moreover the sudden loss of population would naturally be more dramatic in industrial areas employing a large proportion of immigrant, mainly Italian, labour. As the *institutrice* at Livet noted:

Since the first rumours of war the many Italians of our *commune* have been anxiously looking for ways and means to return to their country. All the rented accommodation at Livet has suddenly become vacant. The town, usually so lively with its Italian workers, has taken on a sad air.[3]

Again, the migration of young men from village to town had been a feature of French rural life since the mid-nineteenth century.

The loss of young men from the villages in August 1914 was real enough however. The tiny village of Villard Reculas, high up in the Oisans, lost twenty-five men, some 24 per cent of the total population, to the mobilisation. Of the remaining thirty-two males, seven were under the age of eight and fifteen were over sixty-five. Thus some 40 per cent of the remaining males could be classed as 'able-bodied' for the purpose of agricultural labour.[4]

Indeed the shortage of agricultural labour was of immediate concern to civilian authorities in August 1914 and it was to remain a major problem throughout the war. This was not a new phenomenon. Already, by the turn of the century, voices had been raised expressing concern about the effects of depopulation on the rural economy, and about the poor state of agriculture as a whole. By 1900 it was estimated that France was short of about 100 000 agricultural labourers.[5] Each summer, with the approach of another harvest, the question of labour shortage was renewed in the local press. This concern transcended political differences. In July 1914 both *La Croix de l'Isère* and *Le Droit du Peuple* carried lengthy articles on the theme of rural depopulation and the implications of labour shortage.[6] French agriculture was thus in no condition to face war. The loss of just one or two men from some village *communes* would be serious enough. The sudden departure of some 20 to 25 per cent of the rural population would have drastic consequences.

Added to the shortage of labour was the effect on the economy of the military take-over at the beginning of August. All railways were appropriated for military use and there was an immediate requisition of horses, cars, carts, lorries; in short, anything that might be of use to an army on the march. The serious economic problems that civilian authorities faced throughout the war stemmed directly from this. The fact is that the French High Command had made little or no provision for the effects on the agricultural and industrial economy of a rapid mass mobilisation of men and material. Possibly because of the basic misconception of the length of the coming war, no attention was paid to the effects of indiscriminate mobilisation. Men from all walks of life and of all occupations, apart from certain key personnel attached to *préfectures*, railwaymen and specialists in the coal mines, were to be called up. Initially there were to be very few 'reserved' occupations.

The mobilisation of men and draught animals therefore severely exacerbated the existing labour shortage in agriculture. The immediate concern was to finish the gathering of the harvest, which in most cases had begun before the end of July. On 7 August the *préfet* issued a circular to *maires* of rural *communes* asking them to make a list of all available labour, survey the needs of local farmers, distribute labour accordingly over the *commune* and vote credits on the municipal council for the utilisation of temporarily unemployed town workers, including non-mobilised foreigners.[7] Foreign labour was not welcomed in the villages at the beginning of the war and only eleven *communes* in the *département* accepted it during August. There were some objections, too, to the use of urban *chômeurs*.

In fact, helped by particularly fine weather during August and frantic last-minute attempts by peasant *mobilisés* to break the back of the work before their departure, the first harvest of the war was gathered remarkably quickly. The majority of *instituteurs'* notes for this period indicate that, despite the shock and disruptions, activity in the fields had not slackened. By the third week of August the only *communes* still registering difficulties were in the areas of larger farms to the north-west of the *département*. Undoubtedly labour shortage was much less of a problem on the smaller farms in the Oisans and Vercors regions. As one old *cultivateur* pointed out: 'we in the mountains are used to hard work in the summer. The women, children and the old have always helped gather the harvest. This terrible crisis has meant simply that those left behind have had to work even harder.'[8]

All the same it was a considerable achievement and it was seized upon in the local press and by civilian authorities as proof that the *Union Sacrée* was working in practice. Particular mention was made of the *Dauphinois'* determination to make the best of things and of the unselfishness with which those unaffected by the mobilisation came to the aid of those less fortunate, 'unprecedented in a region so renowned for its strong peasant individualism'.[9]

It was the wholesale mobilisation of craftsmen and professionals vital to the rural economy – mechanics, wheelwrights, blacksmiths, millers, veterinary surgeons and so on – that caused the most serious problems during the first months of the war. To this was added the transport problem consequent upon the militarisation of the railways, the restrictions on mobility imposed by the state of siege and the fact that poor-quality horses and carts, rejected as unfit by the military, very soon needed urgent attention. The corn harvest, once gathered, needed to be threshed, milled and transported as flour to the bakers in the towns. The *département* possessed a total of 3872 threshing machines, water, steam and windmills on the outbreak of war.[10] By the end of September 1914 the *préfet* estimated that some 70 per cent of thresher owners, 65 per cent of blacksmiths and over 80 per cent of millers had been mobilised.[11] In the hardest-hit areas agricultural activity was thus paralysed and many *communes* were totally isolated for commercial purposes during the first months of the war. With machinery lying idle for want of adequately trained operatives the upshot was that the harvest was in danger of being left to rot, and the implications of this for bread supply in the towns were serious indeed. For example, on 7 August the *maire* of the small town of Renage calculated that the five bakers in the town had only six days' supply of flour between them.[12]

The mobilisation of just one vital specialist could cause great difficulties. The village of Goncelin, for example, was fortunate in that it lost only 10 per cent of its male population in the initial mobilisation. As a result, thanks to the mutual aid of farmers, the harvest from the outlying areas was safely gathered by 10 August and the two threshers in the vicinity were working full time. All went well until the owner of the mill, a bachelor in his mid-forties, was mobilised on 14 August. The shutting down of the mill put an effective brake on all harvest work and by 18 August the three village bakers were predicting the exhaustion of flour reserves by the last week of August. In the event the crisis was overcome by the municipality buying in the services of the miller of nearby Le Touvet.[13]

In some *communes*, particularly in remote areas, it was simply the lack of petrol, requisitioned in huge quantities by the army, which caused threshing machines to cease functioning before the harvest was finished. However at Malleval this particular problem was overcome by the village's one private car owner siphoning off sufficient quantities from his vehicle to maintain the thresher for the two days needed to finish the work.[14] There are varied sources of information detailing economic activity in 103 rural *communes*, roughly 20 per cent of the total for the *département*, during the month of August. Only six of them fail to mention any of the diverse difficulties outlined above. The situation was not helped by the premature mobilisation at the end of August, some three months ahead of time, of the military class of 1915.

In the short term, at least, it was industry and commerce which suffered the most dramatic effects of the militarisation of civilian life, with a multiplicity of factors combining to create a near paralysis of the local economy. Throughout August and September an absurd paradox obtained: at a time when villages were desperately short of farm workers there was a large pool of unemployed or under-employed labour in the small industrial towns. In Vienne, where the departure of Italians and mobilisation of Frenchmen had reduced the population by 20 per cent, there was a total shutdown of all the textile and engineering factories by mid-August causing 4500 *chômeurs*.[15] In the textile town of Voiron 90 per cent of all factories and workshops stopped working on 2 or 3 August and were still closed two weeks later.[16] At Grenoble some fifty enterprises employing more than ten people had closed by 22 August. Taking into account the departed foreigners as well as *mobilisés* and the unemployed, the town was occupying only one-third of its pre-war workforce.[17] All in all, by the end of the month, the *département* as a whole numbered 11 937 unemployed industrial workers of both sexes, approximately one-fifth of the pre-war industrial population. In addition to this some 8000 partially-employed workers were occupied for only 50 to 75 per cent of the normal working week, with correspondingly reduced wages.[18]

Given the lack of forethought and the prevailing view that hostilities would not last very long, it is difficult to effect a coherent analysis of the type of industry or enterprise most affected by the mobilisation. As in agriculture the loss of skilled workers and specialists was crucial and was a major cause of shutdown in both industry and commerce. Much depended therefore on the age structure of the workforce at the beginning of the war and the attitudes of individual *patrons* or directors. It was indeed possible for a small factory or workshop to continue functioning with half or even a third of its normal workforce provided that a sufficient number of skilled operatives remained. In this respect the small engineering concerns employing a high proportion of time-served skilled machinists in their late forties or early fifties were in a reasonably fortunate position.

The mobilisation of the *patron* or of important foremen and chargehands was the biggest single reason for closure. This tended to have far more effect in the small and medium-sized enterprises operating as family firms than in the larger collective societies. Delegation of responsibility outside the immediate family was far more restricted in the smaller firms. The mobilisation of the *patron* was the prime reason given for the closure of three small engineering works and iron foundries in Vizille. The *fonderie* Favretto Frères, for example, despite having sufficient blast-furnace operatives and a backlog of orders to maintain production for two or three months, was forced to close because there was no foreman or supervisor, these responsibilities having been exercised by the proprietors, both of whom were mobilised on 2 August.[19]

Many enterprises were caught in the same way and the *préfet* cited the mobilisation of the *patron*, leaving the enterprise without sufficient direction or effective supervision, as a prime reason for the closure of some 40 per cent of small and medium-sized enterprises.[20] In some cases it was not the lack of foremen or chargehands which caused the *patron* to close his enterprise on mobilisation, but his sheer reluctance to hand over responsibility for the duration. An extreme example was Jean Bourdis, the director of the *soierie* Casimir Marder at Moirons. Mobilised on 5 August, he insisted on shutting down his factory, thus causing the unemployment of 580 female workers as well as several non-mobilisable skilled operatives and mechanics, an act of selfishness perhaps, but one justified by Bourdis on the grounds that the war would only last a couple of months and that any hardship would be shortlived.

It seems that the textile industries were hardest hit by the mobilisation, despite the fact that around 80 per cent of their workforce consisted of women. The reason for this of course is that nearly all the mechanics, maintenance engineers, foremen and chargehands were men. The loss of such personnel was obviously crucial in an industry where, on average, each spindle or loom had to be serviced, unblocked or otherwise repaired and maintained two or three times a week.[21]

Many proprietors, however, shut down their enterprises not for selfish or personal reasons, but because the militarisation of transport facilities deprived them of essential raw materials and the possibility of expediting finished goods. The lack of raw materials was the more serious problem. Orders could always be despatched piecemeal, and in some cases by lorry or horse and cart. It was the vital commodities normally carried in bulk by rail which were lacking in August. At Marseille, the biggest and closest *entrepôt* for South-East France, the mobilisation of dock workers, coupled with the Military's take-over of railways, had caused giant stockpiles of raw silk, dyestuffs, grease, oil and coal by the middle of the month.[22] It was not just the lack of railway transport which was causing problems. The state of war had deprived French enterprises of products of the German chemical industry, for example sulphates and various types of resin which were necessary for paper manufacture. The invasion of North-East France, which of course was to become the theatre of war for the duration, affected the country's richest coal fields, a serious problem since coal was so vital to much of French industry.

In fact the situation on the railways began to improve slightly after the initial mobilisation period had ended. The Rives–Valence line for instance, totally closed to passenger and commercial traffic during the first two weeks of August, began operating one train daily in both directions for these purposes from 20 August (this compared with six trains daily before the war).[23] However use of railways for non-military purposes was still very restricted. The military governor also imposed restrictions on the type of commodity that could be transported by rail. From the end of August the only type of paper which stationmasters were allowed to receive was that used for newsprint. This badly affected the *papeteries* making paper bags for grocery shops, paper sacks for sugar refineries and so on. There were also inconsistencies which are not easy to explain: railways were allowed to transport combustibles like coal, anthracite and oil, but forbidden to carry firewood or faggots with which to light them.[24]

The transport and raw materials problem persisted throughout 1914 and consequently factories continued to close intermittently in October and November as their reserves became exhausted. However by the end of the year the railways were operating at something like 50 per cent of their normal peacetime capacity, and this improvement continued into the spring of 1915 by which time stockpiles of essential commodities at Bordeaux and Marseille had been cleared.[25] By Christmas 1914 the steady flow of complaints reaching the *préfecture* from *maires* and industrialists about lack of stocks and transport problems, which in September had sometimes reached fifty per day, was down to a trickle; although this was perhaps as much a reflection of the extent to which they had become resigned to an unsatisfactory situation as a genuine indication of improvement for, like the labour shortage in agriculture, transport difficulties and scarcity of raw materials were to continue to cause problems throughout the war.[26]

Another reason for the under-employment of workers, and in some cases the total shutting down of enterprises, was the bank moratorium. As in England fear, panic and uncertainty at the end of July had caused a run on banks as people rushed to withdraw their money. A number of small-town branches of Grenoble banks, their capital reserves dangerously depleted, had to close for the duration of the war, transferring their reserves and remaining staff to the *Chef-lieu*. The Government acted quickly by imposing a moratorium effectively postponing the payment of bills and the honouring of cheques for one month. A Ministerial Decree of 31 July also limited withdrawals from savings banks to fifty *francs* per fortnight. Many *patrons* were therefore unable to pay for certain essential raw materials and consequently were unable to pay wages to employees.

The general decline in the amount of money in circulation during the first weeks of the war obviously affected local commerce, and not surprisingly there was an immediate shift in patterns of consumption, with a larger proportion of available cash being spent on vital foodstuffs. The customary propensity to hoard essentials at times of national crisis soon manifested itself. There was a rapid emptying of *charcuteries*, *épiceries*, *boulangeries* and *boucheries*.[27] In the larger towns there were lengthy queues outside food shops even before the announcement of mobilisation and the declaration of war.

Small shopkeepers were perhaps fortunate in that in their absence on military service they could call upon wives, mothers, fathers, sisters or even younger brothers to look after the business. Few were forced to close simply because of the mobilisation of the *patron*. It was the combination of military service with an immediate decline in custom which caused traders in non-essential commodities – tailors, hosiers, jewellers, even ironmongers – to cut their losses and close for the duration, a phenomenon more common in villages and small towns than in larger centres with a more diverse clientèle. Indeed commercial life in the more remote mountain villages was totally suspended. At Venosc in the Oisans, for example, the milliner, dressmaker and cheesemaker all closed for the entire length of the war.[28]

In the garrison towns and industrial centres like Grenoble and Vienne many retailers of durable consumer goods and luxury items adopted an *attentiste* attitude, remaining open to see if any profit could be made from the immediate situation. Both towns were major departure points for *mobilisés* who, making last-minute purchases before going off to the front, could afford a fortuitous, if temporary, custom. The inexperienced Louise Perrin, left alone in her husband's ironmongery, had a steady stream of soldiers buying cutlery, plates and glasses for their kitbags.[29] Once the hurly-burly of the initial mobilisation period had passed, however, the effects of industrial unemployment made themselves felt and those who had taken a gamble and remained open faced a tough time between the end of August and the beginning of November, when textile and metallurgical factories began executing orders for the Army Commissariat. Louise Perrin, for example, operated at a considerable loss throughout September and October, but by mid-November her daily receipts had risen to two-thirds of the pre-war average.[30]

Ironmongers and the like could adapt some of their commerce to current conditions. Clearly this was far more difficult for traders in pure luxury items, and of all shopkeepers they were the worst hit by unemployment and the decline in custom at the beginning of the war. Three-quarters of jewellers, milliners and high-quality dressmakers in Vienne closed between the second week in August and the end of October, although by spring 1915, with a return to full employment in the town, more than half of them had re-opened.[31] Even those catering for the cheaper end of the market, with cheap jewellery and clothes for the textile workers and their wives, suffered. At Vienne the jeweller Geoffrey Bouvier saw his sales drop to 25 per cent of their 1913 level by Christmas 1914, while his rival, Leon Paget, had to wait until the beginning of 1916 for his figures to exceed half their pre-war average.[32]

For grocers and purveyors of general foodstuffs in the towns the situation was of course somewhat different. Their major problem was the replenishment of supplies exhausted at the beginning of the war. Apart from bread the biggest demand was for sugar, meat and dairy produce. With the transport problems a number of grocers faced initial hardships, but the situation did improve during September. Their problems were not helped by a tendency, noted by several *instituteurs*, for farmers to consume more of their own produce and sell less to merchants from the towns.[33] Butchers were also affected by shortages: military requisition of horses and cattle direct from farmers deprived them of the main source of their most saleable meat, particularly horsemeat. *Charcuteries*, with a greater reliance on mutton and pork which were more freely available, fared slightly better. Generally, few purveyors were so badly affected by the conditions of August and September that they were forced to close.[34]

Despite shortages of some commodities there was no official Government attempt at the beginning of the war either to requisition food for civilians or to fix prices centrally. The *préfets* therefore continued to exercise their individual responsibilities in this field. The prime concern of the *préfet* was the maintenance of an adequate and fairly-priced food supply in the major towns like Grenoble and Vienne. The task was not made easier by the *Ancien Régime* aspect of the rural economy after the mobilisation, and transport problems caused considerable local variations in food prices during the first months of the war. In the larger towns attempts by shopkeepers to corner foodstuffs, particularly in Grenoble, caused problems during the days of uncertainty at the end of July and the first few days of August. Shopkeepers in the wealthier *quartiers* of Grenoble were reported selling rice, coffee, sugar and flour at prices 50 per cent above their pre-war level and there were several 'disorders' in food shops.[35]

The authorities took immediate measures against price speculation. On the second day of mobilisation the *Maire* of Grenoble appealed through the press for shopkeepers not to add to the current difficulties by increasing prices, and the municipal council organised sub-commissions empowered by *préfectoral* decree to check the stocks and prices of all foodstuffs in the town. Those suspected of hoarding, speculating or monopolising found their names printed outside the *mairie* under the heading *Guerre aux accapareurs*. Finally the *préfet* had recourse to articles 419 and 420 of the Penal Code, and as a last resort was given powers of compulsory requisitioning from food shops. In fact, once war had become a certainty and the excitement of the first few days had died down, cases of speculation in foodstuffs declined. The *Tribunal Correctionnel* at Grenoble tried sixty-eight cases of fraud, speculation and *escroquerie* by shopkeepers between January and July 1914, seven in the first week of August and only ten between September and December.[36] In the rural areas, by contrast, basic food prices varied considerably, but most villages and small towns experienced an immediate drop on pre-war levels, reaching an extreme of 50 per cent in the rural *cantons* south-west of Grenoble. However by the end of October, with improved transport facilities, prices in rural areas had more or less regained their pre-war level.

In fact it was not until the second half of 1915 that prices of basic foodstuffs rose appreciably. Undoubtedly the shortage of money after the bank moratorium helped prevent an immediate and drastic rise in prices. However public response to appeals to boycott speculators in the towns and the very short shrift given to speculators by the press also played a large part. The drastic resort to forced requisitions was not needed and indeed the *préfet* praised the 'admirable restraint' displayed by shopkeepers in the *département* in his report to the Minister of the Interior at the end of October, adding that the general maintenance of food prices at around their pre-war level was an important factor in the lack of civilian disorders during the early months of the war.

THE STATE AND THE NEEDY

A more likely reason for the general absence of disorders and unrest during the early months of the war was the Government's immediate decision to introduce a uniform system of relief for families and dependants of mobilised soldiers. The need for some kind of social security in the event of a *levée en masse* in time of war had been foreseen in laws of 1905 and 1913, and before the war there already existed a scheme of assistance by which the dependants of those currently *sous les drapeaux*, that is military classes 1911 to 1913, were granted seventy-five *centimes* per day for the wife and twenty-five *centimes* for each child under sixteen years old.

On the second day of mobilisation the President of the Republic issued a decree, countersigned by the Minister of War, extending the current provisions to all classes mobilised. The decree became law on 5 August and in essence it was as follows: for the duration of the war the dependants of all soldiers and sailors of whatever military class who were mobilised for the National Defence and who had been the vital financial mainstays and supporters of their families were entitled to a daily *allocation militaire* of one *franc* plus fifty *centimes* for each child under sixteen years old. The money to pay for this was to come from credits specially voted into the war budget. This news was posted immediately outside all *mairies* and advertised in all the local daily newspapers in the country.

On the same day the *préfets* received a circular from the Minister of the Interior, a lengthy document in thirty-three articles, outlining the basic procedure and conditions of application. In the first instance the claimant must make an application to the local *maire*. The *maire* then compiled a brief report on the economic situation and family circumstances of the claimant and sent this, together with a short statement giving his opinion of the worthiness of the application, to a *Commission Centrale* sitting permanently in the *chef-lieu* of each *canton* of the *département*. The members of this *commission* – there were usually three – were appointed directly by the *préfet* and were drawn from among the *notables* of the locality, usually *juges de paix, percepteurs* and *notaires*. It was they who made the decision whether to accept or reject the applications. When necessary they reserved the right to make further independent enquiries into the personal circumstances of the claimant. In cases of rejection appeal could be made to the *sous-préfet* of the claimant's *arrondissement* who, after considering all evidence and making further enquiries of his own, sent the appeal together with his own opinions on the case to a *Commission d'Appel* comprising five members sitting in each *arrondissement*. Again these were *hautes fonctionnaires* designated by the *préfet*. The decision of the *Commission d'Appel* was transmitted first to the *sous-préfet*, from him to the *maire* and finally from the *maire* to the claimant.

Clearly the whole procedure was complicated, cumbersome and subject to considerable delays. The State had undertaken a huge responsibility and the administrative problems involved in executing fair and just decisions on cases involving such diverse social categories as wives of peasant farmers, agricultural labourers, shopkeepers and industrial workers were to prove immense. With no real precedent on which to rely, and operating in wartime conditions, it is not surprising that the dispensation of the *allocation militaire* became hedged about with anomalies, ambiguities and contradictions that could not fail to arouse jealousies, bitterness and rancour.

The system was open to abuse on all sides. The local *maire*'s role was crucial and it was his opinion on the application which usually swayed the commissioners. In the larger towns the *maire* would employ police to make extensive enquiries into the personal circumstances of the claimant. In the small villages, where the *maire* usually knew the claimant personally, the opportunity to pay off old scores could lead to charges of prejudice and favouritism. The system could also be abused by the claimants. There were many whose children, for whom they were getting a supplement, were working in the fields or, later on, in a factory. There were cases of claimants receiving supplements for dead children and even of individuals making two successful claims in different *communes*. Later in the war one of the most common complaints against the whole system was that the vast majority of claimants were women, while all those who decided the fate of these claims – *maires*, commissioners, *fonctionnaires* – were men.

This is, however, to anticipate many of the consequences. The *allocation militaire* was to become the vital mainstay of a large proportion of the civilian population during the war, and increasingly so towards the end. Initially it was received favourably in both town and village as a clear sign of the Government's well-meaning attempt to alleviate hardship. The most common complaint was about the delay in payment. The news of the introduction of *allocations* was posted in villages and towns on 6 August but it was not until the second week of September that the first payments were made in the more remote areas. In the interim recourse had to be made to the existing local systems of poor relief, private charity and *soupes populaires*.

It was of course in the towns and industrial regions, where the unemployed were unable to find work in the fields, that the need for relief was most urgent. On 10 August the Rector of the Academy of Grenoble was already expressing concern about the fate of workers' wives and their children, calling for urgent distribution of the *allocations*. In his opinion the State owed it to these people to act without delay.[37] At the end of August, replying to a questionnaire sent by the *préfet*, the *maires* of forty-three *communes* where the majority of the workforce usually worked in industry gave a bleak picture of the numbers of poor and needy. At Bourgoin, for example, nearly half the population were 'destitute' as a consequence of the mobilisation of the main breadwinner. At Voiron, where there were 1800 unemployed textile workers, 800 families were truly 'needy'. The average figure that emerges from the results of this questionnaire gives 40 to 50 per cent of families as being completely without resources after one month of war.

As will be seen, a number of wives and mothers for various reasons delayed for a long time before making applications, despite the worthiness of their cases. Those who did apply for relief stood a good chance of acceptance. By the end of May 1915, 48 846 families in the Isère were receiving *allocations*, very approximately one-third of the total number of families, and only 3634 applications were finally rejected as not being genuine cases of need.[38]

One other important area in which the Government needed to act quickly to alleviate financial hardship after the mobilisation was that of rents. Here its chief problem lay in maintaining a careful balance of interests: the Government had to accommodate simultaneously the small private landlords whose incomes often depended largely on rents from their tenants, the industrialists, shopkeepers and small businessmen who rented their premises and, of course, the families of *mobilisés* deprived of financial resources.

Clearly there were a number of imponderables. What, for example, was to be done about tenants who had simply abandoned their rooms or apartments on their mobilisation? Should their accommodation be held vacant in abeyance, or should the landlord have the right to let out the accommodation to someone else during the *mobilisés'* absence? Should he in fact assume that the accommodation had been vacated permanently? What was the position of tenants who had not been mobilised? Were they expected to continue paying rents even though they might be out of work? What was the position regarding the tenant/*mobilisé* who had simply been posted as 'missing'; how long should the landlord have to wait before presuming him to have been killed?

Faced with the impossibility of imposing uniform regulations satisfying all interests in these circumstances, the Government did just about the only thing it could do; it procrastinated by introducing short-term measures. On the assumption that hostilities would not last very long, it announced on 15 August a ninety-day moratorium from the beginning of the war on all private rents up to 1000 *francs* per month in Paris, 600 *francs* in towns with 100 000 or more inhabitants, 300 *francs* in towns of between 5000 and 100 000 inhabitants and 100 *francs* in all other localities. The moratorium was extended to all commercial and industrial rents on 1 September.[39]

These were palliative measures and, when the original ninety-day term of the moratorium expired at the beginning of December and there was no sign of an end to hostilities, a new one was imposed to run from January to March 1915. The real trouble of course was that the longer the war went on, and the longer the payment of rents was delayed, the bigger the problems that would face both landlords and tenants when it all ended. Already in November 1914 *Le Droit du Peuple* was predicting either bankruptcy for landlords or penury for tenants if the Government did not make constructive proposals to end abuses, but it is difficult to see what measures could have been adopted. In the interests of the *Union Sacrée* the Government had to be seen to be acting for both sides. By January 1915 many parliamentarians were privately admitting that the Government had no solution to the problem of rents and was simply putting off the day of reckoning until the end of the war.

WOUNDED SOLDIERS, REFUGEES AND PROBLEMS OF LOCAL ADMINISTRATION

With the general mobilisation causing disruption and chaos in so many areas of civilian life, the authorities could not impose the fiction of 'business as usual' which characterised the first months of the war in Britain. Nor indeed did they try to. Substantial territory in the North-East had been invaded, and the press had successfully inculcated the ideals of National Defence, of war of survival and the need for sacrifice. With working populations in the towns facing mass unemployment for the first time within living memory, the *bouleversements* of the war were immediately felt. For the civilian population living in the war zone, particularly, war was a reality from the start.

Away from the fighting zone, in villages and towns, the immediate feeling after the mobilisation was, in fact, one of unreality. A young village *institutrice*, Marie Rodet, particularly remembered those first few weeks as a period of intense physical effort combined with an unnatural feeling, enhanced of course by the sudden departure of the menfolk, but caused also by worry, anxiety and gloom:

> Our minds of course were on the war. My elder brother had departed, my best friend had lost both of her brothers. Nearly everybody in the village had been deprived of someone dear to them. There were few newspapers in the locality but we were not as innocent or stupid as some people would like to think. We knew that something terrible was going on, but we wanted to know more; how were our loved ones faring? What was it like for them? Perhaps it was a good thing that we had so much work to do in the fields that summer, it kept us occupied.[40]

Even in the villages of the Oisans, where for centuries *colportage* had deprived the local population of its menfolk for many months of the year, the atmosphere was more silent, more empty than usual.[41] In the small textile towns, of course, many of the women who had lost their jobs as well as their menfolk to the mobilisation were denied even the chance to take their minds off things.

However the real impact of the war was not long in coming. On 22 August, exactly three weeks after the announcement of general mobilisation, the first trainload of wounded soldiers arrived at Grenoble, to be followed two days later by another 400.[42] By 4 September the figure had reached 2000 and by Christmas 1914 the *département* was looking after 13 500, most of them despatched directly from the front, the minority as convalescents.[43]

In the first instance the wounded were directed in hospital trains to Lyon, the *Chef-lieu Militaire*, and from there they were sent in four directions in the alpine region: Montélimar, Briançon, Albertville and Grenoble via Vienne and Bourgoin.[44] To prepare for the wounded and supplement existing hospitals, the *Service de Santé* of Grenoble established several temporary military hospitals by requisitioning convents, factory warehouses and, especially, classrooms in various teaching institutions. Of course Grenoble itself could not possibly cater for all the wounded, and trains and motorised convoys of convalescents and wounded were despatched regularly to towns and villages throughout the *département*. In this way Vizille and La Mure each received 300 on 15 September and by the end of the year 220 of the 564 *communes* of the Isère had received a quota.[45]

The chances were that only a minority of these wounded would belong to any of the local regiments. At the beginning of the war the High Command had no real, systematic plan to direct the wounded *en bloc* to their own localities. Administrative and transport problems prevented this. There were also other considerations, not the least being the effect on morale of recently-departed loved ones returning as *grands blessés*. Questions of expediency also determined that the most serious cases, those with severe abdominal or head wounds, could not be moved very far; these were initially lodged in the nearest military hospitals in the war zone or in Paris, and subsequently sent as convalescents to the provinces. By 1916 however, the year of Verdun, there were so many serious cases to be dealt with that, increasingly, *grands blessés* were sent straight from the front. Meanwhile, for the first year or so, the

Isère, nearly 150 miles from the nearest section of the front line, tended to receive only those with less serious head wounds, limb wounds and, later on, gas wounds.

To greet the wounded at Vienne and Grenoble the local *Croix Rouge* organised reception committees to dispense chocolate, cigarettes and other comforts, and teams of *Gardes Civiles* were organised to attempt to implement the High Command's wishes that the wounded should have as little contact as possible, at least initially, with the local civilian population. This was clearly a difficult task. The first sight of wounded soldiers returning from the front had a profound effect. Newspapers had given a day's warning of the first arrival and a crowd of several hundred milled round the station courtyard at Grenoble. Stretcher cases being transferred from trains to ambulances had to run a gauntlet of 'sympathetic', 'anxious' and even 'over-enthusiastic' civilians.[46] This general mood was indicated, on a smaller scale, by *instituteurs* in villages and small towns. At Viriville, where a convoy of 100 wounded arrived on 6 September, the *curé* and *instituteur* organised a reception committee at the *mairie* and all work in fields and workshops stopped. There were manifestations of solidarity, sympathy and patriotism all round. The less badly wounded talked of the superiority of French fire power, the virtues of French artillery and in particular of the '75' field gun. They were bombarded with anxious questions about life at the front, the sort of food they had been eating, what the Germans were like and so on. Naturally the main point of these questions was to discover what it was like for the local *Virivillois*, but unfortunately this convoy, mainly members of Provençal regiments, had had no contact with the *Chasseurs Alpins*.[47]

There is little doubt that for the local population the first real contact with wounded soldiers tended to increase their general uncertainty and fear about the state of affairs at the front. The soldiers themselves would give conflicting and highly subjective views about conditions and chances of military success in the foreseeable future. In any case there was a limit to the amount of information that the High Command allowed them to divulge. They were not, for example, to speak of actual losses, either those of specific French units or those sustained by the enemy. They were governed by the same rigid rules of censorship as were the journalists and war correspondents. In most cases their knowledge of the general war situation was as confused as that of the civilian population. As one ex-*Chasseur Alpin* explained:

What is not often realised is that we soldiers were usually as much in the dark about the military situation as the civilians. Our platoon, our company, our unit, that was all we knew or generally cared about. That was our world during the war. We were told the same things by our officers that the civilians were told by the press.[48]

Another *Grenoblois*, wounded early in the Battle of the Marne and sent to convalesce at La Rochelle, described the reception given to his convoy:

It was extraordinary. Flowers, chocolates, wine, large cards . . . we were fêted like heroes, but we couldn't answer the questions: 'How far are the Germans from Paris? Are we on the retreat? What are the British doing?' They expected us to know far more than we did.[49]

What tended to have more effect on local opinion and to stiffen resolve during the uncertain first months of the war was not so much the first contacts with wounded soldiers, as the arrival in the *communes* during September and October of the first convoys of refugees from Belgium and the invaded areas of North-East France. Certainly the tales that some of these wretched dispossessed families brought with them matched the atrocity stories of the press. There were stories of German soldiers cutting off the hands of babies in reprisal for the murder of a German officer, and Belgian nuns told of convents being sacked, churches looted, priests murdered and nuns raped in orgies sometimes exceeding in violence and brutality any sixteenth-century iconoclastic riot.[50] The pitiable condition of the refugees themselves could also promote the need for unselfishness and necessary sacrifice called for in the *Union Sacrée*. The parading of the worst cases in front of the village population was a common tactic, accompanied in many cases by a short speech from the *maire* of the 'what are our sufferings compared to these?' variety. Most moving of all were the experiences of refugee families which had been split up during the panic-stricken movements of population at the beginning of the war. Daily throughout September and October the local press printed pleas by local *maires* for information concerning the whereabouts of children or aged parents of refugees lost in the flight from the war zone, or enquiries from serving soldiers about the whereabouts of their refugee families.

The lodging and feeding of refugees was a tremendous task. In an attempt to utilise refugees as efficiently as possible, an *Office Centrale de Placement des Chômeurs et Réfugiés* was created by the Government on 28 October 1914. The aim of this body was to match, as far as possible, available labour to labour requirements in the localities. Throughout the war there were steady trickles of refugees but the two main periods of influx were during the initial German invasion and war of movement in 1914 and during the German breakthrough and push towards Paris in the spring of 1918.

Transport problems and the sheer numbers – by the beginning of 1915 the Government had had to deal with nearly three million cases – meant that the majority of refugees were lodged in *départements* or provinces adjacent to the war zone, such as Pas de Calais, Seine, Marne and Somme, while the rural provinces in the South and West received the fewest. By the end of 1915 the Isère had received 5567 refugees.[51] On the arrival of each convoy of refugees, the families were spread out among *communes* in the *département* by the *préfet*'s office. In order to help him apportion reasonable quotas the *préfet* regularly circulated a questionnaire to *maires* on the availability of housing and labour needs in each *commune*. On receipt of the response refugees were despatched to families while each *maire* was sent a list giving the identity of each refugee and told to check the military situation of each and watch out for spies and 'suspects'.

Each adult refugee was entitled to the same rate of *allocation militaire* as the locals, although if the refugee obtained work the *allocation* would be discontinued. The *préfet* particularly stressed the moral need for *maires* to find work for the refugees and make sure that they were not exploited by the locals. They were to be housed wherever possible with local families. If this was not possible then church halls, school classrooms and other such buildings could be converted into dormitories, in which case care would be taken to separate the sexes. They were to be fed either by the locals lodging them (for which the local was paid 1 fr.25 per adult and fifty *centimes* per child per day), by local hoteliers or by canteens organised by the municipality. In principle all refugees were to obtain free medical care. The general aim as stressed by the *préfet* was to 're-create as far as possible the atmosphere of the *foyer*, to make refugees feel as much at home as possible'.[52] For this the good will of municipalities and of local families was essential, and not surprisingly the *Union Sacrée* was repeatedly invoked to this end.

A display of good will was also expected of the refugees. It was not always easy, of course, to assimilate refugees in local conditions. Those lodged in the mountain *communes* of the Vercors and Oisans, for instance, found it particularly difficult, especially in winter, to cope with the cold climate and harsh farming conditions of the mountains. Indeed the majority of refugees, coming from industrial towns and conurbations of the North-East, took some time to adjust to rural ways of life. All able-bodied adults were expected to help out with work and make themselves generally useful in the locality. To oversee the work, payment and behaviour of the refugees a *Commission Consultative* was established in each *canton* of the *département*, comprising six members, two of whom were to be refugees. The *Commission* took a dim view of refugees who, without good reason, 'remain idle at this time of crisis'. Those who refused to work or showed bad will would have their *allocation* stopped until such time as the *Commission* decided that their attitude and behaviour had improved.[53]

The initial response by the population of the Isère to the receipt of refugees in October and November 1914 was generally good, and by the beginning of 1915 the *préfet* was able to inform the Minister of the Interior that 'our population has shown remarkable solidarity and unselfishness in the matter of housing the poor unfortunate refugees from the invaded areas'.[54] Out of more than 300 *communes* which had received the initial influx only two, La Terrasse and Varces, showed evidence of 'bad will'. In both cases the *maire* had written to the *préfet* explaining that the locals refused to lodge refugees despite all attempts at enlisting their co-operation for the national effort. Reasons given were that the refugees were usually 'dirty, immoral and vermin-ridden' and mainly town-dwellers totally unused or unsuited to agricultural work. The *préfet*'s reply was that if the locals refused to show the good will and co-operation displayed by the rest of the population, then recourse would have to be made to military requisition and forced billeting of refugees on individual houses. In the event forced billeting was not necessary in 1914 and the two *communes* admitted their refugees in February 1915.[55]

Quite obviously the tasks of local administration in the *communes* were considerably more complex in time of war than in peacetime. The main burden of administration fell on the municipal council, and in particular on the *maire* or his *adjoint*. The problem was that these people in the smaller towns and villages were subject to the same rules and conditions regarding military conscription as the rest of the population. As a result the crucial role of *maire* was filled by aged civilians elected for peacetime purposes (there being no municipal elections during the war) or by *remplaçants* from the municipal council chosen according to the number of votes received for the office of *maire* during the 1912 elections. Nearly a quarter of *maires* or *adjoints* were mobilised in August 1914, and in some cases the local municipal council was down to three or four members. The average age of *maires* remaining at their posts was sixty-nine years.[56]

Few of these people were suited by either experience, temperament, profession or age for the exacting tasks to be expected of them during the war, yet the role of *maire* was arguably the most important and crucial of all civilian occupations throughout the period of hostilities. In addition to normal peacetime functions, the *maire* had to liaise with the *Intendant Militaire* on the requisition of food and animals, supervise *allocations* and issue identity cards and, later in the war, ration cards. He had to allocate refugees to local houses, supervise teams of prisoners of war and soldiers on leave working in the fields, deal with complaints from local inhabitants about requisitions and lack of war news, inform families of bereavements, supervise local police functions, maintain law and order and organise charity collections for the war effort. In addition to this he had to act as a general liaison between military authorities and local inhabitants, organise schooling and educational facilities, arrange temporary hospitals, survey prices and commerce to guard against speculation and fraud, balance the *communal* budget and in general keep the local population as well informed as possible about war news. Above all he had to maintain a high level of morale in the name of the *Union Sacrée*. For none of this did the *maire* or his *adjoint* receive any salary or any form of remuneration. The longer the war lasted, the more the tasks and responsibilities of *maires* and *adjoints* multiplied, and it is hardly surprising that towards the end of the war the number of resignations on grounds of old age, infirmity or sheer exhaustion increased considerably.

The role of *maire* therefore required energy, dedication and an almost superhuman ability far above the average and, in general, the *maires* performed prodigious feats in the interests of the National Defence. There was nothing to stop the *maire* resigning, of course, since he owed his position to election in the first place, but subtle pressures were exerted on him by the *préfet*. The poor old *Maire* of Champier, for example, eighty-six years old and clearly senile, attempted four times to resign between November 1914 and his death in 1917. Each time the *préfet* repeated the standard formula: 'I am counting on you, the country is counting on you, to keep at your post and continue to show your great patriotism at this hour of need. You will find, I am sure, great reserves of strength to carry out your honourable tasks.' In vain did the poor old man get his mobilised grandson to write to the *préfet* explaining that he had already done his duty for France in the wars of Louis Napoléon in 1855 and 1870.[57]

Part of the problem about resignation was that there were few people willing or able to act as *remplaçants*. In the case of a resignation the *maire* had to write to the *préfet* who then, if he agreed, ordered the *maire* to convoke the municipal council and delegate a list of possible members to replace him. If, as was often the case, no one came forward, the *préfet* had to write to the *Conseiller Général* to designate a person capable of fulfilling the *maire*'s functions.

In the event there were only two resignations in 1914, and it seems that the decision of *maires* to remain at their posts was due as much to the belief that the war would not last long as to any extended pressure or emotional blackmail exerted by the *préfet*. One old *maire* who had finally had enough by the spring of 1918 described the pressures he had been under:

It was impossible to satisfy everybody. I was caught constantly between the population of my village and the military author-ities. If fodder requisitions were inadequate it was I who had to face the wrath of the farmers, but it was also I who got the blame from the *Intendance* for not meeting the quota. It was I who had to explain to the wives of *mobilisés* why they were refused an *allocation*. I was always having to explain why the municipality allocated supplies of coal to some households and not to others. I am sick of charges of favouritism and corruption. In addition to meeting all my responsibilities, I have had to try and fit in work on my own farm. I have continued as best I can, but I always thought the crisis would not last long. But now, after nearly four years and no end in sight, I have had enough. Someone else will have to take over. It is a thankless task.[58]

The most thankless task of all was that of bringing bad news to the bereaved. This was the *maire*'s official responsibility although, as will be seen later, some delegated this to the local *institutrice*. On occasions like this the full pomp and ceremony would be employed. In small towns and villages the *maire* would don his mayoral sash and medals and, dressed in formal black, would proceed to the door of the bereaved's house, often accompanied by the *curé*. There were many variations of course, depending on whether the *maire* knew the family personally, but the standard speech would include reference to the great sacrifice made by the son of the *commune*, that he died bravely, and of course that his death was not in vain. Indeed it was because he gave his life for *La Patrie* that the bereaved wife, mother, sister or father was exhorted to redouble efforts for the war. The way in which this sort of news was received by the bereaved families must of course be left to the imagination.

3

Recovery and Acclimatisation, 1914–16

THE BEGINNING OF INDUSTRIAL MOBILISATION

On the morning of 15 August 1914 the director of the iron foundry Experton–Repollier of Renage received a visit from a captain of the *Intendance Militaire* stationed at the headquarters of the 14th Military Region in Lyon. The captain's brief was to research the capability of local industries to furnish certain essential military commodities. On this particular day the search was for large quantities of urgently required shovels and pick-axes, existing stocks in army stores having been rapidly exhausted by the mass departures for the front. With most of its skilled labour mobilised the foundry, which specialised in the manufacture of wooden-handled edge tools, had been operating at one-third of normal capacity during the first two weeks of August and the old *patron* had envisaged a total shutdown in the near future.

On his tour of inspection of the foundry the captain asked several important questions: 'What is the full productive capacity of the foundry? What are the possibilities of twenty-four-hour production? Who supplies the wood for handles and what is the situation as regards skilled and semi-skilled labour in the locality? In the event of a military order being placed with you, how quickly would you be able to meet the high quotas?' The *patron* replied that it would be a fairly simple matter to convert his three American iron-pressing machines to pick-axe production, and that in addition to his regular wood supplies he knew of several sawyers and wood cutters in the locality who would be glad of work. The only problem was the lack of skilled workers and machine operatives. 'Don't worry about that,' said the captain, 'the army can secure a *sursis d'appel* [deferred conscription] of any essential workers from the reserves and territorials.' Two days later the *patron* received an official order for 200 000 pick-axes to be produced and despatched in job lots of 10 000 per week. In addition the military governor

provided a team of four skilled workers, natives of Renage, on an
indefinite secondment. Within a week the foundry, which normally
employed fifty men, was a hive of activity, with sixty-five
employees working day and night to meet the production target.
'The *Intendance*', wrote one of the local *instituteurs*, 'has come to the
rescue of the *chômeurs*. There is enough work at La Maison
Experton to last, if need be, until the end of December. Work has
been found for sixty labourers, wood cutters and sawyers.'[1]

On 29 August the large engineering factory of Bouchayer et
Viallet, normally Grenoble's biggest industrial employer, received
an order from the military engineers for curved bomb shelters and
metal sentry boxes, providing work for more than 500, and within
three months activity at the factory was more intense than it had
ever been before the war.[2]

Before the first month was out, therefore, the army had begun
placing large orders for essential supplies with various individual
enterprises. It was not, however, just heavy engineering or metallurgical commodities which were in short supply. Such an unprecedented *levée en masse* required products of leather and textile
industries such as boots, uniforms, flags, sheets, blankets and so
on. At the beginning of October the *Intendance* at Lyon listed the
following as requirements of first priority: hatchets and scabbards,
bolts, nuts and pins, cotton for shell fuses, powder and cardboard
for cartridges, canvas and tarpaulins for tents and kitbags, wood
and asbestos for fireproof shelters, trench stanchions, tyres for
army vehicles, metal boxes for cartridge cases, steel for helmets,
leather for saddles, cauldrons and saucepans for canteens and,
presumably because of the extra clerical activity associated with the
administration of a large army and navy, vast supplies of writing
paper and pencils.[3]

All this of course was in addition to the normal requirements of
war: guns, swords, ammunition and, above all, missiles of all
shapes and sizes. By the end of September the cry was out
throughout France: 'shells, shells'. On 28 September the directors
of Bouchayer et Viallet received a command from the War Ministry
to install as soon as possible a forge capable of producing 1000
shells a day. By the end of the year the first 1000 had rolled off the
production line and by the beginning of 1918 the firm was producing 9000 shells a day for the '75' field gun. It had increased its
factory space by 50 per cent and its workforce from 800 to 2750.
Other Grenoble-based factories followed suit. The firm of Neyret

trebled its workforce to 700 by the end of 1915 on shell production alone, while at Livet the Usine Keller received its first order for shells on Christmas Day 1914 and was employing 1200 on producing ammunition for heavy artillery by the beginning of 1916.[4]

Such a massive increase in shell production naturally had a spin-off effect. In the northern suburbs of Grenoble the paper manufacturer Fibrocol, which had shut down on the mobilisation, was converted to the production of cheddite for shells and saw its workforce double to 750 by mid-1915 and quadruple to 1500 by the beginning of 1918.[5] Shell fuses were made in textile factories such as the *soierie* at Beaurepaire, which re-opened in November 1914 exclusively to produce fuses and by the beginning of 1915 was providing work for eighty-five *tisseurs* and *tisseuses*, twice its pre-war labour force. Shells and grenades had to be packed carefully in boxes, and since straw was commissioned by the army for other uses shredded paper had to be found. The paper manufacturer Peyron, at Vizille, turned over half its production to this end in May 1915 and by the end of that year was able to invest 35 000 *francs* in a special American paper-shredding machine.[6] A common practice was for the big industrial enterprises working directly for the *Intendance* to farm out orders for special parts to local specialists on a piece-work basis. Thus Joseph Grand, a machine-tool engineer at Vizille, spent the entire war, from January 1915 onwards, producing copper and bronze shell cases exclusively for Bouchayer et Viallet; his workforce increased from six to fifteen and worked round the clock on twelve-hour shifts from November 1915.[7]

As the number of casualties grew the *Intendance* turned to textile manufacturers for the provision of blankets, sheets and bandages for the military hospitals. At Vienne, the leading textile centre in the *département*, sixteen firms formed themselves into the *Union de la drap Viennoise* with each enterprise turning over a part of its production exclusively to sheets for the army. The leading firm, Picolat et Collon, for example, executed 2972 separate orders between October 1914 and the end of 1915. The textile factories of Voiron produced seven tonnes of cotton wool and over one million metres of bandage during the same period.[8]

Clearly, at a time when general mobilisation had caused economic disruption, the increasing and diversifying demands from the army for war material soon began to act in a beneficial way. They also contributed to the rather confused picture one has of economic activity during the first months of war. 'The Dauphiné has become a kind of Babel', wrote the geographer Raoul Blanchard in 1916.[9] The initial orders from the *Intendance* were for huge quantities of standardised items which the larger enterprises were best equipped to fulfill. It was not always easy for small textile and metallurgical firms to adapt or convert their machinery to military production and it was not until mid-1915 that they really began to benefit from direct orders from the army or spin-offs from the large war factories. Since the larger firms tended to be concentrated in major centres like Grenoble and Vienne, the decline in industrial unemployment was patchy: fairly rapid in the two biggest towns, far slower in places like Rives and Vizille. By the beginning of December all the major textile factories at Vienne were engaged in war work and the *sous-préfet* was able to report that under 100 workers were still unemployed.[10] By mid-January 1915, 80 per cent of Grenoble's metallurgical and engineering concerns employing more than ten people had received orders from the *Intendance*.[11] At Vizille only the two largest textile firms and paper manufacturers were working on military contracts by 31 December, although this had reduced the official unemployment figures from 782 to 301.[12] None the less the overall decline in industrial unemployment in the *département* was fairly impressive, dropping from nearly 12 000 to just over 3000 by the end of 1914, and to 400 by July 1915, reaching a figure of sixty-seven men and ninety-five women still without permanent full-time work (mainly refugees finding seasonal work in agriculture) by 1 May 1916.[13]

Can one speak therefore of the beginnings of industrial mobilisation so soon after the beginning of the war? The term has been liberally applied by historians of France, Britain and Germany, and the usual starting point has been taken as the stabilisation of the Western Front into the trench system by the beginning of 1915 and the resultant shell shortage that was acutely felt by all three belligerent countries. In France real industrial mobilisation is said to have coincided with the arrival of Albert Thomas as Under-Secretary of State at the Ministry of War, in charge of armaments and munitions, in May 1915.

In fact, very early in the war, industrialists, politicians and journalists of both the Right and the Left expressed the urgent need for the army *Intendance* to provide orders to private enterprises in order to alleviate the unemployment problem in the industrial areas. On 11 August 1914 the President of the *Chambre de Commerce* of Paris appealed to his colleagues in the provinces to do their utmost to ensure that factories and workshops continued to work and that those which were closed re-opened to provide work for the greatest number of workers possible. To achieve this it would be necessary to solicit orders from the *Intendance* as soon as possible.

Against this background of concern for solving the problem of unemployment and the realisation, after the Battle of the Marne, that the war might develop into a war of attrition, Millerand, the Minister of War, called a conference of the leading industrialists at Bordeaux on 20 September 1914. He revealed that the massive consumption of shells during the first six weeks of the war had been totally unforeseen and unprepared for, and that shell production was henceforth to be the order of the day. All metallurgical and engineering enterprises, big and small, were to be enrolled in a vast programme of production for the war effort. Industrial mobilisation can therefore be said to have started at this point. The main question was who was to have overall control of armaments production: the State or private industry? Clearly, in time of war, a rational system had to be evolved for allocating defence contracts to industry, and for control of labour supply, prices, raw materials and transport. A straightforward way to achieve this would be for the Government to requisition large-scale metallurgical enterprises for the duration. The Government's right of requisition already existed before the war, according to laws of 1877 and 1911, and by the eve of the war the production of armaments was primarily in the hands of State-owned enterprises. Requisitioning had been enshrined in the Republican tradition since the *levée en masse* of 1792–3. To industrialists, however, the idea of requisitioning, with its implications of price fixing, removal of executive power and, above all, strict limitation of profit, was unacceptable.

At the beginning of industrial mobilisation a form of compromise was reached. In official propaganda the State maintained the right to control arms production and, indeed, guns and heavy artillery continued to be made mainly in State factories. In theory private industry, under orders from the State, produced material for the National Defence. In practice, however, executive organisation remained in the hands of private industrialists. The nucleus of private organisation of arms production was the division of industry into cartels or *groupes de fabrication*. The head of each *groupe* received bulk orders from the Ministry of War for production of arms and munitions and farmed these out to industrialists in the *groupe* in the form of a sub-contract. The heads of the *groupes* met regularly at the conferences of the Under-Secretariat of State for Artillery (subsequently the Ministry of Armaments under Albert Thomas). Initially, for the production of field guns and heavy artillery, there were three main *groupes* and, for shells, fifteen.[14]

From the beginning, therefore, industrial mobilisation respected private ownership of the means of production and, although subsequently modified by the Socialist Albert Thomas, this fundamental principle, with its implications of vast profits, was to be maintained throughout the war. This was, however, a different form of capitalism from that of peacetime. In the urgent conditions of war the State took an unforeseen lead in overall administration of the economy to the extent that some historians have seen this as a seminal stage in *dirigisme* and economic planning. Indeed the free market was to a large extent superseded by the State as the main consumer and distributor of transport, labour and raw materials. State demand became the imperative factor and, because of Government controls on essential services and commodities, resumption of full industrial activity depended heavily on the securing of defence contracts.

Representatives of the State and the business community met regularly at the *Commissions Mixtes Départementales Pour le Maintien du Travail* which were established in the localities throughout 1914–15. These were corporate bodies comprising the heads of local industry, administration and transport services, parliamentary deputies and leaders of trade unions, and their purpose was to co-ordinate and administer local general economic activity. One of the first *Commissions* to be established was that for the Isère which first met at the *préfecture* in Grenoble on 19 August 1914. Under the chairmanship of the *préfet*, the *Commission* met approximately every two weeks and initially comprised forty-three regular and nine 'corresponding' members (*maires* of the nine main industrial towns in the *département*). In terms of membership, industry had approximately 37 per cent representation, State *fonctionnaires* 30 per cent, trade unions 12 per cent, academics 11 per cent and politicians and journalists 10 per cent.[15] At the first sitting, amid the chaotic economic conditions of August 1914, two sub-commissions were named to investigate unemployment and measures to facilitate a speedy return to 'normal' economic activity.

Since they discussed and dealt with all areas of local economic activity, the *commissionnaires* assumed considerable administrative power throughout the war and their duties and responsibilities grew apace with the development of industrial mobilisation. Six members were added to the *commission* in February 1915 and nine more in October.[16] Eventually, by decree, the *Commission Mixte* was converted on 25 October 1915 into the *Sous-Comité Consultatif d'Action Economique (SCAE)* with separate sub-commissions dealing with agricultural and industrial affairs. This committee met every fortnight from November 1915 to 27 December 1918.[17] The main tasks that the *SCAE* dealt with concerned the fundamental problems of raw material supply, transport, markets, prices, fixing of wage rates, conditions of work, apprenticeships, placement of unemployed refugees and regulation of the labour supply generally.

THE RECRUITMENT OF LABOUR

The most pressing and serious problem, and the one most frequently discussed by members of the *SCAE*, was that of labour supply for agriculture and industry. As local industries began to re-open in order to execute defence contracts, the availability of skilled workers and specialists was a crucial factor. Already by mid-1915 there was an acute labour shortage in the metallurgical and engineering industries. Even some textile enterprises largely employing females were experiencing labour shortages. In the *soieries* of Voiron, for example, many workers who lived in country districts some distance from the factories had to stay at home to replace fathers and brothers in agricultural work. Certain industries also lost a part of their female labour force to other enterprises which had hitherto used mainly men, for it was the lack of male labour which caused the biggest problem. By early 1916, in the Grande Maison de Velours, the number of male workers had fallen from fifty-five to seventeen, and the Grenoble glove manufacturers had lost 60 per cent of their male *coupeurs*.[18]

How, then, was labour recruited for industrial mobilisation? 'It was necessary', wrote Raoul Blanchard, 'to knock on all doors.'[19] The State played its part by procuring *sursis d'appel* from the army, providing prisoners of war and refugees, and by recruiting foreign labour from French colonies, Eastern European countries, North Africa, China and neutral European countries like Spain and Switzerland.[20] The industrialists themselves had to find the rest. By advertising in the local newspapers, almost daily from the

France 1914–18

spring of 1915 onwards, they attracted old men, *réformés* and *exemptés* from military service that agriculture could not occupy, and ultimately women, many of whom entered the industrial workforce for the first time.

The purpose of the *sursis d'appel* was to allow businessmen to procure on secondment from the army a former employee who had been mobilised (or an adequate replacement) whose skills and expertise were essential to the running of the enterprise. Secondment would initially be for periods of one, two or three months, with the possibility of renewal. Provision had been made for secondment right from the beginning of mobilisation although the procedure for granting *sursis* was not made fully clear at either the *préfectoral* or military governor level. During the first three months of the war, for instance, the *préfecture* daily received anxious letters from *maires*, *instituteurs* and private farmers asking that the *préfet* intervene with the military governor to grant *sursis* to thresher owners, mechanics, blacksmiths, *gardes champêtres*, all of whom were indispensable to agricultural life. Invariably the *préfet* would reply that he was unable to do anything and that requests would have to go through the correct military channels. This meant applying in the first instance to the *sous-intendant militaire* of the relevant military sub-division, whence the request would be passed to military headquarters at Lyon. Often there followed a long delay while the request was being considered. If the *mobilisé* concerned was a *réserviste* (over forty-five years old) or not on active service the chances of a temporary *sursis* being granted were good. If the *mobilisé* belonged to the *armée active* the request would, in most cases, be rejected out of hand.

As more and more industrialists procured defence contracts towards the end of 1914, demands for *sursis* of foremen, skilled lathe-operators and machinists increased accordingly. During the first nine months of the war the Government gave considerable freedom to private industrialists to recruit or employ indiscriminately mobilised workers under the *sursis* system. Provided the *mobilisé* was claimed to be a skilled worker, or deemed vital to the effective functioning of the individual enterprise, and was not in the *armée active*, little attempt was made to check the veracity of *sursis* demands. Clearly the system was open to abuse and charges of favouritism and corruption. Old friends of the recruiting *patron*, members of his family, even *mobilisés* whose families had purchased from the *patron* a false demand for *sursis*, returned to work in the war factories. Predictably the increasing number of shirkers or *embusqués* during 1915 caught the attention of the Socialist press. 'Quite apart from the moral issue of nepotism,' wrote Chastenet in December 1914, 'there is the question of accidents and misuse of valuable machines and tools by untrained personnel who have no right to be working in the factories.'[21]

Even allowing for the obvious bias of the Socialist press on issues of this nature, the question of shirkers in war factories had become such a serious one throughout France by August 1915 that, in an attempt to remove the worst abuses of the *sursis* system and to maximise the efficiency and productivity of labour in munitions production, the Chamber of Deputies voted the *Loi Dalbiez* on 17 August 1915. By appointing commissioners to check thoroughly the professional credentials of each applicant for *sursis*, the law effectively placed the allocation of the supply of an important segment of the labour force in the hands of the State, operating locally through the *Commissions Mixtes* and subsequently the *SCAE*. Subject to military discipline and regulations, the *rappelé* could apply for a prolongation of *sursis* after a year. After the commissioners had checked applications for *sursis*, the worthiness of each demand was considered at the fortnightly meetings of the *SCAE* which would, after discussion, pronounce an *avis favorable* or a rejection of the application. The final decision on *sursis* demands rested with the military governor at Lyon, to whom the *SCAE* sent every application. In practice the military governor altered only about 5 per cent of decisions made by the *SCAE*.

Interpreting the *Loi Dalbiez* most rigorously, the *SCAE* used the following basic criteria when assessing applications: the skill and experience of the applicant, his age (whether he belonged to the *armée active* or not) and the economic importance of the enterprise wishing to employ him. Demands from November 1915 to December 1918 came from diverse sections of the local economy and not just those industries engaged directly in war work. During this three-year period there were 995 demands, 459 of which were rejected. Not surprisingly the majority of those rejected were applications from those not engaged either in work necessary for the National Defence or in jobs important to the local economy. For example 88 per cent of applications for *sursis* of butchers, bakers and other small shopkeepers were rejected. Forty-nine per cent of applications came from the region's biggest employer, the textile industry, which also had the largest proportion of acceptances.

Although the *Loi Dalbiez* tightened up considerably the system of granting *sursis d'appel* and succeeded in removing most of its abuses, it was only natural that in application it tended to favour the urban industrial areas and that its stipulations were more stringently interpreted in requests from office workers, shop-keepers and building workers. Not one of the fifty-six demands from various shopkeepers in village *communes* in the *département* was accepted, and only those office workers normally working in industries currently engaged on defence contracts, or in the Grenoble glove industry, stood a reasonable chance of being granted a *sursis*. The reason given for rejection in such cases was normally 'does not exercise a profession deemed sufficiently important'. The majority of applications rejected from the metal-lurgical and textile industries were on the grounds that the *mobilisé* was 'too young' or in the *armée active*.

In a situation where the recall of a *mobilisé* to his normal civilian occupation meant not only a considerable improvement in the financial affairs of a working-class family, but also in some cases (where the *mobilisé* transferred to munitions production direct from service in the trenches) the possible difference between life and death, the deliberations of the *SCAE* on questions of *sursis* were of crucial importance to the families concerned. Around two-thirds of the time at each fortnightly meeting was spent considering *sursis* demands, each meeting averaging around one and a half hours. The investigating commissioner's report, on which the discussions were based, gave straightforward factual information with no attempt at offering an opinion on the worthiness of the demand. Often, however, his report was accompanied by letters from members of the family of the *mobilisé* concerned.

There is only one example of outside pressure being brought to bear successfully on the decisions of the *SCAE* on questions of *sursis*, and that concerned the provision of law enforcement officers in the *communes*. Immediately after the announcement of the *Loi Dalbiez* the *préfet* issued a circular to the *maires* or their *adjoints* in the *département* asking them to list, in order of priority, personnel whose recall from the army was absolutely vital to the running of the local administration. Out of thirty-six replies, thirty requested the urgent recall of the local *garde champêtre*. Justifying his particu-lar demand, the *Maire* of Vizille pointed out that the population of his town had increased to 4500 after one year of war and that security and law enforcement was left in the hands of just one sexagenarian *garde champêtre*, the sole survivor of a pre-war team of six. At Chasselay the *maire* stressed the need for an extra *garde champêtre* to help search surrounding forests for deserters from the nearby military camp. *Maires* in several outlying *communes* noted that the work of the former *garde champêtre* was now being done by his wife, or that retired *gardes champêtres* were having to control two, sometimes three, *communes*. As a result of these requests fourteen *gardes champêtres* were placed on *sursis d'appel* in September 1915 but, again, the larger towns were favoured. Grenoble received four and Vizille two. Applications from the most remote villages were rejected.[22]

While *sursis d'appel* helped to provide much-needed skilled labour for industry, unskilled and untrained labour, particularly for agriculture, had to be sought elsewhere. On the farms, as has been seen, the harvest work of autumn 1914 had been accomplished by mutual aid and the use of temporarily unemployed town workers. During the dead season of the winter months the question of labour shortage on the farms had been pushed into the background, it being widely assumed that by the return of the busy season in 1915 hostilities would be over. As spring 1915 approached, farmers, *maires* and journalists turned their attention once again to the problems of agriculture, accentuated now by the rise in industrial employment and the forthcoming mobilisation of the military classes of 1915, 1891, 1890 and 1889.

One measure proposed by the Ministry of Agriculture in conjunction with the War Ministry was the provision of military *permissions* by which mobilised French soldiers would be granted a furlough of between fifteen days and a month to enable them to return to farms and help out at particularly busy periods. On the face of it this could have been a popular measure, but the practical difficulties of implementing it were considerable. The Military High Command could not afford the loss of large numbers of peasant-soldiers, many of whom were in the *armée active* on frontline duty, all at the same time. Moreover, with interminable delays on the railways, travelling time would reduce fifteen-day leave periods to nine or ten days' availability for farm work. The *permissionaire* would arrive at his village tired and, particularly if his unit had recently undergone a spell in a front-line trench, physically unsuited to heavy agricultural work.[23]

Another way of using agricultural *permissions* was to take *permissionnaires* from among army reservists and auxiliaries stationed at military depots situated in each *département*, form them into teams of between five and ten and allocate them for fifteen-day periods to *communes* where farmers were experiencing particular problems over lack of labour. From February 1915 the *permission-naires*, only a minority of whom would be natives of the *départe-ment*, would be fed and lodged with the farmer concerned and would receive a daily wage of 1 fr.50. The problem was that military labour organised in this way could only afford temporary help. Not all *mobilisés* were peasant farmers, of course, and many of the *permissionnaires* working in the villages of the Isère during the spring and summer of 1915 were former office workers, shop assistants and unskilled industrial workers totally unused to hard physical labour on the farms. Many of them were in late middle age. Bad weather could also reduce the effectiveness of teams of *permissionnaires*. In the village of St Vincent-de-Mesage, for exam-ple, the teams assigned to local farmers accomplished only four days' work during a particularly wet fortnight in January 1916, and the *mairie* was besieged by complaints from local farmers about money and food wasted on soldiers who just 'sat around and played cards'.[24] Many old farmers distrusted teams of military labourers from the start and a number of *instituteurs* and *maires* in the more remote villages in the *département* indicated that, with the approach of the harvest period of autumn 1915, farmers would prefer to rely on 'the spirit of 1914'. If the harvest could be successfully gathered during the disruptive conditions of mobilisa-tion, then hard work and mutual aid would certainly suffice after a year of war. 'We prefer to rely on our own efforts,' wrote an old *paysan* of La Cote St André in July 1915, 'we need no outside help. Let us alone to do the work we know best. We will manage.'[25]

Despite the problems of using military labour on farms, the question of *permissions* continued to be discussed in the press during 1915 and 1916 and the local military authorities persisted with their use. In June 1915, for example, *Le Droit du Peuple* published a lengthy article concerning the need for the Military High Command to show good will to peasant farmers by allowing auxiliaries regular paid holidays every two to three months to work on local farms. 'This', according to Chastenet, 'would serve the double purpose of ensuring food supply in times of need, and reassuring the peasants who are bearing the brunt of the sacrifices that the country is thinking of them. France is an agricultural country. To antagonise the peasant is to endanger France itself.'[26]

By the end of 1915 the problem of the shortage of farm labour was so serious that the *SCAE* had authorised a special 'agricultural section' comprising academic agriculturalists and *maires* of large *communes* to consider agricultural problems, particularly those of labour supply. In July 1916 the *préfet* reported to the Minister of Agriculture that the *département* was short of more than 3000 urgently-needed farm workers.[27]

An alternative to the use of military labour was the use of German and Austrian prisoners of war to work on local farms. This would overcome the problem of the temporary nature of *permissions*. On 7 April 1915 the Minister of Agriculture sent a circular letter to all *préfets* advising the use of POWs in teams of twenty which could be moved from village to village as and when necessary. The letter suggested that farmers pay a daily wage of forty *centimes* for each prisoner plus food and lodging provided by the farmer or, if the farmer could not provide the latter, a maximum wage of 1 fr.50. If the prisoner did his work badly the commander of the troop guarding the team could halve the daily wage.[28]

Among local authorities, such as the *préfet* and *sous-préfets*, deputies for the Isère and *conseillers généraux*, the idea of using POW labour in this way was a popular one. The chief advantage was that it was a cheap form of labour; it could be utilised fully during the busy sowing and harvest seasons, and returned to the POW internment camps during quiet periods. It was available as long as the war lasted and it was a supply of labour that was growing with each major offensive at the front. The first POWs had arrived in the Isère at the end of September 1914. By the beginning of 1915 there were some 600 in internment camps and on 1 May 1915 the *préfet* informed the Minister of Agriculture that he had at his disposal 1400 POWs for immediate use.[29]

Among *maires*, farmers and *instituteurs* at local village level the idea was somewhat less well received. A great disadvantage of POW labour was that each team of twenty prisoners required constant surveillance by at least five armed guards and there were simply not enough French guards to reduce or split the teams. This was a particular problem in dispersed hamlets where the deployment of twenty labourers, even at harvest time, was simply not practical. Most farmers required just three or four labourers, not cumbersome and unwieldy teams of twenty, and many could not, even at the cheap rates stipulated by the Ministry of Agriculture, afford to pay so many wages. Again, if the individual farmers were unable to provide food and lodging, the *commune* would have to provide it. With the housing of refugees and the provision of temporary military hospitals, most *communes* would find difficulty in renting barrack-like accommodation for POWs.

The biggest disadvantage of the scheme of using POW labour was the fact that the great majority of farmers simply refused to employ or to have anything to do with the enemy, and *maires* did not want Germans and Austrians in their *communes*. At the end of April 1915 the *préfet* asked all *maires* in the *département* if they were prepared to use POW labour. Despite the pressing need for help on the farms during the busy season, only sixty-five out of 564 *communes* replied in the affirmative and three-quarters of these stipulated 'only as a last resort' or 'with great reservations'. Only seven *maires* replied that there were farmers in their *communes* actually prepared to house and feed POWs. A number of *maires* wrote that farmers were frankly 'astonished' at the very suggestion that they should have Germans in their houses, let alone on their farms. One *maire* wrote that after a long meeting of the farmers in his *commune* to discuss the project he was faced with cries of 'treason' from many of the wives and that he was very nearly assaulted.[30]

Interestingly an analysis of the responses of *maires* to the question of POW labour suggests that the most categorical refusals and most vituperative 'anti-Boche' feelings came from the more remote villages. Nearly two-thirds of the sixty-five acceptances came from the larger, more accessible villages in the *Arrondissement* of Grenoble, while villages in the mountain *cantons* of the Oisans and Vercors rejected the scheme unanimously. One important reason for this is that farms in these areas were smaller, more dispersed and traditionally used less labour than those of the plains. All the same, as the *Maire* of Bourg d'Oisans wrote:

> It is in our more remote mountain *communes* that rumours about the Boche become more distorted. The villagers rarely read the papers, but I have seen them coming down from Huez, Villard Reculas and Venosc to our town for the market. They read the front pages of the papers, they talk to refugees. Is it surprising that they carry back to their hamlets with them wild stories about the wickedness of the Boche?[31]

Of course the *bourrage de crâne* of the press and the hate-mongering propagated by refugees and encouraged by unscrupulous *maires* was largely responsible. For months the local village populations were encouraged to believe that the Germans were sub-human. Now they were being asked to welcome them into their homes, feed and clothe them.

Industry benefited far more than agriculture from the use of POW labour. Factory labour was naturally much easier to supervise, and industrial workers in the textile, metallurgical and coal-mining industries were more used to working alongside foreigners. A case in point was the Compagnie des Mines de La Mure with mines at La Mure and La Motte d'Aveillans and a total workforce of around 2500 coal-face and 1000 surface workers. The company was the most important provider of coal and anthracite in the Dauphiné. Traditionally its labour force was fluctuating and unstable, with a large percentage of foreigners, mainly Italians, and local, seasonal labour amongst its face workers.[32] Because of the urgent need to ensure a steady supply of coal in France and the strong possibility that the major coal fields of the North-East would be immobilised by being in a theatre of war, the majority of French coal miners had been granted an immediate *sursis* or had been mobilised *sur place* at the beginning of the war. As a result the company had not suffered greatly from the general mobilisation. However, at the onset of winter and with the mines of the North-East of France out of action, demand for coal in the Dauphiné increased considerably, and by 17 December 1914 the mine at La Motte was short of 120 face workers. The rapid deployment of refugees from the North-East, many of whom came from mining communities, helped to ease the labour shortage in the spring, but with the general mobilisation of Italians from May 1915 onwards the problem became serious, particularly among face workers. Between the end of March and mid-May the La Mure mine alone lost 168 of its face workers, around 10 per cent of the total.[33]

The problem with recruiting labour for the mines was that the work was hard and dangerous, the shifts were long and wages lower than those being offered in textile and metallurgical factories working on defence contracts.[34] To meet the need for face workers the company took advantage of the availability of POWs and began planned recruiting of French colonials, Spanish and Chinese. At La Mure the first contingent of 121 POWs were being employed in August 1915 and by April 1916 there were 434. At La Motte POWs accounted for more than 255 of all mine workers by the beginning of 1917. Since the directors of the company estimated that it cost them less than five *francs* a day to employ each POW, this represented a considerable saving on labour costs.[35]

There were no incidences of anti-German feeling reported amongst the French miners or the local population. Indeed the *Commissaire de Police* for La Mure was slightly concerned about the apparent passivity and indifference with which the POWs were received. He attributed this variously to the 'internationalist' sentiments which had existed among the working-class community, to the strong Socialist element on the municipal council of La Motte d'Aveillans and above all to the fact that the POW miners were doing a disproportionately large share of the rough and dirty work.[36]

The major problem with the employment of POWs and foreigners in the mines was the fact that they were generally far less productive than their French counterparts. By the end of 1915 the director of the mines noted that POWs were averaging only two truckloads of coal per shift, compared with five truckloads produced by French miners. There was also a high degree of malingering and a rise in voluntary absenteeism amongst the POWs, while many of the specially recruited Spanish workers started to look for higher-paid work in textile and metallurgical factories after a month or so.[37] Of course some of the POWs working at the coal face had recently been wounded in action and, in any case, the majority of POWs and foreign workers were not used to mine work.

The coal mines were the biggest employers of POWs locally, but some of the larger metallurgical factories were able to make use of POWs for particularly heavy or menial tasks: cleaning machines, sweeping floors, heavy lifting duties and so on. At Livet, for example, Keller et Leluxe employed two teams of fiteen POWs at fifty *centimes* a day and housed and fed them in a specially constructed dormitory on the outskirts of the town, about half a mile from the factory. Their arrival in the town initially provoked far more hostility than in the mining communities and the local authorities took care to ensure that they had the minimum amount of contact with French people either at work or in the town. They ate separately in the canteen after the other workers had finished their meal break, and at the beginning and end of each shift they were marched in single file to and from the dormitory building. This twice-daily procession through the main street of the town was a possible danger point for demonstrations and physical violence. During the first month after their arrival in November 1915 they had to run the gauntlet of angry abuse; cries of 'murderers', 'rapists', 'child killers', were heard and three times during the first week there were fights and scuffles. However, since the prisoners were not allowed into the town at night, disorders never became serious and after two months the daily sight of German prisoners marching through the town was accepted as normal.[38]

By mid-1916 all the major metallurgical factories, and many of the larger textile enterprises working on defence contracts, were employing foreign workers of various origins. However the great influx of workers from Spain, Belgium, Switzerland, Poland, China and Greece was still insufficient, and on 18 April the *SCAE* estimated that the Fourteenth Military Region was still short of 11 000 workers. Increased emphasis was to be placed on colonial labour: Annamites, Moroccans and Kabyles. From mid-July 1916 regular consignments of colonials arrived at Grenoble and Vienne stations. Placed under the control of the *Service de Contrôle du Main d'œuvre Colonial et Etranger*, these were despatched in small groups to the larger war factories. The Arabs were considered to be more suited to agricultural work, while Annamites were used mainly on shell production in Grenoble and sheet and blanket manufacture in Vienne and Voiron. Colonials were treated with almost as much circumspection as were POWs. Having been divided into teams, they were each given an identity card and travel permit and subjected to rigid security controls from the local *maire*.[39] Those working for the large industrial enterprises like Bouchayer et Viallet were housed, like the POWs, in dormitories and given the dirtiest and most unpleasant tasks. However they were paid at normal rates for unskilled labour.

Ultimately industrialists in receipt of defence contracts had to advertise locally for labour, either directly through the press or by the posting of vacancies on large billboards in towns. They also recruited through the *Office du Placement*. Initially women were slow to come forward and, indeed, most industrialists in metallurgy and engineering were reluctant to employ them, turning to women only after other possibilities had been exhausted. Prejudices against the use of women in hitherto male-dominated industries died hard.

A common objection was that women were congenitally unsuited to coping with assembly-line production in munitions factories and that they were simply not strong enough to be employed in heavy lifting duties. Some *patrons* masked their sexist prejudices by emphasising racial ones, predicting grave moral consequences if young, innocent women and girls were exposed to long hours on the factory floor in the company of men, especially of colonials whose morals were always 'suspect'. This 'moral' objection was also expressed by local trade union spokesmen in metallurgical and engineering industries, masking what was undoubtedly their main fear, that large influxes of female labour would lead to a dilution of the workforce and have a damaging effect on wage claims. There were also the 'hygienists', fearful of the physical safety of women who would be exposed to the spread of diseases in chemical industries and susceptible to accidents in heavy-engineering factories.

Most of these arguments lacked any real conviction in an area whose major industries were connected with textiles and where women had outnumbered men in silk-weaving and clothing factories since the late nineteenth century. What carried far more weight was the *nataliste* argument in which 'paternalists', church leaders, intellectuals, industrialists, journalists and politicians of both Left and Right found common expression in a concern for maintaining the *femme au foyer* where her chief role was the raising of children. This was a potent argument in a country where, for some decades, great concern had been expressed about the birth rate. War and the great loss of male lives obviously brought into sharp focus the implications and dangers of a stagnating or declining population, and in the later stages of the war the *nataliste* lobby gained considerable influence.

It was Albert Thomas himself who was instrumental in mounting a propaganda campaign in favour of employing women in munitions factories. From the beginning of 1916 he regularly issued statements publicised through the local press, stating the patriotic duty of industrialists to recruit women and emphasising the virtues of female labour. Since the military authorities could release only a limited number of men from auxiliary service, and since there was a delay in arrivals of colonial and foreign workers in sufficient quantities, industrialists would have to overcome their prejudices.[40] However even Thomas had to acknowledge the major disadvantages of female labour: it was not likely to be specialist or skilled, and it was not strong enough to do certain types of work. Complaining about the lack of initiative shown by industrialists in arranging training courses for women, Thomas implored the *patrons* not to treat women as a 'sub-proletariat' on the same footing as colonials and unskilled foreigners: 'they are French, they are willing, they have a patriotic duty to work for the National Defence and you have a patriotic duty not to exploit them'.[41]

It was the couching of the employment of women in patriotic terms that helped swing the consensus of opinion among journalists and industrialists in favour of large-scale recruitment of women. Moreover demand for shells and for the labour to produce them grew dramatically during the Battle of Verdun, from March 1916 onwards. Weighing carefully the *nataliste* argument and the needs of the National Defence, Chastenet, in *Le Droit du Peuple*, exhorted *patrons* not to overlook the advantages of employing women, and appealed to their humanitarian sentiments. 'Many women, young and old, need extra money to support their families. They have given their husbands, brothers, sons and fathers to service for the country. Play your part by hiring them for the National Defence.'[42] Even *La Croix de l'Isère* reluctantly came to admit the patriotic need to hire women on shell production.[43] By mid-1916 the recruitment of women had become a regular discussion topic in the fortnightly meetings of the *SCAE*, and towards the end of the year the *Chambre de Commerce de Grenoble* published a long article in praise of the qualities of women as factory workers.[44]

Despite this intensified propaganda, the percentage of women working in munitions production in the *département* did not rise dramatically during 1916. It stood at approximately 20 per cent in September of that year and did not reach 30 per cent until the autumn of 1917. More than half of the women were working in Grenoble-based factories. The larger enterprises generally proved more willing to hire women than smaller ones. Of the fifty-six munitions manufacturers in Grenoble in September 1916, only fifteen were hiring women, all of them with a workforce of more than forty.[45] There were some exceptions: Keller–Leluxe at Livet, for example, despite seeing its workforce increase from 250 to 1350 by mid-1917 was, by that date, still employing only nine women inside the factory, with twenty more working on piece-work at home.

Not surprisingly the type of work done by women was that requiring the least skill or specialisation: manufacture of fuses or charging of cartridges, grenades and shells. However in the larger factories there were, as early as 1916, some incursions into male specialisms. At Bouchayer et Viallet, for example, five teams of ten, each under the supervision of a male foreman, were employed on the turning of shell cases, for which they had spent two weeks in training. At the usine *Grammont* at Pont de Chéruy thirty of the fittest and strongest women were employed alongside men in lifting and stacking heavy shell cases. At Diederichs of Bourgoin there were even female crane operatives and a female shift supervisor before the end of the year.[46] Generally, however, it was not until the last months of the war that women assumed more responsible positions in munitions production.

The average shift in munitions factories lasted ten to ten and a half hours, for which the average pay in June 1916 was 4 fr.50 for women and 6 fr.50 for men. These rates varied by up to one *franc* per shift according to the size of the enterprise, locality and actual occupation. Again, the larger firms paid higher rates: Bouchayer at Grenoble was paying its women 4 fr.75 per shift for turning shell cases, 4 fr.50 for fuse making and four *francs* for lifting, stacking and loading. At the other extreme, women working on fuse manufacture in the Société de Décolletage in Vizille received only 3 fr.50 per shift. These rates could be increased by up to a *franc* per shift on the piece-work system operated in the larger factories. It was also customary for employers to provide free overalls and safety helmets.[47]

Despite these fluctuations and the fact that almost everywhere in munitions factories the pay of women averaged only two-thirds that of men for equal tasks, munitions work still offered between one and two *francs* per day more than the great majority of women's jobs in textile and service industries and about twice as much as most shop work. Why, then, despite the incentive of higher wages, did women seem reluctant initially to apply for munitions work? One major industrialist blamed the reluctance on the novelty of the work and the conservative attitudes of women: 'they are too susceptible to rumours about accidents and unpleasant conditions of work. Young women seem to prefer the cleaner and safer atmosphere of shops and offices. They are scared to venture into the unknown.'[48] However, if rumours about accidents were rife, so too were the rumours of wage rates that could very nearly double the average shop girl's weekly income. Chastenet, writing in *Le Droit du Peuple*, was nearer the mark:

Outside of places like Grenoble and Vienne it is difficult for women to make twice-daily journeys to and from work. A journey time of up to two and half hours per day on top of an eleven-hour shift, six days per week, leaves too little time for rest and leisure.[49]

Paul Mistral, in the same newspaper, advocated more crèche facilities to encourage young mothers to work on munitions.[50] Perhaps the most perceptive contemporary explanation came from the *Commissaire de Police* of Grenoble:

Many shop and office girls regard heavy work in armaments factories as being beneath their dignity, despite the higher wages. This also extends to many of the women working in textile factories. These at least are well established and have a certain status as part of the tradition of our area.[51]

Even if young girls were not affected by attitudes like this, perhaps their mothers were. Throughout 1915 and 1916 the *préfecture* received a number of plaintive letters from young women in their late teens complaining of a variety of social and family pressures preventing them from working in munitions factories. Some, from the more remote villages, merely reflected traditional parental anti-urban fears and prejudices akin to the *nataliste* and 'hygienist' arguments of the intellectuals. Others, like this example from a nineteen-year-old native of Allevard Les Bains, illustrate well the dilemma of the young girl caught between familial duty and the temptations of a new and independent income:

My father and brother are both mobilised. Since the beginning of the war my two sisters and I have been helping my mother run our bakery. We have worked hard and my mother pays me one *franc* a day. Many of my friends have found work at the Société Anonyme des Forges at Allevard and are getting as much as four *francs* a day. I have many times written to my father and asked permission to work there. Both he and my mother keep refusing. My father insists that I have a duty to stay at home and help my mother with the bakery. My mother says she does not want me mixing with the people at the factory. I know that she and my sisters can run the bakery without my help. I do not know what to do. If I get a job at the factory, I would have to leave home. I don't want to do that, but when I read the posters saying that I should help in the National Defence, and when I hear of the money my friends are earning, I feel rather bitter.[52]

Class prejudice against female munitions workers, at least during 1915 and 1916, was undoubtedly widespread and might help to explain the reluctance of shop and office girls to leave the comparative security of their occupations. It was not likely, however, to concern female textile workers in towns like Vienne or Voiron, domestics or those women who had lived such a hand-to-mouth existence as weavers or *gantières* (glove makers) *à domicile*. These women were accustomed to long hours of unpleasant work. Nor was it likely to deter the increasing numbers of war widows left alone with families to support, and for whom the *allocation militaire* was not sufficient.

The fact remains that it was not until the last year of the war that applications for jobs in munitions factories increased significantly. It might well have been that the 'short war' illusion persisted, the belief that the war would soon be over and that it was hardly worthwhile for textile workers and shop girls to give up their jobs with no guarantee that they could return to them once the war was over. For it was, in 1916, still automatically assumed by the majority of industrialists and journalists that female work in munitions factories was only temporary, and that immediately the war was over they would be laid off. It might also be that economic pressures to seek higher wages in few forms of employment took some time to develop: it was not until the winter of 1917 that price rises in basic foodstuffs began to take real effect.

4

The Acceptance of War, 1915–16

PROPAGANDA AND THE 'NORMALISATION' OF THE WAR

Throughout 1915 and 1916 the local press maintained the illusion that the war would be won by the Allies in the foreseeable future. This would still be a matter of months rather than years, however, and any attempts at more specific forecasts were censored. Indeed, with the ending of the 'war of movement' in 1914, press reportage of military affairs in general became increasingly vague, partly because of restrictions imposed by military censorship and partly because of the static nature of the war from 1915 until mid-1918. Only the great offensives mounted by the Allies excited any significant comment in the headlines. After the victory of the Marne in September 1914 the headlines themselves became slightly more muted, with the sensationalism of the early weeks of the war giving way to a rather more sober appraisal of events at the front, although phrases like 'brilliant success for our armies' were still fairly frequent. Thus the French offensives in Champagne and Artois in 1915 were presented as a series of attacks rather than as a giant co-ordinated effort to break through the German lines. When these were repulsed, or petered out, emphasis was placed on German losses, which of course continued to be wildly exaggerated.

When the Germans began their attacks around Verdun on 21 February 1916 the local press reacted slowly. The first mention of the battle was a printing in *Le Droit du Peuple* of the the brief, terse, official communiqués, with no extra comment. The battle had lasted two weeks before the historic significance of the fortunes of Verdun began to be emphasised. On 6 March *Le Petit Dauphinois* reassured its readers that '130 000 Germans are already dead'. As the fighting continued through March the battle remained front-page news in the now familiar pattern: greater coverage was given to the beating back of German attacks, while French losses were described as 'successful resistance' or 'Germans make limited advance, but their losses are terrible'.[1]

When the Battle of Verdun settled into a pattern of attrition from mid-March onwards it ceased to occupy the daily headlines, being relegated to two or three inches of column space in all the local newspapers, with the occasional major coverage of a specific event, or eulogies of the 'hero' of Verdun, Colonel Driant. By the end of April reference to Verdun was absent for days, sometimes weeks, on end, and until mid-summer 1916 war news was virtually curtailed to a simple repetition of the official communiqués. The monotony was relieved by the British offensive on the Somme which, on 5 July, both *Le Droit du Peuple* and *Le Petit Dauphinois* reported as being a 'great success for our allies', with 'thousands of German prisoners taken'. Two days later *Le Droit* described British losses as 'insignificant', and on 9 July *Le Petit Dauphinois* published a long article glorifying the 'brave tommies'. The press continued to use the exploits of the Russians as a diversion from the disasters on the Western Front and, perhaps, to maintain an interest in military news. Towards the end of July it was the ill-fated Brusilov Offensive which came to the rescue, and headlines such as 'Russian advance proves irresistible' and 'our Russian allies are invincible' replaced references to the Somme which had, of course, by now become an unmitigated disaster.[2]

Thanks to the censor, therefore, the local population's grasp of the progress of military affairs was invariably out of date and often wildly inaccurate. It was from the beginning of 1915 that the full weight of the censor's blue pencil was felt. Of course it was not just reportage of events at the front which was censored. The list of instructions given to local newspaper proprietors for the whole of the war by the *préfet* and military governor amounted to a formidable attempt, the longer the war went on, to limit public awareness of the conduct of affairs by the governmental and military authorities: 'It is advisable for us to hide from the local population the real excesses of this terrible war', wrote the *préfet* to the director of *La République de l'Isère* on 16 December 1915.[3] Clearly the censors had learnt their lessons from the sensational journalistic excesses of the first months of the war. The 'miracle' of the Marne had not been followed by a rapid Allied advance to Berlin, it had led to stalemate on the Western Front. The war had not been won by Christmas, and the public must therefore prepare itself, or be acclimatised and prepared, for a situation in which hostilities might continue for some time; hence the strict clampdown on any references to internal weaknesses in Germany or over-exaggerated reports of French successes, lest these arouse undue expectations. Needless to say reports of 'premature' peace initiatives by Socialist conferences like those in London and Zimmervald in 1915 and Kienthal in 1916, and even diplomatic initiatives like those by President Wilson and the Pope in 1916 and 1917, were carefully surveyed. The censors had to maintain a careful balance between emphasising the sacrificial nature of the war in accordance with the maxims of the *Union Sacrée* and the interests of *jusqu'au-boutisme*, and the need to prevent the full range of horrors becoming public knowledge for fear of damaging morale. Hence the careful surveillance of the printing of casualty lists, with all reference to regiments and places of origin of the dead being cut. Villagers in the Dauphiné would, in due course, know when a member of their local community had been killed, wounded or gone missing, but they must not know the extent of casualties for the region as a whole.

The general war effort must be seen to be progressing smoothly. Accidents and explosions in munitions factories in France must be kept secret as far as possible. The extent of knowledge of economic disruption caused by the war, particularly in regions close to the war zone, must be strictly limited. There must be minimal awareness of shortages and food supply problems and of exports of coal and vital foodstuffs from the Isère (obviously to avoid hoarding and price speculation as much as to sustain morale). Generals who had been deliberately popularised and idolised by the press from the beginning of the war must have their reputations protected, so changes in the High Command, like the 'promotion' of Joffre and the 'disgrace' of Mangin in 1916, must not be made public knowledge. Above all France must be seen to be fighting the 'just war' in defence of Christian and liberal values and must be portrayed as fighting it 'cleanly'. Thus, while reports of German use of poison gas at Ypres in 1915 were not discouraged, absolutely no reference must be made to French attempts to develop their own methods of chemical warfare. Similarly the French army must be presented as treating German prisoners humanely, with no references to death sentences, arbitrary executions or other persecutions of German soldiers. Interestingly, while it could be publicly acknowledged that there were male spies working for the enemy, mention of female French spies was to be officially discouraged.

Indeed, as producers, factory workers and guardians of the family, the female sex must be portrayed in an ideal light. As the majority of the civilian population they were the backbone of the nation in time of war. They must therefore be idealised as arch-patriots. This of course was in keeping with Albert Thomas's propaganda campaign for female labour in munitions factories during 1916, but long before then the image of women deprived of their menfolk, guarding the *foyer* and raising their children while patiently, stoically awaiting the return of their loved ones, was deliberately fostered in the local press. Most attention was paid to women in villages, for the female farmer, working from dawn to dusk alongside her children and elderly relatives, fitted perfectly with the image of stoic endurance in time of sacrifice that the propagandists wished to encourage. 'The women of France are performing miracles,' said *Le Petit Dauphinois* in August 1915, 'they have responded to the needs of our country in its hour of danger just as readily as our soldiers. Never have we seen such courage.' 'In the fields our brave women are doing the work of two men', noted *La République de l'Isère*.

The idealisation of the female accorded well with the image of civilian France in wartime as a giant matriarchy. Hence the increased use of familial metaphors: the *Union Sacrée* had gathered all disparate elements into the 'bosom' of *La Patrie*, every village, every *commune* in France had given its 'sons' to service for the country. Every family had been touched directly or indirectly by the war. What village could not boast its patriotic peasant mother who had seen her two or three sons off to the front, and then her husband mobilised in the reserve? By November 1915 nearly every *commune* had received its quota of 'brothers in sacrifice', refugees from Belgium or North-East France. Added to this were mounting incidences of the supreme sacrifice. By November 1915, in the worst year of the war for French casualties, more than four-fifths of the *communes* of the Isère had lost at least one of its 'sons' killed in action at the front, while nearly every *commune* had a *mobilisé* wounded or taken prisoner.[4]

Historical analyses became commonplace. Journalists and pro-pagandists of all kinds referred increasingly to Joan of Arc, the symbol *par excellence* of the spirit of outraged France driven to almost superhuman motivation. The double image of the country girl fired by mystical visions, and of the family grouped together in time of crisis, was most forcefully invoked in general propaganda posters appealing for courage and maintenance of morale, and in more specific posters calling for contributions to *emprunts de guerre*.

The great events of modern history were a godsend to the secular Republican press in particular. The great revolutionary wars were invoked. The Marne was compared with Valmy, the dark days of September 1914 with those of 1792. Socialist journalists went to extremes, making use of the anniversary of the beginning of the *Commune* as a supreme example of patriotic revolutionary energy being mobilised in France's hour of need. Even the terminology of the Great Revolution was employed: certain days were earmarked as great *journées* for special contributions to the war effort: *Journée des Poilus*, *Journée des Réfugiés Belges*, *Journée des Régions Envahis* and so on.

It all added up to the propaganda image of a peace-loving, peasant-dominated France roused to fury by the aggression of the barbaric Teuton. France had become one large family united in sacrifice. It has already been seen how, in 1914, propagandists quickly turned the war of defence into one of aggression and liberation. The task for propagandists in 1915 and 1916 was to inculcate into the civilian population the *esprit guerrier* on the assumption that this would help France and its allies to bring the war to an early and victorious conclusion. However it also had to maintain morale by acclimatising the civilian population to the stalemate situation of trench warfare. To mobilise opinion, to maintain a constant state of alert while simultaneously anaesthetising it by trying to normalise the war, was obviously not easy.

Increased use of the *feuilleton* (serial), such a popular feature of the pre-war press, undoubtedly helped to normalise the war situation. By mid-1915 all the local newspapers except the clerical *Croix* were running their own daily serials, and their subject matter ceased to be drawn from examples in the current war, reverting to tried and trusted *policier* or *crime passionnel* themes. No opportunity was lost, however, to employ heavy and rather crude symbolism. The detective, against the odds, would patiently, doggedly, follow his prey to the very end, a veritable *jusqu'au-boutiste*. The villain, in most cases, would be a foreigner, usually of Central European origin. The wronged party in the *crime passionnel* would tend to be a woman, French, and very often of peasant stock. Not suprisingly, when most good journalists and writers were mobilised, the quality of these serials, usually over-long, clumsily allegorical and ranging from the rabidly chauvinistic to the downright banal, showed a marked deterioration as the months went by.

Of course the vicissitudes of the local press remained largely outside the purview of the inhabitants of villages and small remote townships. Here the *Bulletin Communal*, now virtually reduced to a summary of the front pages of the newspapers, continued to provide the only real war news, apart from that disseminated by soldiers on leave and convalescents from the front. The main task of maintaining propaganda for the war effort in the rural areas fell therefore to the forces of public and private education, and of the Catholic Church.

THE EDUCATION SERVICE AND THE *INSTITUTEUR PUBLIC*

In Zola's famous dictum, 'France will be what the *instituteur* makes it'. In a very real sense the *tenue* or 'conduct' of rural France throughout the war can be seen as a vindication of the educational policies of the early Third Republic. Even allowing for varying degrees of ability and influence which the *instituteurs* and *institutrices* exerted in their localities, their triple role as educators, propagandists and administrators of communal life must be considered, next to that of the *maire*, as a pivotal one and their achievement, bearing in mind the disruptions of the Education Service during the war, were, by any standards, remarkable.

The evolution of the primary school teacher's responsibilities in the Isère from the 1880s onwards had followed the typical Republican pattern as exemplified by this newspaper comment:

> It is the *instituteur* who must form the spirit and the strength of the young generation. He must furnish France and the Republic with citizens worthy of the ideals of liberty and resolute patriotism. The *instituteur* should be not only the educator of children, but also the political educator of *communes*. In each of our parishes a voice must be raised against that of the *curé*.[5]

In July 1914 the teaching personnel in public primary schools in the Isère comprised 737 *instituteurs* and 1493 *institutrices*, and in private schools 83 and 368 respectively, roughly one for every 185 inhabitants.[6] Socially and geographically they came preponderantly from the rural areas. Of 1024 *instituteurs* and 933 *institutrices* who retired from service between 1866 and 1917, 550 came from peasant families in the mountainous areas to the east of the *département*. Only seventeen migrated from Grenoble and Vienne and less than a hundred came from small towns like Vizille, La Tour du Pin and St Marcellin.[7] Nearly two-thirds of them made their careers either in their native *communes* or in a nearby *commune* in their native *canton*. Only fifty-seven had originated from outside the *département*.

Politically the primary teaching force also fitted the Republican stereotype. In June 1911 the *préfet* estimated that more than half of the *instituteurs publics* subscribed to the Socialist *Le Droit du Peuple*.[8] Not surprisingly, with a tendency towards the political Left, and with constant emphasis on defensive patriotism in their teaching, the *instituteurs* of pre-war France increasingly attracted the attention of education and police authorities concerned that in the use of the common catchphrase *'aimez la France, détestez la guerre'* too much emphasis should not be placed on pacifism.

In the event their fears were to prove groundless, but it is small wonder that the patriotic and energetic devotion to duty of primary-school teachers during the mobilisation period was greeted by the authorities as something of a 'divine surprise'. By October 1914, 379 *instituteurs* in the Isère, some 45 per cent of the male primary teaching force, had departed without a murmur of dissent. 'From the first day of mobilisation', noted the *préfet*, 'our *instituteurs* called to the army have given us an example of courage and fortitude.' 'Far from causing obstructions,' reported *Le Petit Dauphinois* in November 1914, 'the mobilised *instituteurs* have shown by their *élan* a desire to banish the enemy which had hitherto been regarded as unthinkable. The anti-militarist of yesterday has become the standard-bearer of the quest to preserve our civilisation.'[9]

One should, though, beware of implying too dramatic a change from the peace-loving patriot to the model of bellicosity. Not all *instituteurs* and *institutrices* had placed the same amount of emphasis on defensive patriotism before the war, and certainly not all of them became ardent advocates of war during the hostilities. However it must be noted that throughout the entire war there was only one case of an *institutrice* in the Isère being arraigned for overtly pacifist views. Those teachers who remained at their posts therefore proved patriotic. It is hard to find evidence to contradict this self-congratulatory assessment by the Rector of the Academy of Grenoble after ten months of war:

> The French *instituteur* has played a fundamental role in our achievements since August 1914; a resolute mobilisation, the enthusiastic ardour and physical endurance of our soldiers, the patient resolve of our people without despair, a free but firm adhesion to civic as well as military discipline. Our brave *instituteurs publics* have formed and fashioned three-quarters of the armies of the Republic.[10]

Because of the encouraging behaviour of the *instituteurs* and *institutrices* during the mobilisation period, it was apparent, once the smoke and dust of the first months of campaigning had died away, that the central question was not so much the morale and patriotism of the teachers, but how they were to be most effectively used in maintaining morale and essential services in their localities. That they would play a vital role in this respect had been acknowledged from the outset. A Ministerial Decree of 1 August 1914 ordered all non-mobilisable teachers to remain in their localities and not take vacations elsewhere, despite the fact that the *rentrée* was still two months away. Since the rural teachers traditionally helped out with the harvest in the Dauphiné this was, in most cases, an unnecessary exhortation.

As educators of the young, teachers were ideally placed to impart propaganda, and in this they certainly did not lack instructions or guidance from above. The aim, according to a ministerial circular of July 1915, was that all areas of teaching should be submitted to the influence of the war. Morale and opinion must be mobilised around the 'moral force' of the country. The central theme of course was the national unity of France.

In every lesson some reference was to be made to the war. Children must be told clearly what their fathers, brothers and uncles were doing for France:

> What teacher, at the present time, could let a single day pass without speaking of the war? The children know that something terrible is happening. Explain to them the reasons for this war, that the German people have become insane, proud, arrogant, literally mad. They believe that their sole purpose in life is to help their country to dominate the world. Our brave *poilus* are

therefore defending not just France, but civilisation itself. Represent therefore the great nobility of the French *poilu*. Recite the acts of heroism. Read to your classes the letters of the soldiers. The children will find in them the three French virtues: love of *La Patrie*, courage and good humour.[11]

In music lessons patriotic songs were sung, such as '*La Marseillaise*', '*Le chant du départ*' and '*Les Hymnes des Alliés*'. There was no better way to teach children about the war than through geography and history lessons. Emphasis in these subjects changed from a world aspect to a concentration on France. Geography lessons, for example, consisted mainly of following the movements of the army on a map, using flags. Attention was paid to the great national resources of France and the vital need to defend them. In history pupils were taught the historical traditions of France and her role as the chief defender of liberty. Children were told that the invader had always come from the East. This obviously required a certain falsification of history. Popular imagery, therefore, substituted the Germans and Austrians for the Spaniards and the English. Whole eras in French history had to be omitted or glossed over. The Hundred Years' War, or the Habsburg–Valois rivalry of the early sixteenth century, clearly did not fit conveniently into the scheme of things. Not surprisingly, events in the current war were distorted. Verdun, for example, became a brilliant French victory with half a million Germans killed.

The teaching of languages also changed. German was dropped in favour of English and there was a much greater emphasis on Latin and Greek because of the stories of acts of courage and patriotism contained in the classical texts. As regards the French language, its establishment universally throughout France had of course been a fundamental aim of the educationalists of the early Third Republic, and this was given a renewed emphasis throughout the war. Subjects for French composition became increasingly concerned with the events of the war. Children were asked to remember their *vacances de guerre*, to write about their friends and families, brothers, fathers, uncles at the front. They were asked to write their own war poems, imagining themselves as soldiers at the front, or they were given a selection of situations and asked to write essays or compose dramatic reconstructions on them. For example: ' "The Germans have killed a small boy aged seven whom they found playing in a field with his toy gun" or "The Germans have invaded your town". Describe their actions and your feelings and those of your family towards the invaders.'[12]

Considerable importance was attached to physical education. The boys had to prepare for the rigours of military life. The girls had to be tough enough to follow their mothers into the fields. All types of sporting and fresh-air activities were encouraged: gymnastics, boy scoutism, rugby, soccer, swimming, cycling, walking and marching. To create and develop a strong and vigorous race, basic hygiene had to be emphasised. Starting at the youngest level, the *Inspectrice Générale des Ecoles Maternelles* went so far as to state that hygiene is the basis of the National Defence. Not only children, but also mothers in rural areas should be properly acquainted with, and educated in, good standards of hygiene.[13]

If the campaign for hygiene, against dirt and disease, was one element in the desire to safeguard the future of the race, an especially urgent consideration in wartime, so too was the campaign against alcoholism. Before the war this had largely been the preserve of the *nataliste* lobby. The connections between excessive drinking and a declining population had been a staple of moral and civics lessons in church and lay schools since the turn of the century. At the start of the war the military authorities had attacked the famous French institution, the *bistro*, and also the wine sellers, café proprietors and purveyors of all kinds of alcohol, as being a threat to the war effort. By 1915 and 1916 the local press was alleging that women and children, as well as men, were taking increasingly to spirits. Notable among them were the female munitions workers who, according to *Le Petit Dauphinois* and *La Croix de l'Isère*, with good wages in their pockets and their new sense of freedom, were following their male companions' example. It was not only the right-wing and clerical newspapers which were concerned about alcoholism: 'We are fighting two wars,' wrote Chastenet in *Le Droit du Peuple* in October 1915, 'against German militarism which would destroy us from without, and against alcohol which will destroy us from within.'[14]

Indeed instances of drunkenness amongst juveniles and adults did increase during the first two years of the war, but nothing like as dramatically as was suggested in the press. None the less the education authorities were sufficiently worried to redouble their efforts in the war against alcoholism. The report of the Inspector of the Academy of Grenoble for 1915 stated that, unfortunately, much of the good influence that school exerted on the young ones was often cancelled out by the bad example of their families, where the consumption of alcohol was very high, particularly in remote rural areas.[15] The aim therefore was, by consistent and determined teaching, to transmit some of the anti-alcohol propaganda through the children to their parents. By the beginning of 1917, 65 per cent of the primary schools in the Isère had organised their own anti-alcohol leagues, and anti-alcohol propaganda conferences for parents and teachers had been arranged in the *chef-lieu* of each *canton*, although, as the Inspector of the Academy lamented, those organised in the mountain *cantons* to the east had been rather poorly attended.[16]

The way the anti-alcohol campaign was conducted, by aiming at the parents through their children, shows how the authorities used school to disseminate important propaganda in the local community, an otherwise difficult task in remote areas where mothers and grandparents were dispersed throughout the community during the day, working in the fields, and where newspapers were scarce. In a letter of advice to the Rector of the Academy of Grenoble in April 1915, the Academic Inspector of the Isère urged that teachers must use their authority and local influence, never ceasing to use the idea of national unity and national defence:

Most parents and grandparents in the villages of the Dauphiné will not have had the same level of education that the young receive today. Teachers should therefore use simple slogans, tracts and brochures in explaining to the children the causes of the war, why we are fighting the war and why we will eventually win the war. The children should then be told to repeat these lessons in their own homes in the after-school hours, borrowing if possible the posters and brochures. In particular, simple dictations should be learnt off by heart in the classroom for the children to recite at home.[17]

Children were also told to copy down whole extracts from soldiers' letters which had been selected for 'particularly striking expressions'. Simple songs were learnt by rote to be repeated around the supper table in the evening. In this way important propaganda messages and themes were driven home to parents in the villages, in particular the reasons for price fluctuations and shortages of commodities like sugar, petrol and coal, the need to

make personal economic sacrifices, the demands on families to
subscribe to the various *journées* and especially the four *emprunts de
guerre*. Above all villagers learnt through their children why it
was important to hold out until the end, to carry on the *entr'aide*
and spirit of co-operation shown in August 1914, to maintain and
redouble their efforts in the fields, not to listen to pacifist speeches
or pay any attention to proposals for a premature peace; why,
in spite of (indeed, because of) the sacrifices of French life, it was
necessary to hold out until the Central Powers were totally and
irrevocably defeated.

It was all very crude and, like the constant barrage of *bourrage de
crâne* in the press, particularly stultifying: 'Recent progress in
teaching methods, especially moves towards a more child-centred
education, had hardly touched the remote areas of the Dauphiné,'
recalled one ex-*institutrice*, Marie Plissonier, who worked in the
village of Lavaldens during the war. She continued:

> In this respect, all that the war achieved in the field of education
> was a reinforcement of old-fashioned, boring dictation and rote-
> learning methods. Teachers were dictated to by the Ministry of
> Education, children were dictated to by the teachers and parents
> were dictated to by the children. [18]

Teaching in schools was, of course, only one of the vital jobs
performed by *instituteurs* and *institutrices* during the war, as Marie
Plissonier recalled:

> As a rough estimate, I would say that classroom lessons occu-
> pied no more than half of my time. Our village received very few
> newspapers, so the Municipality asked me to make several
> copies of the daily communiqués and distribute them to the
> outlying hamlets. Many of our older inhabitants were unable to
> read, so I would construct a map of the theatre of operations
> taken from the newspapers and communiqués and try to ex-
> plain, in so far as I was able, the movements of the armies.
> During the first months of the war I used to do this nightly in the
> school hall, and the sessions were eagerly attended at the begin-
> ning. However attendance gradually declined as the villagers
> lost interest in the day-to-day events of the war, and by 1916 the
> sessions were limited to Saturday evenings. I remember that
> there was a renewal of interest in spring 1916 during the fight for

Verdun, but by early summer this had subsided. I cannot remember the Somme campaign attracting much interest or attention, but that is possibly because the height of the battle coincided with the busy season.

During the long summer holidays I opened a *garderie* for around twenty of our very young children to keep them occupied during the day while their mothers worked. In the winter evenings I organised knitting campaigns for balaclavas, gloves and underwear for our soldiers. I would get the wool from the Municipality although this was always in short supply, and the mothers and grandmothers would come to the school hall where we had a small fire, and we would knit and gossip. I was really supposed to direct and lead the conversation in some way, to talk about the war and the success of our campaigns etc. In fact I rarely did so. I did not feel learned enough to talk with authority about this and, in any case, by the second year of the war most of us preferred to talk about local things, the sort of things that had always occupied us. Some of our less well-educated villagers used to dictate letters to me, to be sent to their husbands or brothers.

Our two *facteurs* had been mobilised, so I also had to help deliver letters. The job I hated the most was delivering bad news to the bereaved. The *maire* would inform me that 'x' had gone 'missing' or had been killed in action. I had to summon the courage to tell the family concerned. People reacted differently of course. Some received the news hysterically, but most reacted with a kind of numbed shock, as if they had expected it in some way. Several times I protested to the *maire* about having to do this, but he always insisted that, as a young woman, respected in the village, I was best qualified to console the bereaved, to soften the blow as it were. Our village of around four hundred people lost thirty of our menfolk killed during the war.[19]

In fact Marie Plissonier was lucky that the local *maire* and *adjoint* had not been mobilised and the municipal council had been reduced by only two. In many *communes* the *instituteur* or *institutrice* had virtually to take over the local administration in addition to teaching. This, as has already been seen, involved dealing with refugees, hospital beds, *bons de réquisition*, lists of poor and needy, postal services and so on. The historian is indeed fortunate that so many of them managed to find time to make notes and reports during the war. In fact every one of the reports conserved in the archives indicates vital extra-curricular activities of some kind, organising *soupes populaires* for example, during the period before the formal institution of the *allocations*.

There was, not surprisingly, a certain sexist aspect to the division of extra-curricular labour within the rural teaching force. If the *institutrice*, like Marie Plissonier, was expected to use soft words and the gentle touch to console the bereaved, to organise knitting campaigns and mobilise village gossip to patriotic ends, it was the *instituteur*'s job actively to develop and encourage the *esprit guerrier* amongst the local male youths approaching mobilisable age. It was he, working in conjunction with the *maire* and the municipal council, who organised the evening rifle clubs, arranged gymnastic displays, invited veterans of 1870 to give guest lectures and so on. 'Twice a week', wrote an *instituteur* of Monestier du Percy, 'the young men of fourteen to seventeen years of age come to the rifle range improvised in the school playground. The sessions last for an hour, and afterwards the older ones take coffee and lemonade while we discuss the latest war news.'[20] Sometimes the *instituteur* would collaborate with wounded soldiers in organising concerts and festivals in the school playground for their profit. Such a concert held at Vizille in August 1915 attracted some 250 people, who were entertained by a choir of the town's primary-school children and songs and recitals composed by various soldiers. After a speech by the *maire* and two *instituteurs* on the usual themes of herosim, sacrifices and *Union Sacrée*, a collection was organised which yielded 375 *francs*.[21]

A highlight in the smaller villages was the return of a local *poilu*, usually an ex-pupil of the local primary school on leave from the front. Despite restrictions on what he was allowed to divulge, and the fact that he was likely to be as ignorant of the actual state of hostilities as the civilian population, the *poilu* could offer some useful advice to the young men in the locality preparing for their own mobilisation. The *instituteur* could also use him to liven up his lessons in school for the younger children, with tales of derring-do and the heroic exploits of the local *Chasseurs Alpins*. To the older boys, specially invited to the lessons, he could offer practical advice on such matters as the best way to preserve body heat in sub-zero temperatures, how to keep down the rat population in the trenches, the best way to while away the long periods of inactivity during rest periods from front-line trenches and so on.

The more garrulous *poilus* might spend the evenings of their leave in the local café, as at Sechilienne or Livet, being plied with drinks and recounting their exploits in the trenches.[22] This of course depended on the disposition of the *poilu*, and as the war dragged on the free drinks paid diminishing returns as it became harder to find *permissionnaires* willing to talk about the war at all, let alone in enthusiastic terms. Like Henri Barbusse's *poilus*, many just wanted to forget, temporarily at least, their experiences. Moreover the civilian population, sated with war talk, were losing interest. As one *Grenoblois* recalled:

> I had no interest in glorifying the war. I was asked by my old teacher to tell a class of children about my recent experiences at Verdun. I refused, not wanting to disillusion them. I knew that if I told them the truth they would not be interested and probably would not believe me anyway. In any case I would be reported to the military authorities and my leave would be terminated.[23]

There is indeed some indication that by 1916 children were becoming bored with constant war talk and war lessons. 'My pupils are becoming listless,' complained an *instituteur* at Rives in June 1916, 'they no longer ask enthusiastic questions as they did a year ago.'[24]

The demands on the local *instituteur* and *institutrice* were therefore great, although much of what was actually taught in class required an intensification and adaptation of existing subject matter and methods, a matter of adjusting degree and emphasis rather than a fundamental change. It was, in theory, a fairly straightforward task to adapt the curriculum and organisation of the most centralised education system in Europe to the demands of war propaganda. What complicated the task beyond measure and made its accomplishment difficult to achieve was the sheer disruption and dislocation caused to the Education Service, which suffered considerably from the effects of general mobilisation. The most serious problem was the mobilisation of male teachers. Much of the influence the primary-school teacher exerted upon the community, and hence the likelihood of propaganda efforts succeeding, depended of course on his or her personal popularity and long-standing relationship with the local inhabitants. As has been seen, roughly one-sixth of the entire primary teaching force of the Isère had departed, and while it can be imagined that the removal

of a particularly unpopular or incompetent teacher might have been
greeted with a collective sigh of relief, the lack of adequate, experienced replacements could seriously impair the propaganda effort.

As in industry, replacements had to come from the ranks of old
retired teachers or, predominantly, from new female recruits to the
profession. This in itself was no problem since the trend from the
turn of the century had been for females to replace males in
primary teaching. The real problem was the lack of adequately
trained or experienced *institutrices* in the Isère during 1914, 1915
and 1916. This was aggravated by the Education Service's re-
deployment programme. A disproportionately large percentage of
instituteurs had been mobilised from the larger towns like Grenoble,
Vienne and Voiron, and priority was given to the towns by
relocating experienced teachers from the villages. Thus it was the
more remote rural areas which suffered most from mobilisation at a
time when demands made upon the local teacher were greatest. In
exchange for a well-established, popular and experienced teacher,
usually a native of the locality, many villages had to accept
nineteen- or twenty-year-old probationary *institutrices* or, in some
cases, pupil teachers who had yet to finish their period of training.
Even this was not sufficient to make up the numbers; in 1915 five
instituteurs were taken out of retirement and forty-three *institutrices*
were given their first post, and in 1916 there were forty-nine new
institutrices and five re-employed *instituteurs*. Of the new *institutrices* during the first two years of war, only thirty had the *brevet
supérieur*, the minimum desirable qualification for a primary-school
teacher, and thirteen had no formal qualification whatsoever
beyond the basic *brevet élémentaire*. These were nearly all posted to
schools in rural *communes* in the *département*.[25] By the end of 1916
the primary teaching force in public education was eighty-six down
on it summer-1914 figure.[26] Indeed the pre-war figure was not
regained until 1919.

The average salary of probationary *institutrices*, class five, in
elementary primary schools was thirty *francs* per week by the end
of 1916, and for those teaching in *écoles supérieures*, forty-three *francs*
per week, which compared favourably with the thirty to thirty-five
francs per week, including bonuses, which could be earned on
munitions work. The onerous conditions of work, complexity and
immensity of the duties required, and the considerable administrative tasks, undoubtedly deterred many would-be *institutrices*. Marie
Plissonier claimed that she would never have entered the profession

during the war had she been able to foresee what was involved. Moreover young women from the villages had, more than ever, to work on the farms and help out in the home at a time of serious general labour shortage.

Another serious problem was the requisitioning of school buildings for use by the army as warehouses, lodgings for POWs and refugees and as temporary military hospitals. By the end of August 1914 fifty-seven schools, nearly half of them in rural areas, had been taken over for the duration, and although some were returned to the Education Service in 1915, thirty-two of them were still *hors de combat* in mid-1916. This meant that the school had either to move to another location, which in small villages was scarcely possible, or to share the premises with the military authorities, which would often mean all the classes being taken in one or two small rooms while the children shared the building with wounded soldiers and convalescents, clearly an undesirable state of affairs from the point of view of morale. If other premises could be found they were likely to be inadequate, without proper facilities for teaching or basic hygiene. In extreme cases several classes ran concurrently in the same small room with children perched on desks or sitting on the floor. The disruptions produced some absurd teaching situations from the point of view of pupil–teacher ratios, and mixed age and ability teaching. In the village of Clavans, for example, one young *institutrice* of six months' standing had simultaneously to occupy, interest, educate and maintain discipline among a class of seventy-five children ranging from the age of six to fifteen, the older ones being a group of Belgian refugee children.[27]

To maintain standards as well as successfully disseminate propaganda would, in the circumstances, have required a degree of experience, devotion, strength of character and personality, levels of willpower and energy bordering on the superhuman, certainly beyond the capacity of the average twenty-year-old novice *institutrice*. Naturally some teachers cracked under the strain. The Education Service had added to the burden by maintaining, through the local *maire*, its constant and careful watch over the patriotism and morals of the teacher. It was reluctant to dismiss incompetent classroom teachers during the war because of the shortage of replacements. There were only five sackings in the Isère between 1915 and the end of the war, and the number of disciplinary measures taken against 'unsatisfactory' teachers fell from a pre-war annual average of thirty-one to twenty-three. The Education Service tended simply to shunt an unsatisfactory teacher from village to village. More often than not, because of the hypocritical double standards of sexual morality that prevailed, it was the 'immorality' of the young *institutrice* rather than her inability as a classroom teacher that caused most concern. One can, for example, sympathise with the young *institutrice* from Saint Antoine who, having lost her husband at the Marne, was reported in 1915 as having 'advanced views' and 'cavorting with local *permissionnaires*, not behaving like a woman should'. Apparently by 1916 she was drinking three litres of wine a day and was even seen imbibing in front of the children. Despite her being, by all accounts, a good teacher, with her classes showing real progress, local parents' complaints were such that she was shunted around six villages before the Service, with the partial return of *instituteurs* in 1919, found a pretext to dismiss her from the service.[28]

All in all, then, the role of the village primary-school teacher was a crucial one during the war and there is little evidence that, with a few obvious exceptions, they performed their duties in other than heroic fashion. For once one need not be too cynical when reading the annual panegyric on the *instituteur* in the reports of the Inspector of the Academy, of which this one for 1916–17 is typical:

Who has worked harder for the National Defence than our brave *instituteurs* and *institutrices*? With no complaints they have thrown themselves into their duties and responded, year in, year out to the needs of France during her gravest crisis. In the villages particularly, they have done the work of five or six people. When the hour of victory finally comes our people, our statesmen and politicians will have cause to be most grateful and will do well to acknowledge the contribution of our teachers to the victory.[29]

THE CATHOLIC CHURCH AND THE *UNION SACRÉE*

Less influential in the Isère generally, but still important for disseminating propaganda, maintaining morale and giving practical aid to the war effort, was the Catholic Church. Its role and position, however, was far more complicated and less clear cut than that of the laic Education Service. The extent to which the individual *curé* or *vicaire* could be useful in this respect obviously depended on the strength of religious feeling, faith and practice in his particular parish. It is extremely difficult to measure this accurately since there was no precise *sondage* of attendance at mass in the Isère until 1952. Moreover support for church pilgrimages and the like tended to vary according to season, making it difficult to assess fluctuations in religious fervour. Nor can one place much emphasis on numbers of baptisms or confirmations since, by the turn of the century, it had become customary for many parents simply to baptise their children and have no more contact with the church or its officials until first communion, marriage or death.[30] Finally, of course, there is the near impossibility of assessing accurately the degree of private, as opposed to church-going or public, worship. One is left therefore with highly impressionistic contemporary assessments, subscriptions to the clerical press, contributions to church collections and the like.

'The people of the Isère', wrote the *préfet* in 1914, 'can be called Catholic but anti-clerical. Few of them refuse the church sacrament for baptism, first communion, marriage and funerals, but few bother to attend mass regularly. They would rather worship in private than go to church to listen to the *curé*. Many village churches in the Bas Dauphiné are habitually empty, while others for the most part attract only the women. The men seem to be indifferent.'[31]

This was a generalisation. In fact many mountain *cantons* in the Vercors (Corps, Monestier-de-Clermont, Villard de Lans and St Laurent du Pont) seem to have attracted more than half of their menfolk to church services at Easter, and those in the Oisans up to 40 per cent.[32] Most commentators agree, however, that the percentage of women attending various church services and functions was considerably higher. Undoubtedly there still existed parishes where the *curé* held sway over a captive church audience, as in the monastery parish of Chartreuse, but there seems to be little doubt that religious practice in rural areas was on the decline during the Third Republic, as attested by successive lamentations, particularly after 1905, by the Bishop of Grenoble in the *Semaines Religieuses* of the diocese. By 1914, in the industrial towns of the Isère, it seems that amongst the male working-class population indifference to public forms of worship had become the norm, as it had for the majority of traders, shopkeepers and *petits fonctionnaires*, but less so for the *haute bourgeoisie*. Again, women remained considerably more faithful than men.[33]

The fundamental problem of the French Catholic Church during the war was how to accommodate the necessary internationalism and neutrality of the Pope, while simultaneously sustaining its own credibility among the population as an ardent and sincerely patriotic institution dedicated to the upholding of the *Union Sacrée* and the final victory of France. Doctrinally and politically, with Catholics in all belligerent countries, the Pope could neither give his official blessing to the war, nor support one side against another. Thus Pius X and Benedict XV, in devoting the resources and prestige of their position to securing international peace, if necessary a negotiated peace, laid themselves open to the charge of being pro-German or anti-French. The Popes' stance angered the French population and confused Catholics, who believed that right was on their side and that they were fighting a just war against a nation that had violated their territory. This apparent contradiction and fundamental confusion acted as a powerful counterweight to the effectiveness of the nationalist and *jusqu'au-boutiste* propaganda disseminated by the clerical press.

The cleft stick that the church hierarchy found itself in – the desire to support the war effort against Germany and the need to obey the Papacy – helps to explain the notion of *la guerre purificatrice*, the official and intellectual position of the church in France throughout the war. The expiatory nature of the war (*le châtiment de la guerre*) had to be stressed equally with the wickedness of the Germans and the need to destroy Prussian militarism. France's sufferings and sacrifices were a judgement from above. God's church had, for some years, suffered persecution and attack from those who represented the State. France must now suffer fully the sacrifices of war as a form of penance.

It was not just the forces of irreligion as perpetrated by the State for which France was now paying penance. The root cause was the sickness of modern society, four aspects of which were listed by Benedict XV in an encyclical, printed in *La Semaine Religieuse* on 3 December 1914. They were: racial hatred, distrust of authority and lack of respect for the fundamental institution of the family, the class hatred which was seen as the corollary of the industrial age, and, fundamentally, lack of morality and self-discipline, especially among the young.[34] Two months later the Bishop of Grenoble elaborated on this in a pastoral letter to the parishes of his diocese:

It is not God who wanted this war. He is the God of peace, but He has left freedom in the hands of men, and this freedom has been used badly. It has become a formidable instrument of ruin. France, not God, is guilty.[35]

It would of course be a serious mistake for the Catholic hierarchy to proclaim too publicly and place too much emphasis on the guilt of France. A reason must be given for fighting the Germans. This statement by the bishop was the closest approximation of a compromise between the internationalism of the Papacy and the nationalism of patriotic French Catholics:

If France has been tainted by the modern sickness, Germany has it in abundance; a militaristic ruling caste, a class-riven society, a degenerate and immoral youth and a desire to impose her values on a Christian world. Since 1870, Germany has created in France the doctrine of anti-clericalism.[36]

Against this the church needed to substitute the theme of divine protection, a form of 'just war', for that of revolutionary Jacobinism. This was difficult, of course, in view of the neutrality of God and the Papacy. However, in the process of paying penance for the sins committed against the church during the Third Republic, France would rediscover its 'soul'. It would become 'purified'. God would bestow His mercy on the country, for after victory a new start would be made. France would thus be rebuilt, morally and socially. The war, in acting as a cleansing agent, would rid France and Europe not just of the evils of Prussian militarism, but also the worst evils of modern civilisation. France and, by implication, Europe generally, would return to God. In a war which would be short but terrible, France would, in other words, be leading a crusade for the return to the fundamental values: a stable family life and love of God.

Thus, by reiterating traditional themes and arguments, the French Catholic hierarchy took up its official position on the war. The idea of war as chastisement was of course a staple of church ideology. It was to be stressed emphatically after the *débâcle* of 1940 and during the Vichy régime, and had been used after the defeat of 1870. For decades the church had preached against what it saw as the evil excesses of modern civilisation: the rural depopulation and the drift towards godless, overcrowded, alcohol- and vice-ridden towns, the decline of patriarchal values of the family, the bitter class conflict perpetrated by Socialist ideology, the immorality and growing indiscipline of young people, the decline in church attendances, and so on.

However, with the outbreak of war church leaders could claim to be vindicated, for, during the first few months of hostilities, reports came from a number of sources suggesting increased attendance at mass. The bishop exclaimed joyfully:

Who has failed to notice at Grenoble and Vienne, as everywhere, a great revival of religious feeling and faith. More people are going to mass, people are praying publicly, especially in the evenings. What a beautiful sight. At the front and in the rear, the people of France have returned to God. [37]

The obvious point to make about the religious revival during the early months of the war is that one should not try to make too much of it. It was surely to be expected that, at a time of heightened uncertainty, anxiety, tension and fear for the fate of loved ones should induce people to pray; an orthodox manifestation, as it were, of the general mysticism of August and September 1914. It is also difficult to distinguish genuine religious conviction in the use of religious terminology employed by propagandists of all persuasions: the *Union Sacrée*, patriotic 'faith', the 'soul' of *La Patrie*, the 'miracle' of the Marne and so on. Louise Perrin, herself an ardent and practising Catholic, was rather sceptical about the quality of this new-found faith. In September 1914 she wrote to Henri that:

On Sundays, our church is regularly full, even on weekday mornings before work there are many more people than usual. It is comforting to know that we can all turn to God at a time of need, but I wonder how long it will last. [38]

Henri Perrin, at the front, remarked that many of his platoon comrades were praying, not to save their souls, but to save their bodies. 'We are all scared, terrified. In these times it is natural for all men to pray, even those who haven't been to church for years.' [39] By the end of February 1915, however, Henri was noting that during the long rest periods out of the front-line trenches and away from immediate danger the men were praying far less, 'as if they forgot about God away from the scenes of battle'.[40] J. L. Chastenet, writing in *Le Droit du Peuple* on Christmas Eve 1914, while admitting that the churches had recently been fuller than they had been since the mid-nineteenth century, attempted to put the whole phenomenon into perspective: 'people pray out of fear. As more and more people become accustomed to this war which we hope and believe will soon end, we will see fewer people in church and things will return to normal.'[41]

Indeed this was the church leaders' great fear, that acclimatisation should lead to a return to the old pre-war irreligious and 'pagan' values. From spring 1915 onwards *La Croix* and *Le Dimanche Catholique* regularly exhorted *curés* to redouble their efforts in their parishes, warning that immorality and indiscipline amongst young people, especially in the towns, was on the increase, and linking this with a noticeable drop in attendance at mass. After a year of war the Bishop of Grenoble, who had visited all of the 595 parishes in his diocese, had his own doubts about the sincerity of the earlier resurgence of religious activity:

> Recently, particularly in the valleys and towns, I have noticed that young people are becoming accustomed to the talk of death and destruction. They are getting too used to the war. Several parishes have nearly empty churches at mass on Sundays, whereas a few months ago they were reported as being full. We cannot endure the sacrifices if we start to turn away from God or to forget our religious duties. Let us go back to the serious habits of the first months of the war.[42]

In Vienne, by July 1915, Louise Perrin was noting that attendance at Sunday mass was more or less reduced to the 'old faithfuls'.[43] This was also noted by the *préfet* in January 1916: 'in many villages people have stopped going to mass or attending church functions. They are either praying privately or not at all.'[44] As the clerical press took on a more desperate tone in its exhortations, the *curés* themselves reported difficulties in their parishes. The attendance at midnight mass on Christmas Eve 1915 was less than half that of 1914, noted the *curé* at Roybons.[45] The *vicaire* at Saint Pancrasse, commenting in 1917 on the steady decline in attendance at church since the beginning of 1915 (unrelieved even at particular times of crisis such as the Champagne Offensives of

1915 and the first weeks of Verdun in 1916), complained that his parishioners were becoming more indifferent to religious ceremonies, even to burials of local *poilus* killed in action:

> Since 1914 there have been six of our sons buried in our village. The first two ceremonies were attended by nearly all of our parishioners who were able to come. They listened intently to my speeches and prayed fervently with me. At the last two burials, in December last year, 1916, not only were there far fewer villagers at the funerals, but I noticed that nearly half of the mourners waited outside the church in the way that they used to before the war.[46]

The general impression then is that the new-found religious faith gradually evaporated throughout 1915 and 1916. There is no indication of any sudden resurgence at moments of particular crisis, such as the Verdun campaign in 1916, and the decline was more noticeable in towns than in villages. It was not until the end of the war and the return to peace that the church hierarchy suffered a real crisis of morale, but there seems to be no doubt that the church had failed to sustain the mood of the first few months. Of course 'religious faith' in this context refers to public manifestations of worship and devotion. The number of people who worshipped privately can never be known, but it is reasonable to surmise that religious faith, whether 'rediscovered' or not, continued to sustain the morale, and in some cases the sanity, of anxious civilians throughout the war. It was certainly an essential prop for Catholics like the Perrins of Vienne, whose letters to each other to and from the front are studded with references to God.

Why, though, this apparent decline in public demonstrations of faith, and particularly in institutional forms of worship? The answer must be found in the increasing difficulties the church faced the longer the war lasted. In the first place it was probably more affected than industry, agriculture or the Education Service by the mobilisation of its personnel, for of course it could not call upon female replacements. This exacerbated a crisis of recruitment that had been felt particularly since the separation of Church and State at the beginning of the century. On the eve of the war the Diocese of Grenoble had 319 practising *curés* and 197 pupils in three seminaries. During the war 303 *curés* and sixty-eight seminarists were mobilised, accounting for nearly all the clergy under forty-six years of age. In addition to this thirty-seven professors at the seminaries were mobilised and courses had to be suspended. As a result 157 of the 595 parishes were deprived of their *curé* and sixty-five others lost one, two or three *vicaires*.[47] This left only the old or sick *curés*, many of whom found themselves charged with two or three parishes at a time when propaganda functions were added to sacerdotal ones. The church simply lacked the personnel to take full advantage of the upsurge in religious feeling in 1914. Confessions were irregular, the young and presumably more dynamic preachers had departed, and public prayer sessions in the absence of the *curé* were no substitute for the real thing.

The second and more serious problem stemmed from the ambiguity of the church's position on the war, for this was couched in such a way as to make the *curé*'s task of upholding the *Union Sacrée* in his locality an extremely difficult one. It was one thing for the Archbishop of Lyon or the Bishop of Grenoble to proclaim publicly in the Catholic press the need to undergo chastisement and great sacrifice in order to pay for the sins of France; it was quite another for the local *curé* to convince his parishioners that the church was not out simply to use the *bouleversements* of the war in order to reconquer lost souls or attract converts. It needed a particularly influential *curé* with a strong personality to counter successfully the *rumeur infâme*, according to which the church was partly responsible for the war and wanted the defeat of France. The logic of this accusation was that the *curés* had wanted the war in order to bring chastisement, and that this would only be fully achieved if France was defeated. The problem for the *curé* was that the terms of reference employed by the church in pronouncing a *Union Sacrée* were contradictory and self-defeating. Logically the *curé* could only preach *Union Sacrée* to his parishioners by reference to past sins and attacks against the church by local Socialists and anti-clericals. In the heady days of August and September, when the *Patrie* was in danger and the mingled moods of mysticism, fear of the unknown, anxiety and sense of outrage fitted well the concept of national unity and harmony, one did not probe too deeply the motives of the clergy, but when the immediate danger to France seemed to have been overcome after the Battle of the Marne, the church's position and its participation in the *Union Sacrée* began to be questioned.

As might be expected, it was in the Socialist press that the first signs of attack on the clergy appeared. It was the clergy's understanding and 'misuse' of the *Union Sacrée* which came under fire. On 2 October 1914 Chastenet, in *Le Droit du Peuple*, proudly proclaimed that Socialists were sticking firmly to the *Union Sacrée*, but accused reactionary *curés* of profiting from the circumstances to dispense their own propaganda. On 14 October *Le Droit* started a daily scandal-mongering column on an inside page entitled '*peut-on le dire?*', in which anonymous snippets of scandal from the localities were printed. Many of these 'anonymous' letters were undoubtedly journalistic inventions, or at least wild exaggerations, but the point is that they served to damage the reputation and weaken the influence of the *curés* locally by confirming suspicions or reawakening old pre-war anti-clerical prejudices. More serious, because it was rooted in fact, was the charge against the *Curé* of Montalieu who, in November 1915, was condemned by the *Tribunal* of Bourgoin to three months' prison and fined two hundred *francs* for uttering defeatist sentiments susceptible of causing panic in the population. Although the bishop defended the *curé* publicly by stating that the Socialists were equally pessimistic or defeatist, he was forced to admit that the *curé* had been 'over-zealous' in stressing the religious aspects of the war.

It was not just anti-clerical journalists who attacked the clergy. The general correspondence of the *préfecture* throughout 1915 and 1916 contains many letters, again most of them anonymous, written to the *préfet* complaining about the attitudes and activities of the local *curé* or *vicaire*. They had a common theme: the *curé* was an 'agent' of the Germans or was using the war either to procure money for the local church or to procure 'souls' in order to indoctrinate them.

It seems that the clergy could not win. Their practical contributions to the war effort were subject to misinterpretations or wilful distortions, while in their sermons even those sincerely patriotic clergymen like the *Curé* of Vizille, who disregarded the more obvious ambiguities of the church's position and opted for a purely patriotic and chauvinistic approach, were accused by Radicals and Socialists of excessive jingoism calculated to warp permanently the minds of the young.[48] Those, like the *Curé* at Bourg d'Oisans, who studded his sermons with too many references to death and sacrifice, ran the risk of being accused, with the *Curé* of Montalieu, of defeatism or, at best, of excessive morbidity.[49]

In actual fact, despite all the difficulties the church faced, it did make some useful contributions to the war effort. The Bishop of

Grenoble envisaged the role of the village *curé* as being the spiritual equivalent of the *instituteur public*:

> He must know how to explain to the women the grandeur of the cause for which their husbands are fighting. He is an agent of liaison between God and the peasants. In his church at weekly mass or evening prayers, he must become the centrepiece of the union of all his parishioners. He must dispense God's mercy, comfort the bereaved and use the influence of his position to act in the interests of *La Patrie* in securing the victory, in particular by organising and encouraging works of charity and by using the pulpit to encourage parishioners to subscribe to *emprunts*, to welcome wounded soldiers and refugees.[50]

The basis of the church's contribution in village parishes was the *œuvre de guerre*, usually a knitting campaign for the soldiers, or collections made at church ceremonies, baptisms, weddings, special pilgrimages and so on. Initially, in accordance with the *Union Sacrée*, these were to be organised in conjunction with the municipalities and the local *instituteur* or *institutrice*. Starting in September 1914, however, the church organised its own form of *œuvre de guerre: L'Association Catholique de Secours aux Blessés et d'Assistance par le Travail*. In the village parishes, clothes, blankets and other such donations were regularly sent to the local church, to be despatched either to the front or to military hospitals. In addition monthly house-to-house collections were made in the parishes by the *curé*, aided by local Catholic ladies. It was this organisation, administered by the church alone, which eventually provoked the charges that the clergy were breaking the *Union Sacrée* by using the war for their own propaganda purposes, and by failing to cooperate with local secular authorities.

The figures for parish donations to the *Association* are revealing, although there are too many variations to consider for definite conclusions to be drawn. Financial donations depended of course on the ability to pay, the degree of competition from other charities and *œuvres de guerre*, the time of year, the persistence and availability of the collectors and so on. Obviously, richer parishes, with more people to devote time to evening collections, could subscribe more than the poorer ones. None the less the variations in figures make interesting reading and do permit some assumptions about fluctuations in morale and strength of pro- or anti-clerical feeling in the localities. There was, for instance, a downward trend in weekly subscriptions to the *Association* between September 1914 and December 1916, even in the village parishes which could be deemed the most religious. There is a noticeable correlation between the politics of the municipality and the total subscription of the parish. The Radical Socialist *commune* of Cras, for example, devoted only two *francs* to the *Association* in September 1914 and nothing at all from March 1915 onwards, whereas a *quête* organised by the *institutrice* in the name of the local municipality and under the auspices of the *Union Sacrée* raised a remarkable forty-three *francs* at the end of September 1914.[51] In the conservative municipality of St Pierre d'Entrement, 133 *francs* were raised for the *Association Catholique* in September 1914 while only twenty-seven *francs* were donated in a house-to-house collection by senior children of the local primary school two days earlier.[52]

Clearly the implication of figures like these is that, from an early date, subscribers in the villages were either adhering or reverting to pre-war traditions, prejudices and allegiances, disregarding the *Union Sacrée* or, more commonly, interpreting it in a fashion that suited them. It was on these *quêtes*, particularly those organised by the church, that the first resumptions of traditional rivalries and political hostilities took place. Indeed, from the end of 1914, *quêtes* and other *œuvres de guerre* organised by the church tended to be set up in competition with those organised by the municipality, or vice versa. In September 1914 at Le Sappey one elderly Catholic lady collecting for the *Association Catholique* was greeted with catcalls and verbal abuse as she entered a café, while another, in the same parish, was told that the Pope was wealthy enough without 'the good, patriotic citizens of this *commune* adding to his riches'.[53] More frequently there were variations on the theme of the church being in league with the Kaiser, as at La Morette in December 1914 and at Tullins in March 1915.[54] Of course vituperative abuse was not the preserve solely of the anti-clericals. One *institutrice* who addressed a small gathering in the village of St Bardille et Pipet, prior to organising a *quête* in the name of the *Union Sacrée*, was told by several hecklers that they would rather subscribe to the devil himself.[55]

The *curé* in his village parish and the bishop writing in *La Semaine Religieuse* both contributed indirectly to the misfortunes of the Catholic Church during the war. Each in his own way made it only too obvious that the church was going to use the *Union Sacrée* for its own ends. Each fed rather too easily the pre-war anti-clerical prejudices of the *Dauphinois*. It is hardly surprising that the first cracks in the *Union Sacrée* came through the old Church–State rivalry, and these cracks began to appear after only a few weeks of war.

THE ISOLATION OF ANTI-WAR OPPOSITION

On 18 February 1916, surveying morale and public opinion in his *arrondissement* after eighteen months of war, the *Sous-préfet* of Vienne noted that everywhere the population was confident about the final outcome. Signs of war weariness were exceptional and confined largely to individuals. In both town and countryside the public, disappointed that the war had not been terminated quickly after the victory of the Marne, had come to accept that hostilities would last some time yet and were 'quietly optimistic that the resources of the Allies and the economic difficulties experienced by the Germans will soon bring the final victory'. The public accepted that the war must be fought to the very end, until German militarism was totally crushed, and that the year 1916 would see events turning finally and irrevocably to the Allies' advantage.

In the *Arrondissement* of La Tour du Pin the state of morale was equally satisfactory and there was a profound conviction that the war would be won by the end of 1916. There was little indication of disillusion about the length of the war. 'With their usual common sense', noted the *sous-préfet*, 'our people have understood that the war will be long and that victory will go to the side which can hold out the longest. They believe that with the help of the British and Russians, and France's ability to provide its own food in great quantity, we can sustain the war better than the Germans.' Mentions of 'peace at any price' were rare and confined to isolated individual cases. The *sous-préfet* agreed with his colleague at Vienne that the speedy introduction of *allocations* for the needy, works of public charity and mutual assistance, profits made by peasant farmers and care and solace given to wounded soldiers and soldiers on leave had contributed greatly towards the mainten-ance of morale.

At St Marcellin the state of morale continued to be 'excellent', although here there was slightly more concern about the unex-pected length of the war. Again, however, the conviction that the

Allies would finally win was 'almost unanimous' despite the
occasional grumble about shortages and rising prices.[56]

Nine months later, at the end of a year which had seen the most
disastrous bloodletting battle in French history, the *préfet* wrote to
the Minister of the Interior that, in general, the morale of the
civilian population of the Isère remained 'satisfactory'. In the larger
towns like Grenoble, Vienne and Voiron there were occasional
murmurings about the need for 'peace at any price', mainly from
soldiers on leave or workers of 'advanced opinions' in textile and
metallurgical factories, but opposition to the war as such was still
isolated and confined to individuals. The great mass of the local
population was still confident that the next few months would see
the final victory although there were some signs of disappointment
in the towns that the past year had not seen the expected
breakthrough. In the villages and small towns there was almost
total unanimity about the need to crush the Germans militarily
before peace could be considered.[57]

The implication of these reports is that the population in both
town and countryside were more concerned about the preserva-
tion of material conditions of existence than questioning the
validity and righteousness of a conflict which had already brought
indescribable suffering to many. These impressions are supported
by a study of the contents of letters between civilians and soldiers.
From the end of 1915 the military authorities, in order to keep a
closer surveillance of the morale of the nation, exercised a *contrôle
postal* in each military region. This involved regular opening of
samples of letters to and from the front, and provides a useful
guide to the state of morale generally and to day-to-day preoccupations of both soldiers and civilians.[58]

In the Fourteenth Military Region there were certain similarities
of opinion between the front and the rear. In their letters both
sectors showed only a transitory interest in major events of the war
– Verdun, the Somme and the Brusilov Offensive – reaching the
similar opinion by mid-1916 that the unexpected length of the
Verdun campaign was a good sign since the Germans had counted
on a swift victory and a clear march to Paris. Morale generally
seemed to fluctuate simultaneously in both sectors with respect to
the events of the war. There was, for example, a simultaneous
acceptance of the likelihood of a third winter campaign by August
and September; there seemed to be unanimous optimism and faith
in the Romanian intervention on the Allied side. There was,

however, a slight divergence at the end of the year as soldiers appeared to be more resolved than civilians to face the rigours of a third winter of war. Soldiers and civilians alike remained preoccupied with material conditions or day-to-day existence. Throughout the year the majority of complaints from soldiers concerned lack of *permissions*, the bad state of the trenches, particularly in winter, boredom with life away from the front line, and so on. Local news and gossip figured strongly in the letters of civilians. Agricultural matters (prospects for the harvest, current local prices) and complaints about requisitions and lack of labour dominated village letters. In a number of cases complaints about requisitions developed into complaints about the local administration generally. Jealousy, either between one family and another or between neighbouring villages, was a feature of the letters, particularly on the subject of refugee quotas and requisitions which appeared to have been unfairly distributed by certain *maires*. In the letters from townspeople local gossip also predominated, but there was more discussion about wages in munitions factories. A detailed study of the 400-odd letters exchanged between Henri and Louise Perrin in 1915 bears this out. More than 85 per cent of Louise's letters were concerned with family preoccupations, local gossip about neighbours in Vienne, and practical business affairs, for instance asking Henri for important advice on managing the ironmongery. Only a very small minority of her letters made any reference to current military events or international affairs. Not one of them questioned the validity of the conflict or the reasons for the war.

In general there was increasing civilian concern with economic factors throughout 1916. Significantly *jusqu'au-boutisme* – a conviction of the need to fight the war until ultimate total victory – was a constant and firmly-entrenched theme in all the correspondence. Most remarkable is the almost total lack of reference to pacifist propaganda or Socialist slogans. There were only rare mentions of such concepts as 'no peace with annexations'. Alsace and Lorraine, for example, were never mentioned, it being assumed that they would automatically return to France after the victory.[59]

Close inspection of sources likely to be more in tune with local opinion in towns and villages – letters from *maires* and individual farmers and workers, anonymous letters to the *préfet*, reports of local police *commissaires, instituteurs'* reports – does suggest that direct opposition to the war, particularly in rural areas during 1915 and 1916, was isolated and confined to individuals or small groups.

Instances of pacifist sentiments developing among the population and favourable reactions to peace initiatives suggested by Socialists, pessimists or anti-militarists were rare during this period and there is no evidence of pacifism assuming a collective identity sufficient to alarm the authorities unduly.

By themselves, individual examples of anti-war feeling have little significance. In any war there are bound to be voices raised against violence and bloodshed, questions asked about the reason for fighting, criticism of Government and military authorities' direction of affairs and so on. In the small towns and villages isolated anti-war expressions were recorded soon after the Marne crisis of September 1914. The point is that they elicited no sympathetic response from the local population and therefore remained isolated.

Anti-war or anti-militarist expressions might be expected to carry some weight if they were uttered by soldiers on leave from the front, for the *poilu* on active service was still regarded as a local hero. However, at St Verund in May 1915, a local *mobilisé* newly-returned to begin a seven-day leave was booed and molested by an angry crowd after making a violent anti-war, anti-Government speech: 'at the front, my comrades and I will soon turn our guns on our officers. We are the dupes of the capitalists, of the English and the Russians. There will be revolution soon if they don't put a stop to this slaughter.' A *garde champêtre* and two local youths had to intervene to prevent him being severely mauled by the crowd. In the opinion of the *Commissaire de Police*, the people of the community had shown their usual good sense in rejecting his 'advanced Socialist opinions'.[60]

In fact it was incidents between soldiers on leave and local civilians which were most likely to give expression to anti-war feelings. Such incidents increased throughout 1915 and 1916. At Vizille in August 1915 three *permissionnaires* were arrested for beating up a drunken textile worker who had handed them a Socialist poster calling for an immediate negotiated peace and an end to hostilities. Significantly they were released from prison the following day to continue their leave, while the worker was 'taken to Grenoble for investigation'.[61] It was, however, more often the soldiers who uttered anti-war expressions and the civilians who performed the citizen's arrest or otherwise jostled or molested them. At Sechilienne in June 1915 a young infantryman on his first leave from the front was beaten up by a group of youths awaiting their own mobilisation, for having suggested that the Germans were no worse than Frenchmen, and that the real enemy was the French High Command. According to a local *institutrice* who recorded the incident the war had 'turned the brain of this once popular and respected member of the community'.[62]

The hero's welcome for the *poilu* on leave could soon turn to bitterness and hostility, as in the case of Gilbert Rostaing, a native of Livet et Gavet. He returned for his first leave in June 1915 and was fêted and plied with drinks and bombarded with questions about his experiences at the front, in the usual manner. Initially his reticence and reluctance to talk about the war was tolerated but when, on his last night, having apparently drunk too much, he gave forth a torrent of abuse about the 'lies' of the newspapers, the inhumanity of the French officers and *jusqu'au-boutistes* of all kinds, he was forcibly ejected from the café. The local *institutrice* remarked that it was just as well that he returned to the front the next day, for during the following weeks his mother received a series of anonymous poison pen letters.[63]

As these isolated examples suggest, those who dared to speak out against the war in local communities were treated as outsiders, perhaps a continuing manifestation of the tendency of communities to close in upon themselves which was noted at the beginning of the war. Of course it was the soldiers who were experiencing the horrors of war and the civilians had yet to experience real economic deprivation. It is also worth remembering that those of the most 'advanced opinions' – the young men aged from twenty to thirty-five years – were nearly all on active service. The women and children left at home were less likely to be critical, and the old men of the villages, many of whom had seen active service in 1870, were more likely to be *revanchiste* or *jusqu'au-boutiste* in their opinions.

Potentially more serious, because more systematic, was the propaganda campaign noted in many *départements* throughout 1916, intended to induce farmers to sow less or stop cultivating at all in order to sabotage the war effort and thus hasten the end of the war. It seems that in the Isère such propaganda emanated mainly from *permissionnaires*. Thirty-one *maires* or *adjoints* from rural communities indicated in correspondence with the *préfet* during the last four months of 1916 that peasants were being harassed to this end by *permissionnaires* or outsiders from local towns, and the *Commissaire de Police* of Grenoble captured seven handwritten tracts on this theme in September.

Again, the campaign met with little success amongst the local peasants mainly because, as the *commissaire* noted, 'the local farmer is understandably reluctant to forego profits which have increased considerably since the beginning of the war'.[64] Many of those who distributed such propaganda were denounced by the peasants themselves to the local military or police authorities. Others were simply ignored. Only one example of the campaign having succeeded can be traced and this involved a peasant woman near Pontcharra who had just lost both her sons at Verdun. It is significant that the campaign was directed mainly at war widows, and the propagandists seem to have misjudged the local mood for, as one widow put it, 'would you have me forfeit my one consolation for losing my husband? The end of the war will not bring him back and I have to raise my two children somehow. We have made far too many sacrifices for the war to end without total victory.'[65]

Jusqu'au-boutisme therefore was a strong force in the villages and small towns throughout 1915 and 1916. What, however, was the reaction in the working-class centres in the larger towns to the more institutionalised demand for a negotiated peace which the Socialist Party was to put forward from 1915 onwards? With a circulation of around 12 000–13 000 during 1915 and 1916 in towns like Grenoble, Vienne and Voiron, *Le Droit du Peuple* certainly did not lack an outlet, despite the strict censorship of anti-war articles. Moreover the phrasing of some of the isolated anti-war slogans in smaller towns, calling for a 'peace without annexations or indemnities' or a 'just peace based on principles of international freedom', do indicate Socialist inspiration. The irregularity and non-uniformity of press censorship throughout France made it difficult for the authorities to stifle the publicity of peace slogans and, on occasion, *Le Droit* itself was allowed to get away with surprisingly 'dangerous' headlines from summer 1915 when, adhering to the minority position on the war, Chastenet mounted a campaign for a negotiated peace. Since many of the pacifistic articles censored from *Le Droit* had been freely published in *Le Populaire du Centre* at Limoges and *Le Midi Socialiste* at Toulouse, it was, as the military governor pointed out, practically impossible to prevent the spreading of Socialist anti-war slogans in the Isère.[66] The best that could be done was the imposition of a close police surveillance of all Socialist activities in the *département*.

The authorities' task was not made any easier by the fact that one of the well-known Socialist deputies for the Isère, Raffin-Dugens, took up early in the war a violently anti-war position, making himself notorious in the Chamber of Deputies by his attacks on the Government's *jusqu'au-boutiste* policies and by speeches directed against his former 'comrades' who had become ministers in the 'bourgeois' Government. In November 1915 he was criticising the High Command for sending soldiers into battle like 'lambs to the slaughter'. In 1916 he led a campaign demanding that the Government stop the war, asking whether it was worth all the sacrifice in men and money.[67] He participated in the Kienthal Conference in April 1916 and on his return was heavily censored in the Chamber for referring to German Socialists as 'comrades'.[68] In Grenoble on 28 May 1916 he addressed a private meeting of 200 Socialists, telling them about Kienthal and about the anti-war position of the minority Socialists. Half of the audience were women and there were several *permissionnaires* present. He talked for three hours on the need to convince people that 'Poincaré and Delcassé were as much responsible for the war as the Kaiser', and on the need to organise an effective campaign for a negotiated peace. According to the *commissaire* the speech was 'coldly received' and not applauded. Most of the audience apparently found Raffin-Dugens's speech too violent and exaggerated.[69]

Throughout the first half of 1916 the Socialist Party held weekly meetings in Grenoble. These would be more like *causeries* or discussion groups, with anti-war issues being discussed by Paul Mistral, Raffin-Dugens or Chastenet. Such discussion groups do not seem to have had much effect. They were rarely attended by more than twenty to thirty people, a good half of whom were women, usually the same people each time. Occasionally young children were noted in the audience. It was not until June 1916 that the *préfet* saw fit to report their activities to the Minister of the Interior.[70] On 26 June the minister replied that the *préfet* was to advise the military governor immediately of all 'pacifist meetings', but before applying the Law of 1849 the *préfet* must warn the organisations that any meeting whose object or effect was to weaken the morale of the population would be rigorously forbidden.[71]

This clearly had the effect of limiting the number of meetings, but did nothing to stop the flow of handbills and posters in Grenoble, the product of a peace campaign mounted by the Socialists and the leaders of the *Union des Syndicats Ouvriers de l'Isère* during the autumn of 1916. Targets were the walls and entrances of munitions factories, railway stations and main market squares. However the campaign was easily dealt with by the police by the simple expedient of tearing down the posters almost as soon as they had been put up. Thus small squads of police on bicycles were organised to tour the town between six and seven in the morning to remove the posters before workers leaving the night shift or coming to work on the day shift had a chance to see them. There was, as yet, no evidence of posters appearing inside the factories. The police themselves mounted a counter campaign urging workers and citizens to destroy all anti-war propaganda and report suspicious activity to the police.[72]

Such Socialist anti-war propaganda as did survive the police campaign was poorly received in Grenoble. There were no re-corded 'incidents' as yet in the war factories and, on the streets, peace campaigners ran the risk of assault. Five such incidents were recorded at Grenoble during the second half of 1916. Campaigners, some Socialist, some in their late teens, most of them men in their early fifties, were usually given short shrift by the women of the town, who simply accused them of being *embusqués*, a pejorative term which, applied in this context, was the equivalent of the English 'white feather'.

At Vienne, with its proximity to the textile and military conurba-tion of Lyon and its history of militant Socialist activity, there were, surprisingly, few indications of pacifist demonstrations or slogans throughout 1915 and most of 1916. It was not until September 1916 that the *Commissaire de Police* signalled a serious attempt at a peace campaign in the town. This emanated from Geneva. Copies of a violently anti-militarist Anarchist newspaper, *La Semeur*, were addressed to Richetta, a French-Italian Anarchist who had worked in the Vienne textile industry since 1910. According to the *commis-saire*, if this was diffused in large numbers it could represent a real danger to France. During the same month the police received several complaints from local inhabitants about receiving unsoli-cited anti-war propaganda through their letter boxes. To assess the strength of anti-war feeling in the town, the *sous-préfet* allowed Richetta to address a joint Anarchist–Socialist meeting on 24 October 1916. It was attended by twenty-three people, two of them soldiers and seventeen of them female textile workers. The violence of the speakers and the extreme revolutionary position taken by Richetta, calling for the overthrow of the Government, an immediate end to the war and so on, seem to have scared off many in the audience, nearly half of whom left after only a few minutes. By the end of the meeting, noted the *commissaire*, there were more police than workers in the audience.[73] Two days later police entered Richetta's home and seized piles of newspapers, handbills, posters, tracts of Anarchist literature and propaganda for the *Comité Pour la Reprise des Relations Internationales*. Richetta, surprisingly, received a mere two hundred and fifty *francs* fine.[74]

That anti-war propaganda had failed as yet to have any impact inside the factories of the major towns is indicated by the total lack of reference to peace campaigns in the strikes and industrial disputes in the Isère between the outbreak of hostilities and the end of 1916. Indeed the decline in the number of strikes is in itself remarkable, even bearing in mind the mobilisation of the majority of Socialist and Syndicalist militants. In the first seven months of 1914 there were fifteen strikes in the *département*, and during 1917 there were seventeen. Only ten strikes were recorded in the two and a half years between August 1914 and December 1916. The trend was, however, upwards: two in the first five months, three in 1915 and five in 1916. Four of these took place in textile factories in Vienne, three in Grenoble (one in a glove factory, two in munitions factories), one in a textile factory at Voiron and two in munitions factories at Livet et Gavet. These ten strikes involved a total of 3376 strikers, more than 75 per cent of them females. Of the ten strikes, six had as their cause and aim a straightforward wage increase, two had the aim of reinstating sacked colleagues and one, at the *ganterie* Perrin at Grenoble, resulted from the demand by skilled *coupeurs* for the sacking of twenty *coupeuses* 'imposed' on them by the *patronat* because of the shortage of male skilled labour. One searches in vain through the police records for anti-war or Socialist and Syndicalist propaganda. There is, moreover, no correlation between the nascent peace campaigns in Grenoble and Vienne during 1916 and industrial unrest. Indeed the only strike recorded in Grenoble during the last quarter of 1916 was a five-hour stoppage at Bouchayer et Viallet on 9 November when eighty *munitionettes* successfully demanded the recall of a popular forewoman who had been dismissed for excessive 'leniency'. At Vienne there was no strike at all between the end of May and the end of December 1916.[75]

Perhaps the strongest indication that direct opposition to the war was not yet a serious threat to the authorities in the Isère comes from the recruitment figures for 1915 and 1916 in the Military

Sub-Division of Grenoble. Instead of rising during these two years, the number of *insoumis* declined dramatically. In August 1914, as has been noted, just under 1 per cent of *mobilisés* failed to report. For classes 1915, 1916 and 1917 the percentage dropped to approximately 0.5, 0.4 and less than 0.1 respectively. Throughout 1916, for example, the total number of *insoumis* was a mere thirteen, eleven of whom were residents of Grenoble.[76] Of course the mobilisations of successive classes in the second and third years of the war were far less hurried and unwieldy than the great *levée en masse* of August 1914, and the police and military authorities were far better placed to supervise and pinpoint potential *insoumis*. The elaborate preparation amongst the older boys in schools and the regular evening small-town rituals associated with the formation of the ensuing military class all played their part in ensuring successive smooth mobilisations. There is no evidence of any peace campaign having been mounted to exhort young *mobilisés* not to register or report for duty and, as has been seen, any contacts between the jaded, war-weary and disillusioned *permissionnaires* and the young potential *mobilisés* were limited, whether by methods of social control instigated by villagers and townspeople themselves or, of course, by the military authorities or the local *maire*, one of whose many functions was to ensure the smooth departure of each military class.

It is clear that, after nearly two and a half years of war, the civilians of the Isère were still holding out, despite the fact that there can have been few families who, by the end of 1916, had not been affected in some way by the war, either by bereavement or by serious injury to, or prolonged absence of, loved ones and relatives. The foregoing chapters have attempted to provide some reasons. Propaganda in all its forms, the mobilisation of the church for the war effort, the efforts of the local *maire*, the rigid controls on security and censorship imposed by the military authorities, the effective use of social control, all played an important part in constructing the image in the public mind of a collective purpose. At first the need was to defend the *Patrie en danger*. Subsequently it was established, largely because the sacrifices already made were too great to be wasted, that the war had to be fought until total victory was achieved. Underlying this was a continuation of the 'short war' illusion. The population had come to see the war as a succession of stages, each one lasting roughly six months. The next stage would, it was believed, be the last, the one that would provide the vital breakthrough. All that was needed was one last offensive, one last sacrifice. Of course the authorities also prevented the civilian population from knowing just how much of a sacrifice had already been made.

However, even if the civilians had known the full extent of the casualties and dreadful conditions at the front, would this really have made any difference? This of course is the vital, unanswerable question about civilian morale during the 1914–18 war. The implication of the evidence, however unpalatable, is that it would not. That the civilian population was fundamentally materialistic in its attitude to the war was not lost on the authorities. The immediate decision to introduce an *allocation militaire*, the moratorium on rents and rigid controls on bread prices were crucial, not just as an exercise in good will, but in ensuring that the population was able to overcome the shock of mobilisation and the first stage of the war. Then, when the war settled into a pattern of attrition, with its succession of stages, came the resumption of full-scale economic activity with the prospect of full employment and increased wages for many.

As long as prices did not rise too much and shortages were not too severe for the majority of local civilians, the country had in a sense returned to normal in the spring of 1915. During the two crucial years of 1915 and 1916, when French forces often seemed to bear the brunt of casualties and sacrifices on the Western Front, the civilian population seemed to show at the most only a transitory interest in outside events, returning as it were to the mentality of the parish pump, resuming excessively parochial attitudes. Village gossip, petty local jealousies, many arising from incidents entirely unconnected with the war, predominated locally to the extent that the war itself tended to become boring. The war had thus been accepted. In this sense public opinion, in so far as it can be quantified, occupied a middle ground, impervious both to excessive *bourrage de crâne* and to anti-war propaganda. It is small wonder that soldiers on leave from the front often found that the inhabitants of villages and towns far removed from the war zone lived in a different world. It was as if the war had completely passed them by.

5

Total War and the Civilian Population, 1917–18

The prolongation of hostilities into a third and fourth winter naturally entailed an intensification of local economic activity. 'Grenoble', wrote Chastenet in February 1917, 'has become a veritable industrial centre thanks to the tremendous efforts of our industrialists, merchants and workers.'[1] By January 1917 there were ninety-three factories in the Isère working full time on direct munitions production (not counting sub-contractors), employing a total of 13 517 people. By mid-1918 the number of private and State-owned munitions establishments had increased to 157.[2]

The total number of establishments in the *département* working on all types of production connected with the National Defence is virtually inestimable. During the protracted Verdun campaign it had become clear to army leaders, politicians, journalists and industrialists that war on such a scale necessitated a full and total mobilisation of all possible resources and industries for the war effort. In early 1917 the War Ministry compiled a comprehensive list of all forms of industry and commerce that might be pressed into service for the State. Divided into three categories – necessary, useful and superfluous – those listed in the first two comprised fishing, forestry and agriculture, mining, food industries, printing, textiles, chemical industries, rubber and paper industries, clothing, porcelain and glassware industries, leather and tannery, carpentry, metallurgy, construction industries, transport, liberal professions (doctors, lawyers, teachers, intellectuals) and even hairdressers and concierges. The widest group was that covered by *commerce divers*, including newsagents, ironmongers and manufacturers of household goods.

Obviously by 1917 there were few areas of civilian life which were not affected in some way by war production. Some indication of the scale of increased economic activity connected with the war effort can be provided by the general rise in population of the industrial towns. Grenoble, for instance, had a population of 77 500 in 1911. By the end of 1917 the municipality had issued 27 000 coal cards for the civilian population of the town which, on the basis of three persons per card, gives a figure of 81 000. Added to this are the number of military personnel mobilised *sur place* on munitions production and the regular average of 10 000 soldiers stationed at the garrison, which gives a total of around 94 000 inhabitants. By April 1918 the population was estimated at more than 100 000.[3] At Pont de Claix the installation of two large factories for shell production more than doubled the population from 1021 in 1911 to 2158 by spring 1918. Vizille saw an increase of 1700 inhabitants by the end of 1916 and in Vienne the rapid revival of the textile industry after November 1914 saw the population rise by 5000 by spring 1918.[4]

Clearly, just as military personnel and civilian opinion had to be mobilised for one last effort, so too did local economic activity. In truth the years 1917 and 1918 saw an economic and social situation that was in many ways the logical outcome of the problems and obstacles that had been encountered during the initial stages of industrial mobilisation. It was in early 1917 that severe shortages and unprecedented price rises began to be felt seriously by industry and by the local civilian population. If the Allied blockade of Germany had stimulated the export of luxury silk and gloves from Grenoble, the French chemical industry suffered from lack of essential raw materials from the Rhineland and the Ruhr industrial basin. Food industries in particular suffered from the effects of the German submarine campaign in 1917 as imports of refined sugar declined. Production of chocolates and pâtisserie in the *département* was reduced by mid-1917 to around 85 per cent of its pre-war level.[5] The manufacture of liqueurs, for example, already affected by the efforts of the anti-alcohol lobby, virtually ceased because of the sugar famine. The most serious general shortage was that of coal, resulting from the invasion of the mining areas of the North-East. Oil and petrol were also in increasingly short supply because of the German submarine campaign. Transport difficulties, although eased somewhat after 1914, continued to cause problems, while the acute labour shortage, particularly in agriculture, had not been resolved.

AGRICULTURE, REQUISITIONING AND THE FARMERS

It was the decline in agricultural production and its attendant implications for food supply which gave the authorities most cause

for concern. Shortage of labour, the effects of requisitions, shortage
of manure and the constant rise in price of products vital to
successful farming had, in several areas, caused whole farms to be
abandoned. After a survey of the cereal-growing areas of the
département in May 1917 the *Intendance* estimated that only about 70
per cent of the land was being farmed efficiently. In fifteen
communes more than two-fifths of the farms had virtually ceased to
function. This was not so much a case of lack of good will or lack of
patriotic endeavour: 'in many cases', noted the *Intendance*, 'children, old men and women on the farms are simply exhausted'.[6]
'At least until the middle of 1917', remarked Raoul Blanchard, 'the
State made constant demands upon farmers without giving them
anything in return.'[7]

The authorities attempted to deal with the labour shortage by
intensifying measures which had been adopted with varying
degrees of success in 1915. In January 1917 the military governor,
in conjunction with the *SCAE*, devised a programme of agricultural
work for 1917, attempting to regulate production.[8] An estimated
total of 15 600 men (refugees, *permissionnaires*, men of the oldest
military classes on *sursis* and, predominantly, POWs) were put to
work in teams: 500 in February, 3800 from March to May, 7600
from June to August and 3700 in September and October.[9] Priority
was given to assistance for wives of mobilised soldiers working
alone. It is interesting that many more farmers proved willing to
accept prisoners on their farms and in their homes during 1917 and
1918 than they had in 1915, partly because of the increasingly
desperate labour shortage and partly no doubt because of a
modification of anti-German feelings (although about 15 per cent of
farmers offered these services were still refusing them totally by
mid-1918).[10]

The amount of labour made available by the State to help with
agricultural production still did not meet the needs of all farmers.
The *préfet* estimated that the *département* was short of 2000 men for
the harvest of 1918.[11] At the end of July 1917 the Director of
Agricultural Services produced a long report advocating increased
propaganda through the daily press, education authorities and the
formation of agricultural *syndicats*, on the need to produce more, to
use all available labour more intelligently, and on the advantages
of using electricity for threshing cereals. Whole schooldays were
devoted to demonstrations by teams of experts on *motoculture*.
Children were invited to devise huge posters exhorting peasants to

cultivate more. *Instituteurs* were ordered to give evening conferences in the villages explaining why it was virtually a crime against
La Patrie not to cultivate as much land as possible.[12] In short, no
effort was spared to employ all types of propaganda to mobilise the
farming population for one last effort.

Requisitioning and price fixing were the bugbear of the peasant
during the First World War. The framework for requisitioning in
time of war had been provided by laws of 1877, 1890, 1901 and
1911. Concerned fundamentally with food supply for the army and
civilian population in the towns, the authorities issued a bewildering series of decrees on requisitioning, price fixing and quality
control of foodstuffs, wine and tobacco during the war. By the end
of 1918 these occupied two large and closely-typed volumes.

Initially the authorities were reluctant to use requisitioning
methods for corn and flour to feed the civilian population, and
most requisitioning, of horses, wagons, petrol and so on, was
confined to military use. With the lengthening of the war, however, the gradual decline of agricultural production forced the
Government to elaborate requisitioning and price-fixing measures,
and a decree of 16 October 1915 allowed for the compulsory
requisition of corn and flour for civilian purposes, fixing a maximum price of thirty *francs* per quintal of corn. Penalties for refusal
to comply could reach fines of 500 *francs*. Even then, requisitioning
and price fixing of goods was considered only as an extreme
measure (striking, as it did, at the heart of free enterprise), and the
stated aim of the decree was to 'stop speculation and maintain the
normal price of bread'.[13]

The problem of course was that, since the free-market retail price
of corn varied between thirty-two and thirty-five *francs* per quintal,
farmers were discouraged from cultivating corn and, left to themselves, would naturally choose cereals like oats and barley, which
cost less to produce and whose sale price was constantly rising. A
decree of 14 March 1916 fixed a corn requisition price of thirty-
three *francs* per quintal. However, as shortages began to be felt, the
authorities gradually took more extreme measures. On 20 April
1916 maximum prices were fixed for sugar, coffee, oil and petrol,
potatoes, milk, margarine and dry vegetables, and on 4 January
1917 *carnets du sucre* were introduced providing for a maximum of
750 grammes of sugar per head per month. As the situation
worsened during 1917 laws and decrees regulating, rationing and
fixing the price of essential foodstuffs came thick and fast. The

price of cheese was fixed on 11 January, *pâtisseries* were forced to close two days per week from 20 January, meat was to be served only once a day in restaurants from 25 January, penalties for wastage of food were introduced on 2 February, sale of meat was forbidden on two days a week from 14 April and, finally, in January 1918 bread cards were introduced, fixing individual consumption at 300 grammes per day for adults. After lengthy and heated discussions in the Chamber of Deputies, the ultimate law on civilian requisitioning was passed on 3 August 1917. For the length of the war and three months afterwards, the civilian and military authorities were empowered to requisition all objects deemed necessary for heating, lighting, feeding and clothing the civilian population, and all objects needed by industrialists and merchants working in the interests of the National Defence.[14] The maximum penalty for false declarations and evasion was fixed at two years' imprisonment and a five hundred *francs* fine.

Not only was the very concept of requisitioning and price fixing anathema to the peasant farmer, but the way requisitioning was implemented provoked jealousies and local rivalries damaging to the principles of the *Union Sacrée* and to civilian morale generally. *Commissions d'Evaluation* were established in each *commune* or group of *communes*, consisting of between three and seven members, both civilian and military. Care was taken to ensure that farmers were adequately represented. At Goncelin, for example, the *Commission* comprised one captain of the *Intendance*, one notary, one *instituteur* and three local farmers.[15] The job of the *Commission* was to liaise with the local *maire* in inspecting the material or crop to be requisitioned, and to fix quotas for the *commune*. The *maire* himself was responsible for distributing individual quotas to farmers, based on information which he was supposed to keep at the *mairie*. The commissioners did not always do their job well. To serve on a *Commission* was not deemed an honour, it was usually regarded as one more time-consuming administrative chore to add to the ever-increasing list of obligations and duties that local *fonctionnaires* were subjected to during the war.

Since the free-market price for potatoes, wine, corn and hay was invariably higher than the requisition price, a number of farmers attempted to sell their produce in neighbouring *communes* before their requisition quota was imposed on them. It was also possible for the *maire* to act in collusion with farmers in his *commune* either by encouraging false declarations or by ensuring that the worst quality produce was made available to the requisitioners. Sometimes an entire *commune*, municipal council included, was accused of showing bad will and being unco-operative. At Maiseau the *maire* wrote to the *préfet* in March 1918 that the *commune* was unable to furnish any potatoes because of the bad harvest. Investigations by the *Commission d'Evaluation* revealed that the *maire*, his *adjoint* and several farmers had regularly been selling hay, straw and potatoes to private merchants in nearby St Nicolas.[16]

The most common complaint was that requisition quotas had been unfairly and unevenly distributed and that the *maire* had taken no account of the size and capacity of individual holdings, or that neighbouring *communes* had been favoured with lighter quotas. Many farmers also claimed they had been taken advantage of because they were female and old. Some letters of complaint were written from the front by indignant soldiers acting on behalf of their semi-literate, aged mothers. One soldier from Claix, for instance, claimed that his aged, widowed mother had actually to go to a neighbouring village to buy hay at an inflated price because the *Intendance* had deprived her of nearly all her stocks. 'It is scandalous that I and my comrades at the front should endure three years of hell while the *embusqués* at home take advantage of weak, defenceless old women. This would certainly not have happened if I had been at home.'[17]

In all there were seventy-nine cases of forced requisitioning on individual farmers and thirteen official reprimands issued to *maires* for non-compliance or bad will in 1917, and eighty-eight and nineteen respectively in 1918.[18] A number of *maires* claimed in their defence that they were confused by the apparent ambiguity of the regulations on requisitioning and price fixing and did not know what was really expected of them, and thus they were unable to put the decrees into practice effectively. Considering that a copy of every decree was lodged in the *mairie* of each *commune*, this is surprising. Perhaps it was the sheer volume of laws, decrees, regulations and amendments that was confusing. The important point about the imposition and abuses of requisitions is that just at a time, during 1917 and 1918, when journalists and politicians were paying lip service to the need to uphold the *Union Sacrée*, to encourage the peasantry to produce more, to call on them to make one last effort and, above all, not to do anything to endanger their good will or lower their morale, the *Intendance*, the *Commissions d'Evaluation* and often the *maire* himself were, in many cases, producing the opposite effect.

PRICE RISES, SHORTAGES AND RESTRICTIONS

Townspeople, particularly, were becoming increasingly concerned about price rises by early 1917. The rise in prices throughout the war was not uniform. Bread prices, thanks to the efforts made by the Government, remained basically stable until the last year of the war, but the price of potatoes, butter, cheese and coal had nearly doubled by February 1917 and trebled by the end of the year. There were of course slight local variations, and it must be borne in mind that prices of basic foodstuffs had always fluctuated according to season and vagaries of climate. However the continuous price rise noticeable from mid-1915 onwards was unprecedented within living memory, and academics, journalists and industrialists sought to explain the phenomenon and to suggest remedies.

By early 1916 the members of the *SCAE* were sufficiently concerned to commission a full-scale twenty-two page report on the rise of prices at Grenoble. The basic reason for the rise, according to the report, was that the war had upset the balance between supply and demand. While the number of producers had diminished (had been mobilised), the number of consumers had increased (mobilised soldiers, imported labour working in factories). The decline in production was caused by the lack of labour, the militarisation of transport facilities, the invasion of the North-East and the decline of essential imports. Meanwhile the demand, particularly for meat and wine to feed a grossly inflated army, had risen dramatically. The average daily ration of meat for mobilised soldiers, for example, was 350 to 400 grammes per day, considerably higher than that which they would normally consume at home. Aggravating this, according to the report, was the fact that spending power had increased in the form of rising wages for munitions workers, and the introduction of *allocations* which 'for a considerable part of the population has actually brought an increase of resources over their pre-war level'. There was therefore too much money in circulation. As proof of this, the report quoted receipts of cinemas, theatres and concert halls in Grenoble for January 1916, which had risen eight times over the figure for January 1915.[19]

The implication that munitions workers and certain recipients of *allocations* should take much of the blame for price rises was supported by a number of articles published in contemporary academic journals. The argument was that new highly-paid workers had no tradition of saving and desired only to spend their money as fast as possible, thus unnecessarily inflating demand. An extreme version even blamed female munitions workers for attempting to achieve equality of wages with males.[20] The alternative view was that speculators and middle-men were the real architects of price rises, and it was factory workers, particularly those not working on munitions production, who were the hardest hit.[21] Predictably, the local Socialist press was quick to defend workers against the charge that they were using their 'new-found wealth' irresponsibly. Attacking the *SCAE* report on 12 March 1916, Chastenet wrote: 'the view that the workers spend too much money on luxuries is absurd. They have no time to indulge in frivolities, they are too busy spending all their hours at work earning enough to keep pace with prices. What we need are good Jacobin measures: maximum prices and an all-out war on speculators and hoarders.'[22]

Indeed speculation and hoarding were once again causing a serious problem, after having been dealt with fairly successfully during the early days of August 1914. The *préfet* again resorted to methods of social control by asking *maires* to form vigilante groups in their *communes* and by publicising on posters in the towns, and in the press, the names of shopkeepers and all private traders who attempted to take advantage of the situation. *Instituteurs* and *maires* were detailed to form *Comités de Surveillance des Prix* from June 1917 onwards, and some 70 per cent of *communes* in the Isère had such a *Comité* by the end of the year.[23] Individuals were also encouraged to write to their *sous-préfet* or to the *préfet* himself if they had any suspicion or particular complaint, not altogether a wise step since, as can be imagined, there were a number of rather wild exaggerations and false claims in anonymous letters of denunciation. Many people simply used the invitation to air their own private feelings and jealousies; a common one being the age-old gripe that middle-aged male shopkeepers and coal merchants were favouring young, pretty girl customers with large quantities of commodities in short supply. Another common complaint was that in order to obtain tobacco or rice, both of which were in extremely short supply, some customers were obliged to pay double the price for butter, cheese or milk. Price speculation was easier to control in large towns, of course, because of the existence of alternative outlets. There was more opportunity for the shopkeeper to take advantage of shortages in small isolated *communes*, but in doing so he ran a risk, as at La Terrasse in August 1917, where an *épicier* was beaten up and his shop ransacked.[24]

As shortages became more acute during 1917, the possibility of rationing by card was discussed increasingly in academic and commercial circles, occupying the attention of members of the *SCAE* in February and May 1917 and almost continuously throughout the winter of 1917–18, although the censors discouraged too much press participation in the controversy for fear of alarming the population. Once again the introduction of bread, sugar and coal cards was hailed by the Socialist press as a 'good Jacobin measure, since, by curbing the demand of the rich, it should result in a lowering of prices for the good of all'.[25] These were, however, the only commodities to be rationed. Industrialists and merchants, some of whom sat on the *SCAE*, saw this as a dangerous step on the road to total State interference in the economy: 'to restrict demand by rationing interferes with the natural laws of the economy. We already have maximum prices and requisitions imposed by the State. The State should confine itself to ensuring that we have enough good labour on our farms and in our factories, and leave the laws of supply and demand to work in freedom.'[26]

If rationing of foodstuffs offended the *laissez-faire* principles of entrepreneurs, there was at least a favourable general consensus on the introduction of the coal card in October 1917, for here, of course, industrialists were in competition with private consumers. Coal, arguably the most vital commodity for both private and industrial consumption, was in shortest supply throughout the war. Of all shortages that of coal provoked the most serious social tensions and examples of extreme selfishness in both town and countryside. As early as 1 January 1915 the President of the Chamber of Commerce of Grenoble wrote to the War Minister asking him to forbid the export of coal from the Isère and to end State requisitioning of coal, advocating that the State and the Military should get their coal from Britain. The produce of local mines at La Mure and La Motte d'Aveillans should be reserved for local private and industrial consumption.[27]

Coal production was seen by the Government as being of prime importance, and right from the outset of the war the Director of the Compagnie des Mines de La Mure had to apply to the War Ministry, and subsequently to the Ministry of Armaments, for permission to increase prices. Here the company was in direct conflict with *maires*, especially those of industrial towns who had their industrialists and private consumers to think of. Throughout the war, from 1915 onwards, there was what amounted to a running battle between *maires*, particularly the *Maire* of Grenoble who claimed priority in coal deliveries for 'the largest and most important town of the region', and the director of the company.

The coal shortage had already caused the *préfet* to decree the early closure of cinemas, theatres and other places of public entertainment, as well as the restriction of street lighting, from 1915 onwards, but the population was affected in a more fundamental way. It was during this time that the pejorative description of the coal merchant as the 'coal king' gained popular currency. In January 1917 Chastenet, in *Le Droit du Peuple*, asked 'who is the coal king?'

> He is that evil, grasping figure who will see you shiver with cold while he sees that he and his friends are kept warm. He cares little for our brave *poilus* freezing in the trenches, even less for our devoted, patriotic peasants in their remote snow-filled mountain villages.[28]

Of course inhabitants of many rural *communes* were not so badly affected by the shortage of coal because of the availability of firewood from nearby forests, but coal was still needed to heat bakers' ovens and for steam to drive threshing machines. In fact, during 1917, coal rationing of a kind existed in rural *communes* before the introduction of the coal card. The *préfet* authorised the issues of quotas based on an assessment of the number of households in each *commune*. Once again it was the *maire* who was responsible for distributing the quotas amongst families, yet another opportunity to show favouritism, incite jealousies and inflame old passions, although it must be said that the majority of *maires* appear to have genuinely tried to be fair in their distribution. However some could still not resist the temptation to deprive the *curé* or *vicaire* of what appeared to be his rightful share, and there were regular complaints in *La Croix de l'Isère* and *La Semaine Religieuse* on this subject throughout 1917 and 1918. In fact at Vinay the *curé* was accused of having too much coal, lighting large fires in the church vestry while several local inhabitants shivered in near-freezing conditions.[29] There were also three cases during the winter of 1916–17 of *maires* expropriating coal and selling it privately.[30]

The press unwittingly played a large part in aggravating the social tensions attendant upon shortages and price rises, not just with emotive expressions like *charbonnier de roi* and *accapareurs*, but also with a growing desire to identify groups and classes who were benefiting financially from the prolongation of the war. All sections of the daily press agreed that workers in munitions factories were earning unprecedentedly high wages. As the number of strikes and industrial stoppages based on wage claims developed during 1917, newspapers, according to their political and social perspective, made increasing use of pejorative terms like *embusqués* and *nouveaux riches*. To the clerical and conservative press the real *embusqués* were the large numbers of foreign workers – Spanish, Chinese, North Africans and Annamites – who had no vestige of patriotism, cared nothing for the fate of their French counterparts in the trenches and whose main desire was that the war should be prolonged. It was the foreigners who were held responsible for the high wage claims and strike activity. Also classed as *embusqués* were workers recalled from the front, earning 'huge' wages while their former comrades rotted in the trenches for a few *sous* per day.[31] Not surprisingly the clerical press subscribed strongly to the view that workers were largely responsible for high price rises, 'for workers, with their new-found wealth, are offering to pay far above the odds for certain commodities, thus encouraging price speculators'.[32] It was of course but a short step from this view to the clerical argument that the social injustices and high cost of living were a corollary of a decline in standards of morality. This rapid *tour de force* by *La Croix* in May 1918 on the reasons for the decline in standards of living can be taken as an indication that the notion of *la guerre purificatrice* had thus far failed:

This is a war of vandals. People do not economise. The rich do not set good examples and the workers do not know how to save. There are too many goods on display, not enough producers, too much money, too many parasites, too many earners, not enough honesty. Too many foreigners, too many debts, too much luxury, greed and pride. This war has brought out the baseness and selfishness of people.[33]

The Socialist *Droit du Peuple* naturally denied that workers were earning too much and put more emphasis on the dangerous, unpleasant and unhealthy conditions and long hours that men and women had to endure in munitions factories. For Socialist journalists like Chastenet and Paul Mistral the real *embusqué* and *nouveau riche* was the factory owner engaged in munitions production. The fundamental Socialist argument was that the State should have more control over the distribution of defence contracts and that the right of individual entrepreneurs to make vast profits should be severely curtailed. As early as the beginning of 1916 Chastenet was writing of the need to introduce quickly the income tax law which had been much discussed before the war, but had not yet been implemented.

In the Chamber of Deputies Paul Mistral pursued relentlessly the theme of taxing war profiteers and on 1 July 1916 the first law introducing taxation of war profits was passed. Not satisfied with this, Mistral continued to press for a revision of the terms of contract between the *Intendance* and entrepreneurs and for periodic publication of war profits, and on 23 April 1917 the law to which he gave his name, the *Loi Mistral sur la Régime des Fabrications de Guerre* was passed, allowing the State to recoup part of the profits gained by entrepreneurs and to have more control over regulating conditions of work and wages. Mistral also contributed to continuing complaints in the local press and in the Chamber on the number of *embusqués* working in munitions factories; not the foreign workers who were deemed indispensable, but those who, despite the introduction of the *Loi Dalbiez*, were still falsely claiming to be skilled workers. On 7 August 1917 the *Loi Mourier* was passed providing for the return to active service of all members of the class of 1903 and, later on, ex-members of the *armée active* who had not served in combatant units for at least a year.

The one major group in society to escape adverse press comment on its material fortunes was the peasantry. All sections of the press agreed that, if some individual peasants were benefiting financially from the war, the sacrifices they were undergoing throughout entitled them to do so. The tendency, as always, was for urban-based, educated journalists to describe peasant conditions and mentalities in terms and expressions which often bore little relation to reality. Consider, for example, this panegyric by Chastenet on the life of peasants in the mountains in time of war:

It is profoundly moving to visit our remote villages. Here is an earthly paradise. Here there is no selfishness, no hatred. Here our noble people know nothing of the passions, the destruction, the savagery of the human race. Here all is beautiful, pure and clean. If the *Union Sacrée* still exists, it is in the villages, certainly not in the towns.[34]

Compare that with the huge number of letters of denunciation and complaints about *allocations*, requisitions and shortages that the *préfecture* received from villagers throughout 1917 and 1918.

It is difficult to assess accurately the extent to which civilians were able to cope financially with price rises during the course of the war. It is even more difficult to discover who gained or lost financially. The press is not a reliable indicator. Newspapers were heavily censored and were biased, and the tendency of journalists to exaggerate and lump whole groups together into 'classes' is misleading and unhelpful. Certainly one cannot talk of a single 'class' as having benefited financially from the war: there are too many variables. The income of a working-class family, for example, obviously depended on whether the husband was mobilised in a munitions factory or at the front, whether the wife worked, what type of factory they were working in, where it was located (Grenoble, Vienne or one of the smaller industrial towns), how far they had to journey to work, the industrial bargaining power of their union, whether their factory offered piece-work, their health, strength and ability to work long overtime hours to earn bonuses, their particular skills, and so on. All this, of course, has to be compared with their normal peacetime occupation and the rise in prices during the war. As can be seen from Tables 5 and 6 in the Appendix, there were considerable variations in industrial wages throughout the war. The figures are averages and could vary by anything up to a *franc* per day according to the enterprise for which one worked. As can be seen, wages for men were approximately seventy-five *centimes* to one *franc* per day higher in munitions factories.

By the beginning of 1917 wages had, on average, risen by approximately 80 per cent whereas prices had risen by 75 to 100 per cent, so real wages were actually declining. The proportion of his wage that the average male industrial worker had to spend on food per day can be assessed from Table 7. Bearing in mind that the average calorie requirement for working females was some 500 less than for males, one can assume a daily expenditure of around

3 fr. 25 at a time when the average industrial wage in Grenoble was 7 fr. 50 to eight *francs*. Of course, one adjusted one's diet according to the season and to what one could afford. The poorer the household, the larger the proportion of bread and sugar in the daily diet. In this respect the poorest households would be hardest hit by bread and sugar rationing.

So concerned were the members of the *SCAE* at the rise in the cost of living that in March 1917 they asked for a 'typical' working-class budget to be calculated by a local representative of the *Ministre du Travail et Prévoyance Social*. His findings are shown in Tables 8 and 9. They are based on workers in Grenoble, and the report does not indicate how the information was gathered or how many families were interviewed. Clearly the budgets are far too general to permit definite conclusions, but they are certainly useful as a general guide. The budget in Table 8 is clearly that of a prosperous working-class couple earning probably near the maximum possible for munitions work in the locality in March 1917. The near twenty-five *francs* per week surplus of income over expenditure was very generous. It is extremely unlikely that such a couple would have envisaged having such a large weekly surplus before the war. It is not known how many childless couples in Grenoble during the war were in such a happy situation (both working overtime in munitions production), but it is safe to say that they were in a small minority. If any group within the working class formed part of the *nouveaux riches*, it would be couples like this.

There were likely to be far more families in the situation shown in Table 9, where there were children and only the husband worked. Clearly such families had to reduce or adjust their calorific intake and curtail the amount spent on items like tobacco (which for some families was a 'necessity' and for others a 'frivolity'), and there was precious little surplus left for luxuries at a time when a visit to the cinema or theatre cost around two *francs* per person and a cheap suit of men's clothing could cost between fifty and seventy-five *francs*.[35]

A lack of detailed records makes it difficult to draw adequate conclusions about the social and geographical backgrounds of munitions workers. However there are records for workers employed in State-owned armaments establishments in Grenoble, and Table 10 analyses the female workforce at the *Atelier de Chargement des Grenades* between 1916 and 1918. Five hundred and twenty-two women were employed here during the last two years of war. The intake in 1918 was more than double that of 1916, which would corroborate the assumptions made in Chapter 3 about the reluctance of many women to take up munitions work. For example the proportion of female shop assistants, typists and clerical workers who left their jobs for more lucrative munitions work, even by mid-1918, was very low (8.5 per cent). The preponderance of ex-textile workers (49 per cent) is partly explained by the fact that more than half of them had children and had hitherto been working on piece-work *à domicile* and it was not until 1918 that the *Atelier* was able to provide rudimentary crèche facilities. Many of the former textile-factory workers were from the comparatively small number of enterprises which had failed to secure defence contracts from the *Intendance* and were thus unable to pay adequate bonuses for piece-work. More than 50 per cent of those listed under 'other occupations' were ex-domestics working in middle-class households, most of whom entered munitions work only in 1918, which provides more evidence, perhaps, of a rather condescending attitude to munitions work in factories despite the fact that such work could pay twice as much. It should also be borne in mind that by the later stages of the war many middle-class households could no longer afford to maintain domestic staff, let alone pay them at rates comparable with munitions production. Only about 10 per cent of employees were former farm workers or had listed 'no previous occupation'. Of course the pressures to remain working on the farms at a time of great labour shortage were immense. Overall, however, the figures do conform to the assumptions made by recent research that women were redistributed within the industrial workforce rather than entering it *en masse* for the first time.[36]

Around 73 per cent of the workforce at the *Atelier* lived either in Grenoble itself or in the suburbs, within walking distance or a short tram ride away. Not surprisingly there were not many who were either able or willing to travel more than ten kilometres to work every day and most of the workers in this category travelled daily from Vizille or Voiron. Their ability to do so depended on the existence of regular bus or train services, and for such workers the possibility of working overtime, during 'anti-social' hours, was even more dependent on the regularity of transport. It was also, because of the overcrowding and general shortage of accommodation in Grenoble by the later stages of the war, extremely difficult to secure temporary lodgings in the town.

Some 65 per cent of the workforce at the *Atelier* were married women whose husbands had originally been mobilised at the front. Of the total number of women only 13 per cent had husbands who were, either under the *Loi Dalbiez* or because they were above mobilisable age, also working in munitions factories, and only 6 per cent of those so favoured were childless. A particularly poignant statistic is the increasing number of war widows in the workforce. The percentage rose from 2 per cent in 1916 to 6 per cent by mid-1918. The percentage of forty- to sixty-year-old mothers who had lost at least one son in action at the front also rose from 1.5 to 5 per cent. Quite often women in this unfortunate position had no choice but to seek munitions work. One widow of seventy-two, for example, who had lost both her sons, had to travel the thirty-kilometre round-trip daily from Voiron to Grenoble to work in the *Atelier*.

There is little doubt that clerical staff and shopkeepers were among the occupational groups hardest hit by the rising cost of living during 1917 and 1918. At Grenoble's largest department store the 148-strong workforce of July 1914 had been reduced by eighty to sixty-eight in June 1917. Of these eighty, fifty-nine had been mobilised in the army, twelve had retired and nine (three men and six women) had left to find other employment. Of the sixty-eight remaining staff, thirty-one were female shop assistants whose average daily wage in June 1917, including commission, was just over four *francs*, a rise of only about fifty *centimes* over their pre-war figure. Obviously a decline in custom during the first two years of the war affected the amount of commission they could earn and, unlike the munitions and textile workers, they could not supplement their basic wage by production bonuses and overtime work. Taken as a whole, the average wages at the store had risen by only 40 per cent.[37]

One other group who clearly did not benefit financially from the war were the estimated 22 000 female workers *à domicile*. Before the war they had earned an average of between one *franc* and 2 fr. 40 per day making shirts for men and women, lingerie and gloves. During the war the *Intendance* offered them the opportunity of making military uniforms – shirts, caps, tunics, pantaloons, gloves and so on – and by 1917 there were an estimated 18 000 females working at home for the Military in the Isère.[38] The *Intendance* handed large quotas to sub-contractors, who then dispensed orders to their workers. The work was long and hard. By mid-1915, for example, a greatcoat, which could take up to thirteen hours to make, paid a mere two *francs*. Probably the most exploited workers were those making pantaloons at 1 fr. 40 per dozen. Workers had to supply their own cotton and thread, and only by working more than twelve hours a day could they earn even 1 fr. 50.

Workers *à domicile* were eminently exploitable because of the lack of effective syndical organisation outside the *syndicats libres*. Intermediary sub-contractors could thus draw large profits. In June 1915, for example, the *Intendance* paid the sub-contractor 6 fr. 50 for an infantryman's greatcoat, while the worker gained two *francs*. A law of July 1915 brought some improvement in wages by instituting a *Comité de Salaires* presided over by a justice of the peace, and on 30 August the *préfet* installed *Comités* in Grenoble, Voiron, La Tour du Pin and Vienne to ensure that a minimum price was guaranteed by sub-contractors. By mid-1917 it was possible to earn up to four *francs* per day sewing pantaloons or making *bonnets de police*, and a greatcoat now paid as much as five *francs* according to size.

Such workers could of course supplement their income by drawing the *allocation militaire*. Their ability to do so depended on whether they could prove to the *Commissions Cantonales* that the mobilisation had deprived them of their family's chief breadwinner. Not surprisingly the number in receipt of *allocations* increased consistently throughout the war as successive military classes were called up, and this was not compensated for by the early recall and demobilisation, from 1917 onwards, of older *réservistes* and territorials aged forty-five and over. Initially, despite the great number of families deprived of resources at the beginning of the war and the mass of applications in September 1914, many deserving women, believing that hostilities would be only temporary, delayed applying for relief until well into 1915. There were also a minority of potentially deserving cases who initially held themselves aloof from the system, not wishing to be stigmatised as 'needy'. In addition there were some who delayed applying for ostensibly patriotic reasons. Marie Chevalier of Gua, for example, lost out on nearly one year of benefits by not applying until August 1915. Before the war her family had been moderately prosperous, owning two dwelling-houses at a combined value of 3600 *francs* and farmlands to the value of 1800 *francs*. Her husband had been mobilised on the first day and she was left alone to cope with her three young children. As she explained to the *Commission Cantonale*:

I did not join the rush for *allocations* since I believed that we had enough resources to support ourselves until my husband returned. But now, after nearly one year of war, our resources have gone and I can no longer afford to pay the labour needed to help on my farm.[39]

It is not known just how many civilians took such an unselfish and patriotic view, but certainly the stigma of relying on the State did deter a number of women from applying for *allocations* until the later stages of the war. Pride, traditions of independence, self-reliance and long-standing distrust of 'the State' were important factors here and, once again, there was the view that hostilities would not last very long. In some cases it was only the ultimate sacrifice in the form of the death in action of a husband or son which caused women to change their mind and accept that the State really owed them something. This was the case with Marie Pascal of Corps, who did not make her initial application until after her husband was killed on the Chemin des Dames in April 1917:

My husband and I have both served our country well. I have managed to survive by sheer hard work and with the help of my children and neighbours, but now that my husband has given his life for his country, I consider it my right to receive some form of compensation.[40]

Such people were in the minority. So too, undoubtedly, were those, particularly in the remote mountain areas, who were apparently ignorant of their rights under the law of 5 August 1914, despite the mass of printed material publicising *allocations* in every *mairie*. There were three examples of this in the tiny mountain village of Villard Reculas high up in the Oisans, where newspapers were scarcely seen from one week to the next. Here, for example, one young *cultivatrice* did not apply for an *allocation* until mid-1915 because she had misunderstood the regulations, believing that one had to be totally destitute in order to qualify.

Added to all these reasons was the fundamental one that by 1917 it was becoming increasingly difficult to make ends meet, and by the last months of the war the *allocation militaire* had become a veritable institution. According to statistics supplied by the *Commissions Cantonales*, the *Commission d'Appel* and the *préfecture*, there were 107 616 individual applications for *allocations* between

September 1914 and the end of November 1918, an average of around 1380 per month from May 1915 onwards. Only 17 207 were ultimately rejected.[41] By the end of the war, then, approximately 20 per cent of the total population of the *département* were receiving State benefit.

The anomalies, inconsistencies and ambiguities in the way in which the law on *allocations* was implemented make it almost impossible to categorise recipients as financial losers or beneficiaries during the war. Theoretically every family which had lost its main breadwinner because of mobilisation could receive benefit. The issue for families of factory workers in industrial towns was fairly clear cut, particularly when the head of the family had been the only one working before the war. In this sense, the real losers were those wives of *mobilisés* and mothers of small children who had never worked and could not find employment in munitions factories because of inadequate crèche facilities. Such families would see their daily income drop by up to two or three *francs*. It was in the countryside where the difficulties of interpretation and implementation arose. Owner-occupiers of farms had their existing resources thoroughly investigated by the *maire* and the local *Commission Cantonale* before applications were granted. There were no effective centrally-imposed criteria as regards existing resources so that, quite often, an application which might be deemed deserving in one *canton* might be rejected in another.

In January 1917 the *préfet*'s office commissioned a breakdown by occupational status of all recipients of *allocations* in the 213 *communes* of the *Arrondissement* of Grenoble, comprising approximately two-fifths of the population of the *département*.[42] The figures, presented in the form of general totals, mask some interesting local statistics. Obviously the number of recipients would depend on the number of *mobilisés* from each *commune*, but there are variations in the ratio of recipients to eligible cases. In the mountainous *canton* of Bourg d'Oisans, for example, only 72 per cent of those eligible for *allocations* according to the law of 5 August 1914 had applied by January 1917. In the *commune* of Venosc the figure was as low as 57 per cent,[43] while in the industrial town of Vizille it was as high as 91 per cent. Indeed it seems that in the more remote villages the traditional succour of the *bureau de bienfaisance* continued to be the mainstay of the majority of the needy. The implication here is that in remote areas, despite the local jealousies and conflicts, the war had not brought great changes in fortune amongst small farmers one way or the other, at least not by the beginning of 1917.

Thanks to the persistent campaigning in Parliament of Paul Mistral and fellow Socialists against war profiteers, it is possible to trace the fortunes of a number of small and medium-sized commercial enterprises which can be said to have benefited financially during 1917 and 1918. By the law of 1 July 1916 all businesses and commercial enterprises, except farmers selling their produce to the State, which made profits of more than 5000 *francs* a year over and above their normal peacetime profits were liable to a special war tax. Investigations by financial *fonctionnaires* began at the end of 1916 and were to drag on through the 1920s and into the 1930s. The resulting data, which in the case of the Isère were lodged in the *Archives Départementales* at Grenoble, constitute an invaluable source for the economic historian. The records for the Isère alone, listed by *commune* and by business enterprise, occupy more than thirty metres of shelf space in the archives. However the information must be treated with considerable circumspection and, unfortunately, it does not permit a reliable quantitative evaluation for the entire *département*. The records are incomplete and there are important lacunae, particularly concerning some of the larger shell-producing enterprises in Grenoble. One does not know how many enterprises were able to get away without making any declaration at all. Only about two-fifths of the *communes* of the *département* (234 out of 564) are listed in the archives and the conditions of war and the shortage of qualified *fonctionnaires* made a thorough investigation extremely difficult to achieve during the hostilities.[44] Although more thorough investigation was possible after the war, the task was complicated beyond measure by the claims of many businessmen that they had not kept accurate accounts before the war. Indeed some claimed that they had not kept accounts at all until the promulgation of the 1916 law. Businessmen also had an obvious incentive to falsify their records, either by increasing their average pre-war net profits so as to minimise their exceptional war profits, or by minimising their wartime profit figures. A favourite ploy was to claim that the muddled and vague state of accounts of many businesses was due to the incompetence and inexperience of female replacements for mobilised male accountants and general clerical staff. Quite often police reports making use of the opinions of fellow businessmen and local citizens were employed in evaluating the veracity of tax returns, a further opportunity for citizens in the locality to air their grievances and display their prejudices and jealousies. Either way the tax returns were extremely complicated and difficult to verify retrospectively, and there can be no doubt that a number of small businessmen profited with impunity during the later stages of the war.

Bearing in mind all these reservations the archives, for the purposes of this study, are more useful for the evaluation of individual case studies. Not surprisingly the majority of the 330 *communes* not listed as having businesses with exceptional wartime profits were in the more remote rural areas, since farmers were generally exempt from taxation. For example, only four out of twenty *communes* in the *canton* of Bourg d'Oisans were listed as having war profiteers in commerce, while seven out of the eight *communes* of the industrial *canton* of Vif were listed.[45] As has already been noted, many commercial enterprises in remote rural areas closed down for the duration of the war, and some never reopened. In the village of Huez, 1500 metres up in the Oisans, the only commerce functioning by mid-1917 was the local *fromager*, who made a profit of 5600 *francs* during 1917 and 6250 *francs* in 1918.

There is no doubt that sheer chance and geographical location continued to play an important part in the personal fortunes of merchants and businessmen during 1917 and 1918. If commerce tended to become dormant in rural areas, businesses in small 'boom' towns were particularly favoured during the years of full economic mobilisation towards the end of the war. One such town was Chasse in the *canton* of Vienne Nord. In 1911 this town had a population of 1516 and before 1914 it already possessed an important metallurgical factory employing 120 workers. The departure of *mobilisés* reduced the labour force until mid-1915, when the Société des Hautes Fournaux began making shell cases for the *Intendance*. By 1917 the influx of foreign labour had increased the population to 1800, and by the last months of the war the figure was over 1900.[46] The rapid influx of labour had to be fed and housed. Some forty-seven householders in the town, many of them wives of *mobilisés*, were able to supplement their incomes by letting out rooms to the new workers at rates of sixty to seventy *francs* per month. There is no doubt, however, that those who benefited most were the town's two *cabaretiers* (innkeepers): Mme Ansermier, a spinster, and Mme Jullienne, a widow since 1910.

Mme Ansermier had opened a small café and *pension* next to the railway station at Chasse in 1913. She had kept no accounts until 1916 and her normal net profit was calculated at 5000 *francs* per year. Hit hard by the mobilisation, she none the less continued renting out three rooms at eighty *francs* per month per room, and fed twenty people for three *francs* per person per day. Her net receipts for 1915 were 21 600 *francs*, nearly 3000 *francs* down on the 1913–14 figure. As the number of new workers earning good wages increased during 1916, she nearly doubled her receipts to 39 000 *francs* and by the end of 1917 she was feeding forty-five workers daily at five *francs* per meal.[47] Mme Jullienne likewise had a small *pension* within walking distance of the factory at Chasse. In her café she sold newspapers, tobacco and confectionery. Barely able to make ends meet during 1914 and 1915, by mid-1918 she was renting out five rooms at 120 *francs* per month each and her profits for 1918 were calculated at 5500 *francs*.[48]

As has been noted, there were too many variables to enable a precise categorisation of financial gainers and losers from the war. Geographical location, the availability of labour, the age of the employers and employees (whether they were of mobilisable age or not), the availability and efficiency of public transport, the adaptability of small businesses to the war effort, the willingness of young females to enter munitions work, the availability of lodgings in the industrial centres – all were important in deciding the material circumstances of individuals throughout the war. All that can be safely surmised is that there were few who suffered drastically. The *allocation militaire* could just about keep body and soul together, and in a situation where, from 1916 onwards, there were increasing shortages of labour in industry and agriculture, there was always the prospect of increasing one's income. Peasant farmers, for example, might complain about restrictions and requisitions, but as a group they did not suffer sufficiently to provide a pool of mobilisable opinion against the war effort.

6 *

The Triumph of the War Effort, 1917–18

The year 1917 is commonly referred to by historians of France as 'l'Année Terrible', comparable with 1870 and 1940 in the annals of modern French history. To a large degree the local civilian population had been lulled into complacency bordering on apathy during 1915 and 1916 by the general lack of dramatic diplomatic initiatives. True, there had been peace initiatives by President Wilson and the Pope, there had been conferences at Zimmervald and Kienthal, but to all intents and purposes the war situation was not fundamentally different by Christmas 1916 from what it had been in the spring of 1915. There had been no major military breakthrough on either side. Both the major Western Allied powers had undergone their bloodletting campaigns: the French at Verdun, the British on the Somme. To the East the vast Russian army was still able to mount regular offensives, albeit with diminishing degrees of success. All this had undoubtedly contributed to the normalisation and acceptance of the war, and to the civilian population's preoccupation with domestic and local concerns.

However, on the face of it at least, enough happened during 1917 in both external and domestic affairs to divert the attention of the civilian population from their local everyday matters. The fall of the Tsar seriously weakened the ability of the great ally in the East to provide timely diversions from military disasters in the West. The morale of French troops was seriously damaged by the débâcle on the Chemin des Dames and the mutinies at the front during the late spring and early summer. By the end of the year one ally had been rendered hors de combat by the Bolshevik coup and replaced by a new one, the USA, whose commitment to the conflict and ability to provide effective military and economic succour was as yet uncertain. Another ally, Italy, had suffered a serious military defeat at Caporetto, and the proposed conference of International Socialists at Stockholm had failed to provide the basis for a negotiated peace. At home a succession of spy scandals, exposures of corruption, the general lack of a sufficiently energetic prosecution of the war and a mounting wave of strikes culminated in the appointment late in the year, as Prime Minister, of Clemenceau, the thorough-going *jusqu'au-boutiste*.

PRESS REPORTING AND THE WAR 1917–18

The moot question is the extent to which the local population was interested in and fully aware of the implications of these events. Convalescing soldiers, *permissionnaires*, refugees and soldiers' letters from the front could continue to provide channels of communication, but each in its own way was subject to a form of censorship, and of course soldiers at the front were just as unlikely to be fully aware of governmental and diplomatic initiatives and events as civilians at home. There were also meetings organised in small towns and villages by the Education Service but, as will be seen, these were only marginally successful. The press therefore remained an important medium and, for all that it had forfeited much credibility since 1914, it continued in the main to act as a considerable influence on opinion. Surveying private correspondence for June 1917, the Chairman of the *Commission du Contrôle Postal* at Lyon noted that when reference was made to the war or to political affairs, many letters amounted to little more than summaries of newspaper articles and editorials. For example, journalistic expressions like '*maximaliste*' and '*paix boiteuse*' figured prominently in the correspondence of townspeople.

There is little doubt that more people were reading newspapers in 1917 than before the war. The estimated circulation of *Le Petit Dauphinois* had risen from 35 000 in 1913 to 43 000 in mid-July 1917. In the town of Voiron alone (population 15 000) the newspaper claimed a daily circulation of 2500. The readership of *La République de l'Isère* grew from 15 000 to 21 000 by mid-1918, while *Le Droit du Peuple* increased its readership from 12 000 to 14 000, although some 90 per cent of these readers were inhabitants of Grenoble and Vienne.[1] A single newspaper could be passed around to many people in a factory or other large place of work, and the factory population was growing all the time. It was also a tradition for many of the larger cafés in towns to stock a copy of all the local dailies and some of the leading Paris ones. *Permissionnaires*, refugees and wounded soldiers could bring with them copies of dailies from the large provincial centres like Dijon, Lyon, Marseille or Bordeaux. Of course the press was still subject to heavy censorship and journalists were still denied access to the front. The conditions of war rendered almost impossible the task of accurately reporting events in distant countries like Russia and America. The upshot was that the local population continued to be badly and inaccurately informed throughout 1917 and 1918.

Naturally the local press revealed no portents of impending crisis as the year 1917 opened. Indeed *Le Petit Dauphinois* began the year on a positively optimistic note: 'we hail 1917 as the year of victory. France and her allies are more united than ever. The *Union Sacrée* and our determination to fight to the end will see us through.'[2] Albeit from a fundamentally different point of view, Chastenet, in *Le Droit du Peuple*, was equally optimistic. Referring to President Wilson's peace initiative and the Allies' clarification of war aims, he claimed that 'a ray of sunshine will sweep through Europe at last'.[3]

The first news of the Russian Revolution was reported locally on 18 March. The fall of the Romanov dynasty did of course relieve democratic France of a somewhat embarrassing ally. Conveniently forgetting the praise which it had hitherto heaped on the Tsar and the war effort of the Russian autocracy, *Le Petit Dauphinois* hailed the Revolution as a 'revolution for victory', praising the *union sacrée* of all the Russians against Germany. When news filtered through of Prince Lvov's declaration of intent to elect a Constituent Assembly along democratic lines, the whole event was elevated to the status of a 'miraculous achievement'.[4]

Socialist journalists had always been more equivocal about their autocratic ally. In his first report of the Revolution Chastenet devoted an entire front page to an indictment of the 'most savage and repressive régime in history'. This was precisely the same wording with which he had described the Kaiser's régime less than a year previously. He hailed 'with emotion and joy the great work which has just been achieved by our Russian brothers . . . the war can now be confirmed as a truly liberating one. What a great moment this is for Socialists.'[5]

Fundamentally, the non-Socialist press was concerned with events in Russia only in so far as they affected Russia's ability to continue to act as an effective war ally, and the general consensus was that the Provisional Government was now free to prosecute the war more energetically. The publication of Miliukov's reassuring note to the Allies to this effect was thus received with joy. Even the clerical and reactionary *Croix de l'Isère* added its own note of welcome to the new régime.

It is of course too much to expect local journalists, deprived as they were of reliable information about events in their own country, amongst their own troops and in their own Government, to have understood fully the political and diplomatic situation in Russia. The modern reader who traces reportage of events in Russia from the fall of the Tsar, through the Kerensky Offensive, the Kornilov attempt, the Bolshevik coup, the Treaty of Brest–Litovsk and the beginnings of civil war in 1918 is struck not just by the inaccuracies, but by the sheer uncertainty with which local French journalists tackled the news from Russia. This was not for the want of trying. It cannot be said that journalists lost interest in Russia during 1917. Indeed hardly a few days went by without one or another of the local dailies devoting a major article or editorial to events in the East. The problem was that local journalists, and hence the local population, simply did not know what was really happening inside Russia. Reassurance remained the keynote. The Kerensky Offensive, for example, was still being hailed in the local French press as a great success long after it had been revealed in Russia as an unmitigated disaster.

From May onwards the name of Lenin began to figure prominently in the local press. Outside Socialist circles he was hitherto a little-known, rather shadowy figure. Once his advocacy of a separate peace with Germany and his encouragement of desertion by Russian soldiers became known in the West, he was treated by non-Socialists as the worst type of *maximaliste*, in the pay of the Kaiser and rivalling the latter as 'public enemy number one'. Chastenet, in a lengthy panegyric, described the Bolshevik leader, despite his open contempt for Mensheviks, Socialist Revolutionaries and moderate Socialists in the West, as a 'great man, a man of steel who alone can guide Russia to her true Socialist destiny'.[6]

Immediately after the Bolshevik coup nobody really knew who was in power, who the Bolsheviks really were or what their strength was, which is hardly surprising since the position was far from clear even within Russia. On 15 November *Le Petit Dauphinois* spoke of a rift among the revolutionary leaders. Moscow was reported as being at war with Petrograd and, on 16 November, Lenin and Trotsky were said to have been condemned to death and to be in the process of fleeing from Russia. On 18 November the paper reported a 'state of anarchy' in Russia, but on the following day it was finally acknowledged that the Bolsheviks were triumphant. From then on, once the Bolshevik peace proposals had been made known to French journalists, *Le Petit Dauphinois* turned the full weight of its vituperative powers against Lenin and Trotsky, denouncing their 'treason' in lengthy articles during the last week of November. Rumours about separate peace proposals placed French Socialist journalists in a rather awkward position. In *Le Droit du Peuple* on 10 November Chastenet asked, 'should we rejoice or be sad about the situation in Russia? We must not be too hard on the Bolsheviks, their struggle for power has been difficult.' One week later he was portraying the Bolsheviks as the 'Jacobins' of the Russian Revolution, as against Kerensky's 'Girondins'. 'Do not worry,' he wrote, 'the Russians will stay with us.'[7] By Christmas 1917, however, *Le Droit* could no longer ignore the serious news and implications of separate peace. Deploring it, Chastenet simply hoped that the French people would fully understand that this was a logical outcome of the earlier failure of the Stockholm Conference.[8]

The entry of the USA into the war provoked fewer divisions among local journalists, although from the clerical point of view the USA did embody many of the evils of modern society which French Catholics were supposed to be fighting against. In fact surprisingly little was written about the Americans during 1917. To the local journalists, Americans and American history and culture were almost as much of a mystery, and as little understood, as the Russians, despite the traditions of Lafayette and the American and French Revolutions. There was a brief flurry of articles on the German–American diplomatic rift in January and February 1917, then news about America was absent for a couple of months. A general consensus among journalists was that the amassing of large armies by the USA and the sheer difficulty of transporting them across the Atlantic would take far too long to influence the war. It was hoped that the war would be won before the Americans arrived. *La Croix de l'Isère* also voiced a fear which was soon to be echoed in local opinion: the Americans, having made the effort to mobilise troops and transport them, might have an interest in prolonging the war in order to gain some share of the spoils of victory. Paul Mistral, in *Le Droit*, also admitted that readers were worried about American intervention: 'they are saying that America is not ready or prepared for war, it might take them months or even years to prepare'.[9] This uncertainty was not helped by the sheer confusion about the potential strength of the Americans. At the beginning of April, for example, *Le Petit Dauphinois* reported that American military strength numbered 700 000 soldiers. Two days later it was reporting three million and, the day after that, five million American soldiers ready to fight the Germans. By early June this figure had been doubled to over ten million.

It was the Liberal and Socialist journalists who most welcomed the Americans as allies. The great advantage from the point of view of propaganda was that the war could now be fully represented as a true struggle of democratic nations against the dark forces of repressive autocracy. Socialist journalists also particularly welcomed Wilson as a potential arbiter of peace. His projected League of Nations and the principles of national self-determination impressed writers like Chastenet and Mistral, and an entire front page of *Le Droit* was devoted to explaining to readers the importance, meaning and implications of the League.[10] Extreme *jusqu'auboutistes*, however, while welcoming a potentially powerful ally, were less likely to be impressed by the more liberal of Wilson's projections. *La Croix*, for example, denounced the idea of the League as 'a universal republic established on the ruin of all sovereignty; it is the dream of the Jew and the work of the freemason'.[11]

Military and civilian censorship prevented journalists from writing much about the French offensive on the Chemin des Dames in the spring of 1917. In the traditions of *bourrage de crâne*, *Le Petit Dauphinois* did refer to the 'grand and glorious victories of the French army' and provided lengthy praise of the achievements, ability and prestige of Pétain. It hailed the capture of Craonne as a 'brilliant feat of arms'.[12] Only *Le Droit du Peuple* revealed a certain anxiety about the lack of news and the general air of secrecy. In an article entitled 'What is going on at the front?' Chastenet repeated the journalists' favourite complaint about lack of access to concrete information on military affairs. Not surprisingly one searches in vain throughout the local press for the slightest hint of mutinies and the crisis of morale which followed the disaster on the Chemin des Dames.[13]

At least during the early part of the war, the *Union Sacrée* had deprived journalists of the Third Republic of their favourite occupation: revelling in periodic orgies of scandal-mongering, political

polemicising and attacks upon the 'corruption' of the Government
of the day. The year 1917 provided them with a good opportunity
to indulge themselves and, in the process, to reveal the extent to
which the original ideals of the *Union Sacrée* had, to all intents and
purposes, become a dead letter, despite continued lip service being
paid to 'unity of purpose', 'co-operation' and 'unselfishness'. The
spy scandals, attacks on the Government and the appointment of
Clemenceau were therefore given good coverage throughout the
latter part of the year and during 1918. The appointment of
Clemenceau as Prime Minister was enthusiastically welcomed
outside the Socialist press. 'Here at last is the man of iron, the
"Gambetta" of this war who will lead us to a triumphant end',
proclaimed *Le Petit Dauphinois*.[14] This view was shared by *La
République de l'Isère* and, despite Clemenceau's anti-clerical past, by
La Croix de l'Isère. Socialists continued to regard the 'Tiger' as the
vicious strike-breaker of the turn of the century. 'He has never
shed his old anti-Socialist ideas,' claimed Chastenet, 'he represents
the most blind forces of *jusqu'au-boutisme*. With a man like this in
control the war could drag on indefinitely.'[15]

In view of the diplomatic events and continued disappointments, combined with the worsening economic situation at home
throughout 1917, it is not surprising that the local press greeted
1918 in a rather less optimistic fashion than that in which it had
begun 1917. *La Croix de l'Isère* gave a résumé of 1917, enumerating
the defeatist campaigns of the Socialist press and bewailing the
lack of common purpose among the *Entente* powers. It ridiculed
the notion that the German people as a whole could be separated
from the policies of their leaders: '1918 finds us in a troublesome
position which we could hardly have expected a year earlier. We
must fight on to the very end, to total victory and total defeat of the
enemy, nothing less will do.'[16] *Le Petit Dauphinois* referred to New
Year's Day 1918 as a 'formidable date which will be inscribed in the
book of destiny'. There was no mention of the likelihood of victory
that year, simply a renewed call to place faith and trust in the
endeavours of the soldiers.[17] Throughout the cold winter months
Le Petit Dauphinois, in particular, intensified the old device of using
the sacrifices of the soldiers to exhort the civilians to bear their
sacrifices at home: 'the *poilu* will stay firm and resolute if we can
show him that we can support him to the very end'.[18]

As journalists became aware of the German offensive at the end
of March there was a renewed bout of *bourrage de crâne*. During the

last three months of the war, war news dominated the front pages of all the local dailies. By now it was clear to all journalists that a victorious end to the war was not far away although, having learnt from the over-optimistic forecasts of September and October 1914, no newspaper dared suggest a date for the actual end of hostilities.

When the news of the Armistice arrived the local press, predictably, had a field day. *La Croix* welcomed the destruction of the 'nation of bandits' which had done all it could to 'exterminate us by fire, steel and poison. Unable to poison us by gas, they had tried to poison us with Bolshevism.'[19] *Le Droit du Peuple* welcomed with 'deep joy' the news of the 'revolution' in Germany, regretting only that the German people had not overthrown their hated Prussian militarist and imperialist leaders much earlier in the war: 'the way the war has ended vindicates the policies we French Socialists have been advocating for over four years'.[20] For *Le Petit Dauphinois* and *La République de l'Isère* the Armistice was also a vindication of the *jusqu'au-boutiste* approach:

> We were right not to give in to the demands for anything less than a total, unconditional surrender. We have sacrificed much, but it has not been in vain. Our Prime Minister, Clemenceau, and our *Generalissimo*, Foch, have seen us through. This is a great victory for France and the *Union Sacrée*.[21]

FLUCTUATIONS OF MORALE 1917–18

The extent to which the local population was aware of external events and was interested in them can be revealed by a perusal of the civilian and military correspondence intercepted by the local *Commission du Contrôle Postal*, which increased its surveillance during 1917 and 1918.[22] From October 1917 onwards, generals in command of the various military regions also compiled their own monthly bulletins surveying local opinion and morale based on regular reports from military personnel, *préfets*, *sous-préfets* and *commissaires de police*.[23] In addition to this, local civilian authorities intensified their own surveillance of Syndicalist, Socialist and strike activity, activities and attitudes of foreign workers, activities in war factories, and so on. The last eighteen months of the war, therefore, are particularly well documented for the purposes of the researcher assessing fluctuations of morale and opinion.

Considering the diversity of origin of these sources – private correspondence and official reports – it is worth noting that they do not differ on essential points, and a number of observations can be made.

The correspondence suggests that fluctuations of morale were fairly wide during the last two years of the war. Throughout the winter months of 1917 civilian opinion remained preoccupied with domestic and local concerns. Letters from villagers complained about the lack of labour, even during the dead season, and there were increasing complaints from all sections of opinion about rising prices. Not surprisingly the coal shortages were referred to more than anything else in the civilian correspondence: the cold weather and coal shortage were mentioned in nearly 75 per cent of letters.[24] There was hardly any reference to politics or international events. Indeed the war itself (that is, military affairs) was mentioned in only a minority of civilian letters. 'On the whole', concluded the Chairman of the *Commission* at the end of March, 'civilian morale remains satisfactory, the population are anxious about the continuing length of the war, but are still almost unanimous in their opinion that the war will be won in the not too distant future. There is very little pacifist or defeatist talk.'[25]

In April and May, for the first time in many months, military affairs and international events figured prominently in civilians' letters. The Russian Revolution was referred to in nearly 50 per cent of townspeople's letters, but in less than 25 per cent of those from the villages. The main concern here was that the Revolution might enable the Germans to release a large number of soldiers to fight on the Western Front, despite the reassuring tone of the newspapers. There were hardly any references to the possibility of American intervention in the war. Letters dated in the first week of April suggested that much was expected, by soldiers and civilians, of the Nivelle Offensive. Nearly 30 per cent of correspondents hoped that this would be the last, victorious effort. In view of this, it is hardly surprising that the overall tone of correspondence became increasingly pessimistic towards the end of May as it gradually dawned on civilians that the offensive had failed. The drop in morale was far more noticeable amongst the soldiers; there were frequent references to the incompetence of French generals. Some even referred to their 'treason'. There was, however, very little talk of revolution in soldiers' letters, and none at all was noticed in those of civilians. It is fairly clear from the correspondence that not even the soldiers were aware of the full extent of the disaster on the Chemin des Dames.[26]

In June the morale of soldiers and civilians fell even further. References to international, political and military events predominated in townspeople's letters, but still more than 50 per cent of villagers' letters made little or no reference to outside events. Nearly 25 per cent of civilian letters made some reference to the intervention of the USA, but this did not seem to have the encouraging effect on morale that one might suppose. The general consensus was not so much that America might be a powerful new ally, but that the US Government would have a vested interest in prolonging the war. Many letters also complained about the tardiness of American aid in reaching France. There was talk of treason by the French Government, although only in a minority of letters, and there was some reference in soldiers' letters to a revolution which was about to break out in Paris. Again letters from townspeople, particularly those from Grenoble and Vienne, were more depressed in tone than those from villagers. About 20 per cent of letters referred to the proposed Stockholm Conference for a negotiated peace, but the general opinion here was one of distrust, it being thought that the conference was of German inspiration. No mention of the mutinies that had broken out the previous month in several regiments was made in any of the soldiers' letters.[27]

The uncertain international and military situation, the lowering of morale at home and a marked increase in industrial unrest prompted the *préfet*, in mid-June, to write his longest, most detailed and most pessimistic report of the entire war. From April onwards, he stated, morale had fallen to its lowest point since the war had started. There was a general awareness that serious military mistakes had been made during the recent offensive. Too much trust and hope had been invested in Nivelle and the high death rate was not justified. Equally serious was the growing feeling that no new military effort was likely to be worthwhile. The population was also worried about events in Russia and the apparent inactivity on the Eastern Front. Newspaper headlines had not helped but, in the *préfet*'s view, the main cause of the decline in morale was the bad news and defeatist talk of soldiers from the front. Military indiscipline on troop trains, revolutionary talk at railway stations and in cafés, and anti-war propaganda spread by *permissionnaires* on arrival in their local villages gave a bad impression of feelings amongst the troops. What particularly worried the *préfet* was that, whereas a few months previously anti-war talk spread by soldiers on leave would usually receive short shrift from civilians, it was now far more likely to find sympathetic ears.

This was a particular problem in the towns, especially Grenoble and Vienne, whose populations were more 'impressionable, receptive and anxious'. Industrial workers were worried about the length of the war and there was increasing disgust at the huge war profits being made by certain industrialists. This was reflected in a growing number of strikes for higher wages which, fortunately, the *patrons* had hitherto granted. There was also increased Socialist and Syndicalist agitation and frequent anti-war meetings, particularly in Grenoble. The *préfet* was worried that if the workers' demands ceased to be met there might be violence on the streets, which would be very hard to deal with because of depleted police forces. Indeed, if strike movements and revolutionary propaganda spread to war factories in the region, it would be nearly impossible to meet them by force. What was needed, he suggested, was a stricter control of foreigners in the factories and a larger police force. Most importantly, the local town populations must be made more aware that the authorities were doing all they could to ease the economic situation. 'What we really need is a great success for our troops, to show the population that the war will soon be won.'

The situation in the villages, according to the *préfet*, was slightly more encouraging. On the whole farmers were less tired of the war and were bearing the strain better than the townspeople. None the less they were not hiding their feelings that the war had lasted too long. They were fed up with the continued demands being made on them and with getting nothing in return. Lack of labour, requisitions and the overall rise in prices were common complaints. Villagers were proving less and less responsive to the principles of the *Union Sacrée*, but still, compared with the towns, the village populations were continuing to show their habitual *sang-froid* and *resignation*.[28]

Between July and September 1917 the morale of soldiers and civilians improved somewhat. According to the correspondence, the appointment of Pétain with his known concern for the interests and welfare of soldiers appears to have created a good impression among the troops, and this was echoed in many civilians' letters. Preoccupations amongst civilians returned largely to complaints about high prices and shortages. It seems that remote village

populations were at least a month behind those of Grenoble and
Vienne in their appreciation of current military events.[29] An
institutrice wrote to her brother:

> The general mood of our village has returned to that of the dark
> days of September 1914. There are fears, uncertainty about the
> future, lack of reliable news about the war, rumours of revolu-
> tion in Paris which will soon spread to Lyon and Vienne, above
> all, worries about the possibility of yet another campaign. I do
> my best to calm these fears but it is very hard for me since
> neither the *adjoint* nor I have a very clear idea of what is
> happening outside our locality.[30]

By late September, even in villages like this, panic had abated.
The *Maire* of Bourg d'Oisans noted that in their weekly visits to the
market peasant women from small mountain villages and hamlets
in the Oisans had once again stopped talking of outside affairs.
Talk once more was of the price of eggs, requisitions and *allocation*
scandals; 'most seem to have resigned themselves to a fourth
winter of war'.[31] Particularly encouraging for the authorities was
the fact that the Stockholm Conference was now being dismissed,
in correspondence to and from the front, as a sign of German
weakness. 'If the enemy is going to such lengths to negotiate a
peace,' wrote an inhabitant of Grenoble to her husband, 'then they
must be in a very poor state at home. This gives us encouragement
to go on fighting until the ultimate victory.'[32]

By the end of 1917 the near certainty that the war would
continue to last through the winter and until the spring and early
summer of 1918 seems to have been generally accepted by townspeople as well as villagers. '*Résignation*' and '*lassitude*' were the
words most frequently used by *sous-préfets*, police officials and
members of the *Commission du Contrôle Postal* assessing the contents of letters. In October and November some 25 per cent
of letters surveyed referred to the French Ministerial crisis,
the majority of them from townspeople. The appointment of
Clemenceau was received enthusiastically in more than 50 per cent
of letters from civilians. Again, the Chairman of the *Commission*
noted, letters tended to copy the press in depicting Clemenceau as
the man who would restore order and bring total victory for
France. Talk of defeat was very rare in the correspondence,
although there was some anxiety about events in Russia. In

December nearly 60 per cent of letters from civilians made some pejorative reference to the Russian *maximalistes* and the separate peace. Less than 1 per cent appeared to comment favourably on Lenin and Trotsky. Another source of anxiety was the Italian defeat at Caporetto. In many cases letters from border *communes* in the eastern alpine region of the Dauphiné expressed contempt for what was regarded locally as a feeble or half-hearted contribution to the Allied war effort by the Italians, in much the same vein as references to the British effort prior to the Somme campaign of 1916. Another factor here was that a high proportion of the border population were of Italian descent.[33]

During the winter months of 1918 civilians' and soldiers' letters continued to contain abundant references to the international situation. In January some 25 per cent of civilian letters mentioned Wilson's Fourteen Points in a favourable light. The Chairman of the *Commission* did not state whether these were mainly from townspeople, but this does imply that, despite the prevailing *jusqu'au-boutiste* mentality, *revanchisme* did not as yet extend beyond the almost unanimous assumption that Alsace and Lorraine would return to France after the victory. If this is a fair reflection of local opinion then it does seem as if, despite the hate campaigns in the press, the *Dauphinois* did not as yet want crushing punishments inflicted on the German people themselves, as distinct from the Kaiser's régime.[34]

There were fewer references to the Bolsheviks in January and February. They were now considered to be beyond the pale with their separate peace proposals, although there was a brief flurry of disgust once the enormity of the signed peace at Brest–Litovsk in March had become known. Moreover, as a number of letters revealed, aid and support from the USA was finally being seen as an adequately-compensating factor. A minority of civilians' and soldiers' letters referred to the wave of strikes in the locality and throughout France. Since detailed mention of strikes was forbidden in the local press, news about strike activity must have reached inhabitants of remote villages by rumours emanating from strike-affected towns like Grenoble and Vienne. Villagers' and soldiers' letters were most condemnatory in their references to strikes and strikers, particularly since at this time soldiers were receiving something like 10 per cent of the pay of civilian workers in munitions factories.[35]

In April 1918 a new note of anxiety, caused by the German

offensive, was expressed in letters to and from the front. Some letters referred with indignation to the Russian 'treason' and to the British army's retreat before the German onslaught. The tone of townspeople's letters suggested panic, but it would be an exaggeration to state that there was a return to the mood of the dark days of September 1914. Indeed memories of the success on the Marne were invoked, as if for reassurance. Both the military governor and the Chairman of the *Commission du Contrôle Postal* noted that, despite the uncertainty of the current military situation, the vast majority of letters of soldiers and civilians indicated a trust and confidence in Clemenceau and the French High Command. The main reasons for this trust, according to the correspondence, were the 'enormous' German losses, the near unanimous belief that French soldiers were invincible, the fact that France and the Allies finally had unity of command under the Frenchman, Foch, and belief in the determination and iron will of Clemenceau. The only regret, it seems, was that the 'Tiger' had not been in charge of the Government from the beginning. There were by now few references in the correspondence to political scandals, and less than 5 per cent of letters showed any indication of a desire to stop short of a total victory. The very small number of letters advocating peace at any price came from the larger industrial centres, mainly Lyon, Grenoble and Vienne. The village population remained almost unanimously '*résolu*'.[36]

During the early summer of 1918 villagers and inhabitants of small towns maintained their resolute mood, although citizens of Grenoble and Vienne, referring to a wave of strikes during May, displayed continuing anxiety. Some letters from these larger towns were showing increased concern about the length of the war and an impatience with the apparent absence of an Allied breakthrough on the Western Front. In July and August, with the check of the German advance, morale rose considerably even in Grenoble and Vienne. There were more references than hitherto to the Americans as allies, and the general tone of the letters was that this time the Allied counter-offensive would be decisive. Letters from villagers showed more concern for local and every-day matters than they had for several months. 'It is as if', noted the military governor, 'the peasants are now totally reassured about the military situation. They know that the war will be won, they have total trust in our leadership and now they can concentrate on prospects for the harvest.'[37]

Understandably, during the last three months of the war, as the Allied counter-offensive began to gain ground, morale rose accordingly. In September, according to the military governor, the overall state of morale was at its highest point since early 1914. Military affairs predominated in the correspondence, and the word 'victory' appeared more and more. There was now almost unanimous reference to the 'certainty' of final victory, but the civilian population had become so used to disappointments and the protracted nature of the war that even the most optimistic of letters did not envisage an end to hostilities before the spring of 1919. Some of the more pessimistic of townspeople's letters even suggested that final victory would not come until some time in 1920. Generally, now assured of victory, opinion seemed to be prepared for heavy sacrifices still to come. Pacifist or defeatist references were, not surprisingly, extremely rare.[38]

By September 1918 a new note had crept into the letters of soldiers and civilians; hatred of the Germans was now being expressed more strongly and frequently than at any time since the beginning of the war. Extreme *revanchiste* sentiments were noted in some 25 per cent of townspeople's letters although soldiers were, on the whole, less anti-German. Of course the renewed bout of *bourrage de crâne* in the press accounted for much of this, but a major reason was that the German advances earlier in the year had caused a major new influx of refugees throughout France, and they had brought with them more 'atrocity' stories which were augmented by the Allied liberation, during August and September, of regions previously occupied by the Germans. There was some concern from townspeople about having to face yet another winter of war, and there were continuing complaints from all sections of society about prices, rationing and shortages, but on the whole both the *préfet* and the military governor agreed that morale was 'excellent'.[39]

The local civilian population had so learnt to discipline themselves after four years of offensives and counter-offensives, expectations, disappointments and exhortations to give one last effort, that the rapid turnover of events during October and November which concluded the war seems to have taken them by surprise. The realisation that a war which had dragged on for so long was very soon to be over created an overall feeling of stupefaction. Obviously the prospect of immediate peace was the main topic in the correspondence at this time. *Revanchiste* sentiments continued to grow as more and more areas of North-East France were liberated. Distrust of the sincerity of the 'democratic' revolution in Germany was a feature of the correspondence, it being felt that the abdication of the Kaiser and talk of setting up a 'liberal' democracy had happened too quickly to be genuine. Many letters suggested that it was all a cosmetic device by the German leaders to escape the full and just consequences of defeat.[40]

Despite obvious relief at the news of the Armistice, there were few expressions of joy or euphoria in the letters. The mood of November 1918 was in a sense analogous with that of August 1914. Once again, this time after more than four years of war, one was entering the unknown. Uncertainty about the future, the possibility that hostilities might break out again, complaints from many veterans of the older classes about the tardiness of their demobilisation, impatience of the younger classes at the prospect of having to spend many more months in uniform, were all factors contributing to the rather muted tone of the letters. A minority of letters expressed anxiety about the prospects for employment of *démobilisés* and *mutilés*, and about the possibility of the laying off of large numbers of wartime munitions workers, both male and female. There was also the influenza epidemic, which was mentioned in about 20 per cent of civilian letters. Above all, of course, expressions of relief were tinged with the feeling of sadness. At Grenoble, two days after the Armistice, the municipal authorities staged a 'festival of victory'. A *cortège* of *mutilés*, French and American soldiers, and young conscripts of the class of 1920 paraded through the town. There were the inevitable chants of the *'Marseillaise'*. Crowds lined the main streets, flowers were thrown, there were patriotic songs and dances in the main cafés, but, the *préfet* noted, the dominant atmosphere was one of restraint. 'Our population has been through too much, and undergone too many sacrifices. We have held on until the final defeat of Germany, but the *Dauphinois* are fully aware of the price that France has had to pay for this.'[41] At Vienne a similar, but smaller, parade was held. Occasional strains of the *'Internationale'* could be heard, although this was scarcely sufficient to drown the patriotic songs. Again, the *sous-préfet* noted, the overall atmosphere was not quite as buoyant as had been anticipated. In both towns, however, there were no threats to law and order and, surprisingly, very few incidences of rowdiness or drunkenness.[42]

In the smaller towns and villages the atmosphere was even more restrained and muted. Here also there were public ceremonies and rituals. As soon as the official note of the German capitulation had been made known, the *Maire* of Allevard ordered the church bell to be rung, calling in the workers from the surrounding fields and emptying the local factories for a gathering in the town square, where the '*Marseillaise*' and American national anthem were sung, although not the British anthem. On the steps of the town hall he gave a short homily on the deliverance of France, a résumé of all the work that the local population had done for the war effort and of all the sacrifices that had been made, concluding with a list of the dead and wounded of the *commune*. A local *institutrice* noted rapid changes of mood, from initial surprise, 'stupefaction', to relief that it was all over. Perhaps the news took a long time to sink in, or perhaps the litany of sacrifices imposed a sombre note on the proceedings, but there were few signs of outright joy or enthusiasm. The *institutrice* explained this by saying that there had been too many ceremonies and rituals during the war.[43]

At Rives a bonfire was lit in the town square and songs were sung, but it was noted that the most enthusiastic participants in the celebrations were the young conscripts of the class of 1920, for the news meant, of course, that they would not be going off to fight at the front.[44] In those *communes* that had suffered particularly heavy losses of life the celebrations were, not surprisingly, even more muted. The *Maire* of Bourg d'Oisans noted 'nothing really unusual' about the mood of his *commune* during the second week of November. 'Our people remember all the deaths, all the sadness. We are just glad and relieved that it is all over. We will not be holding any celebrations.'[45] An *institutrice* from the village of Lalley noted a curious atmosphere of anti-climax after years of expectations and disappointments.[46] The Socialist *Maire* of La Motte d'Aveillans remarked rather cynically that a number of people had made so much money from the war that they did not fully welcome the peace.[47] Perhaps Marie Plissonier, the *institutrice* from Lavaldens, summed up the village mood most adequately:

We had all worked so hard for the final victory and had suffered so much along the way. There was no formal ceremony in the evening we received the news. I don't think we felt like celebrating too much. All that we had worked and hoped for had been granted to us, but many of us felt that it had taken too long and cost far too much in money and lives to achieve. There was a 'flatness' about the atmosphere. I think we had known all along that we would eventually win the war, particularly after September 1914. After four years we had become so used to war that we had prepared ourselves for another winter of shortages. Besides, many of our villagers were not convinced that an end to the war would mean an end to shortages and rationing.[48]

Clearly the bulk of the local civilian population had remained resolute in its support of the Government's aim of continuing the war to a total victory for France. Despite the years of death and destruction, the pain of family separations, the *bouleversements* and upheavals of war and the economic problems on the home front, the people of the Isère had held firm and proved, in the main, impervious to defeatist or pacifist talk. Morale had certainly fluctuated and wavered during particularly difficult and uncertain periods throughout 1917 and 1918, but it had never cracked and, in the event, although the war effort was sometimes impaired by strike activity, this never reached proportions sufficient to threaten the régime seriously.

RESIGNATION IN THE VILLAGES

Morale in the villages appears to have fluctuated somewhat less than in industrial centres like Grenoble and Vienne. The survey of village correspondence in fact suggests that morale in rural areas never reached a crisis point, and a good case can be made for the argument that the overall trend of village opinion of the war and all its disruptions was fundamentally no different during 1917 and 1918 from what it had been during 1915 and 1916, and that, while it fluctuated, it continued to avoid the extremes of outright patriotic endeavour on the one hand and revolutionary defeatism or pacifism on the other. Of course, as has already been pointed out, the absence of the better-educated, more articulate and potentially more critical members of village populations helps to account for this. It must also be borne in mind that in the more remote and 'backward' villages and hamlets the local *curé*, *instituteur* or *institutrice* would help to compose and write letters to the front and would be unlikely to express overtly anti-war sentiments. None the less one searches in vain through reports of opened letters from villages to the front, or through the letters of *maires*, village *instituteurs* or private farmers to the *préfet* for any reference to, or evidence of, fundamental discontent with the régime. There were, of course, isolated criticisms of various Government administrations and their conduct of the war but, outside the ranks of extreme political activists and militants, only in the occasional anonymous letter to the *préfet* was the very nature and *raison d'être* of the Third Republic called into question. Indeed, even amongst the *Grenoblois* and *Viennois*, such discontented references were rare and again largely confined to anonymous letters to the *préfet*. It is significant that criticisms and attacks on Government policies almost totally ceased after the appointment of Clemenceau was made known.

A second feature of the correspondence is the very rare mention of death and destruction in both villagers' and townspeople's letters. This is extraordinary considering the large numbers of families affected by bereavement by 1917. The rather matter-of-fact tone of civilian letters, particularly those of villagers, was noted by the Chairman of the *Commission du Contrôle Postal*: 'in the main, while the letters of civilians continue to complain about the length of the war, prices, rationing, lack of coal and so on, they exhibit an extraordinary stoicism, an acceptance of human sacrifice. It is as if talk of death is a taboo subject.' Returning to this theme three months later when, for the second time in the war, the Germans were threatening Paris and the immediate outlook seemed very depressing, he commented on the 'ostrich-like' tone of the villagers' letters and remarked that, rather than talk about the deaths and sacrifices of this war, the civilians seemed to be motivated by a kind of 'blind faith' in the outcome.

Blind faith or not, there is no doubt that even in the middle of the crisis period of early summer 1917, at the lowest point of morale during the war, expressions of belief in the final victory of France exceeded by far the fears of defeat. Village letters expressing anxiety or uncertainty about the outcome numbered only just over half of those expressing confidence, and 'anxiety' soon receded in July and August as another harvest loomed.

This implies that even during *l'Année Terrible* all thoughts in the villages must be directed towards the immediate and vitally important agricultural work. This should not be too surprising: harvest work traditionally dominated the village calendar, farmers' livelihoods were at stake and, in any case, the full weight of Government propaganda, channelled through the local administration, the press and the Education Service, was geared to agricultural production for the war. In this context it is noticeable that reported attempts to sabotage agricultural production in order to shorten the war were almost non-existent in 1917 and 1918. Indeed not even during the last, optimistic month of October 1918 did references to external affairs exceed, in percentage terms, references to local or economic matters.

A third feature of villagers' correspondence, and again this is to a certain extent true of letters from *Grenoblois* and *Viennois*, is the general absence of reference to war aims. On the whole the civilian population of the Isère seems rarely to have asked 'why are we fighting?' even during low points in morale. Presumably it was a superfluous question since the priority had never changed since the early days of the war. French people were still fighting to repel the invader and it was almost an article of faith that Alsace and Lorraine would be returned to France. Beyond this, and the assumption that the war would end in a total victory, there were few references to the post-war world until the last month of the war when, as has been seen, stories of atrocities caused a wave of *revanchiste* references. There were increased calls at this time for heavy reparations from the Germans but, again, this was nothing really new: the assumption that 'Germany must pay' went hand-in-glove with the *jusqu'au-boutiste* view. Furthermore, while the Germans were still occupying North-East France and the war had yet to be won, there was likely to be little real interest in the more practical proposals of a League of Nations beyond the vague notion that this must be 'the war to end wars'.

It must not be assumed from all this that the villagers ceased to take an interest in the war during 1917 and 1918. Obviously this would have been impossible bearing in mind the sacrifices that had been made. Even when villagers received fresh quotas of refugees during 1918, there were very few reported references to 'your war' such as had been reported in parts of Provence and Brittany. Deserters in the villages were just as likely to be denounced to the military authorities in 1918 as they had been in 1914. Indeed there were few enough French deserters or *insoumis* to denounce. In the *Arrondissement* of Grenoble only nineteen cases were recorded throughout 1917. There were, however, far more deserters from the Italian army, and many of them had made their way across the border to the villages and towns of the Isère. There were 185 Italian deserters arrested in 1917 and eighty-two in the first quarter of

1918, after the defeat at Caporetto. Many of these sought anonymity in Grenoble and Vienne, working under assumed names in factories.[49] Those who rather foolishly went to the villages would be very lucky to avoid suspicion and denunciation. Again many, under assumed names, found work in the fields. Despite the perenially pressing need for agricultural labour, farmers in twenty-four villages in the Isère obediently noted and reported to the local authorities all suspicious behaviour of these foreigners, leading to their arrest. Particularly vigilant were the farmers of Laval who, throughout 1918, performed citizens' arrests on ten Italian deserters.[50]

The villagers were more severe on French deserters. On 29 December 1917 a twenty-eight-year-old *mobilisé*, Jacob Vial, was recorded as having failed to report to his unit after a twelve-day *permission*. Equipped with his rifle and ammunition, he ensconced himself in the mountains above his home village of Uriage. For food he stole from the various isolated farmhouses in the region and, although spotted several times at night during the following week, he always seemed to vanish when attempts were made to arrest him. At first the more credulous inhabitants of Uriage thought that he was but a reincarnation of the local werewolf which had supposedly terrorised the villagers during the 1880s, and it was difficult for the local *gendarmes* to organise search parties from the village on account of the fear that this legend provoked. On 12 January 1918, however, Vial's mother received this letter from her son telling her of his whereabouts:

> I want to know why these idiots of *gendarmes* continue to pursue me. I owe them nothing. I have done my duty more than they have. They can return to their houses, to their wives and children every night. What do they know of the war? We are all fed up with killing: Germans, French, anybody. All I want to do is go back to my farm and live in peace.

As soon as his widowed mother received this, she showed it to the local *chef de gendarmes* asking him to capture her son as soon as possible. 'I wish him no harm. All I want is for him to be allowed to return to his unit. I have already lost one son in this war. I want him to finish his duty until this whole terrible business is over.' Jacob was captured two nights later by neighbours of Mme Vial and was subsequently sentenced to five years' detention. The *maire* promptly thanked the mother for observing her duty.[51]

In the main, young *mobilisés* of the class of 1919 departed from their villages for the front with much the same ritual and with just as little dissent as their predecessors had done in 1915 and 1916. However, if the villagers seemed impervious to anti-war sentiments, it cannot be said that, barring a few exceptions, they exhibited any more pro-war sentiments than they had since 1914. The key word in correspondence here is *'lassitude'* or war weariness, a feeling that the authorities were continuing to demand too much of the villagers. This is particularly noticeable in *maires'* responses to the organisation of *journées* and in the ability and willingness of the inhabitants of their *communes* to receive new quotas of refugees. The difficulty of assessing and evaluating the actual financial contributions of villagers to *œuvres de guerre* and *journées* has already been pointed out. What is noticeable and revealing is that more and more *maires* throughout 1917 and 1918 were finding it difficult to organise, or find anybody else to organise, teams of volunteers to undertake such work. For example 280 of the 564 *communes* in the *département* failed to respond to the *Journée Nationale des Tuberculeux* organised in May 1917.

The same lack of willingness was noted on the question of receiving more refugees in 1918. As a final resort the *préfet* could always compel the *commune* to receive its quota, but the *maires'* responses to questionnaires on their *commune*'s facilities are revealing. Only about 30 per cent of the rural *communes* can be said to have exhibited an open willingness to receive yet more refugees. Many claimed to have done their share of duty earlier in the war. In this respect some cited the bad, unco-operative behaviour of previous refugees in their villages. Fifty-four *communes* refused point blank to receive any more. 'We are fed up with all this. We sympathise with the refugees, but why can't they be lodged in Grenoble, or Lyon, or Paris?' was one typical remark from the *Maire* of La Motte.[52] Many *maires* complained that refugees were a strain on the coal reserves of the municipality. At Ville Sous Anjou the *maire* wrote that the dispersed rural population in his vicinity had already contributed more than their share to the war effort: 'they do not want to share the intimacy of their private lives and their houses with any more foreigners and outsiders, they prefer to prepare their houses for the homecomings of their own folk from the trenches'.[53]

The campaigns for the third and fourth *emprunts de guerre* in 1917 and 1918 also received a muted response from villagers. Here, of course, the Government was asking for loans rather than donations, repayable at 5 per cent interest. Each of the four *emprunts* organised throughout the war was accompanied by increasingly intense and sophisticated propaganda. Since the *emprunts* were fundamental means of financing the war effort, everything was done to stir the emotions and imagination of the local population. On 26 October 1917 the Minister of the Interior wrote to the *préfet*: 'you must carry out the most active propaganda. Constitute a *Comité Départemental* and authorise the organisation of local *comités* by *maires*.'[54] In the towns the chief propagandists were the businessmen, *patrons*, academics and senior *fonctionnaires*. In the smaller and more remote villages the task fell to the already over-burdened *maires*, *instituteurs* and *institutrices*.

Despite intense effort, the villagers' response to the *emprunt* of 1917 was disappointing, although this was compensated for by an encouraging response from the towns. Of course the *instituteurs* in the villages had to use tact: on the one hand the Government was continually exhorting the peasant to put his money back into the land, now, on the other hand, he was being asked to lend to the State. The Rector of the Academy of Grenoble understood the problem: 'we should not blame the peasants for not wanting to lend money to the State but we must convince them somehow that the more they lend for the war effort, the sooner the victory will be won and the sooner they can get back to normal'.[55]

In fact many peasants thought the opposite to this: the more they lent to the State, the longer the war would go on. 'We have already lent money in 1915 and 1916, this did not bring an end to the war, why should this *emprunt* be any different?' was a typical response from one old widow at Reventin-Vaugris. In the Oisans mountain region, where the campaign met with least success, most of the peasants openly stated that they would prefer to bury their money as they had always done rather than lend it to continue the war.[56] A common response was that villagers simply had little money to lend, burdened as they were with requisition quotas, taxes and punitive mortgage repayments. There was also a counter-propaganda campaign against the *emprunts* organised by the Socialist Rafin-Dugens, although it is difficult to assess whether villagers took much notice of this. More damaging perhaps was the fact that a number of soldiers wrote from the front instructing their parents or wives not to lend money for the war effort. The timing of the *emprunt* was also unpropitious. November and December

1917 were very cold winter months, money in the villages was needed for coal, and the overall level of morale was not good.

The campaign in the villages for the 1918 *emprunt* met with more success. Opening, as it did, in the third week of October, it coincided with the near certainty of a total French victory and an end to the war. This time there were fewer remarks about prolonging the war and fewer attempts at counter-propaganda. In December 1918 the Rector of the Academy voted that only in two, Socialist, municipalities did villagers show any outright opposition to the *emprunt* campaign, although again, as in 1917, he noted that the overall response of townspeople was more encouraging.[57]

Equally apathetic was the general response of villagers in 1917 and 1918 to the increased propaganda campaign to explain war aims, give reasons for fighting and motivate civilian morale in small towns and villages. Once again the main burden of work fell on *instituteurs* and *institutrices*. Most of this was carried out under the auspices of the propaganda organisation *Toute la France debout pour la victoire du droit*. Two hundred and eight conferences were held in the *département* during the last year of the war.

Since there was insufficient personnel to visit all the villages, the aim was that as many villagers as possible should be able to attend conferences in the nearest local towns. They were usually held on Saturday afternoons and evenings. Most of the conferences were reasonably well attended, but mainly by townspeople. Whether because the distance was too far to travel, because of bad weather, or because farmers were exhausted after long days in the fields, most of the propagandists reported a poor turnout by peasants. One *institutrice* noted that, where villagers did attend and ask questions, these were usually couched in terms expressing complaints about their local municipal council and its handling of requisitions, *allocations* and so on, or complaints about prices and shortages. Where the war itself was referred to, questions were usually of the most basic and simple type, such as 'why do our husbands have to wait so long for *permissions*?', 'why is the war lasting so long?'[58]

Instituteurs and *institutrices* also gave specially commissioned lectures in the larger villages during the last year of war. These were really simplified versions of the conferences. By mid-1918 only a few of the more remote villages and hamlets had not staged such a lecture. It was a difficult task for the speakers, who had to explain not just why the war was lasting so long and Germany was still holding out, but why Russian 'defection' really made no difference to the chance of victory and why the Americans were not sending over more soldiers. In addition to this, the rise in prices and shortages had to be explained in simple terms. In order to be able to talk for an hour to adult audiences on these themes, the *instituteurs* and *institutrices* received regular fortnightly bulletins from the *rectorat* summarising the latest military situation and developments in international affairs. Even so a number of speakers found the task beyond them. 'I really cannot talk for an hour on why we are fighting,' wrote an *instituteur* from La Roche, 'I can explain in simple terms that we need to get rid of the invader and regain the lost provinces, that is easy, and our peasants know that already, but I find the more complicated war aims and ideas of a League of Nations most difficult to understand.'[59]

Perhaps the ignorance of some of the speakers did not really matter, for as the *instituteur* noted:

> They don't ask many questions about what is going to happen in the world after the war. The questions they do ask are often of the type which I cannot adequately answer. How can I really explain why the war has lasted so long and why Germany has yet to be beaten? I read out extracts from the various pamphlets supplied to me, but either the audience doesn't understand, or is simply not interested.[60]

Another *instituteur* found it 'hypocritical' to maintain the idea of a continuing national effort in his locality. 'I avoid all reference to the *Union Sacrée* in my lectures since this virtually ceased to exist in our village two years ago.'[61] One *institutrice* from Saint-Priest refused point blank to give a talk on war aims: 'I cannot give talks on why we are fighting. In our locality there have been too many diverse experiences. Some have suffered greatly, others have benefited. This would only inflame public opinion.'[62]

Despite the apparent lack of interest in events which did not concern their immediate families or localities (economic fluctuations, rarity and short length of *permissions*, how long the war will last and so on), the general mood of the populations of small towns and villages, according to responses to conferences and lectures, does not seem to have worried the Rector of the Academy unduly. In a report on the achievements of the propaganda campaigns of 1917–18 he virtually reiterated what the *préfet* had said about the morale of villagers in June 1917:

They seem tired and discontented with the continuing length of the war. The State asked a lot of them and they have responded magnificently, but now one feels that they are simply 'putting up' with the war. They show neither a patriotic fervour nor enthusiasm in the national effort, nor a willingness to listen to unpatriotic or defeatist talk. They are resigned to the fact of war and just want us to win it as quickly as possible.[63]

JUSQU'AU-BOUTISME IN THE TOWNS

It was in the industrial centres, mainly Grenoble and Vienne, that, as the *préfet* noted, morale reached a dangerously low point. In reality there were two periods during 1917 and 1918 when a crisis situation can be said to have obtained: in the early summer of 1917 when news of disasters on the Chemin des Dames appeared to coincide with a wave of strikes, and in the early summer of 1918 when the renewed fear that the Germans might take Paris again coincided with an upsurge of strike activity.

At the end of June 1917 senior personnel of the Army General Staff compiled two separate lists, by *départements,* showing levels of morale in the countryside and in major towns. In the Isère morale in the villages was said to be 'quite good', but in the large towns it was said to be 'bad', with frequent references to peace at any price and particularly poor reports of the behaviour of *permissionnaires*. Both Grenoble and Vienne figured on a list of thirty-four towns in the whole of unoccupied France where morale was so low that especially intense surveillance would need to be mounted on the activities of workers in war factories, combined with an all-out campaign to combat the depression of morale.[64]

Clearly the General Staff thought they had a crisis on their hands in mid-1917. The important question here is the extent to which the activity of minority Socialists and revolutionary or pacifist activity had ceased to be indirect, isolated and ineffective. There was indeed an active Socialist anti-war propaganda campaign in Grenoble throughout 1917. The *Commissaire de Police* noted six minority-Socialist meetings at the *Bourse du Travail* in March, eight in April, seven in June, ten in July, five in August, tailing off to eleven throughout the last four months of the year. The basic theme of these meetings was propaganda for the *Comité Pour La Reprise des Relations Internationales*, calling for a cessation of hostilities and, from mid-summer onwards, propaganda for the Stockholm Peace Conference. Attendance at these meetings varied from fifty-four on 7 March to 210 on 21 June. The average attendance was just over one hundred and significantly, noted the *commissaire*, the same people tended to turn up in the audience every time, and most of them had been attending similar meetings since mid-1916. The speakers also seemed to be largely the same: leading journalists and personnel of *Le Droit du Peuple* like Chastenet, Mistral, Rafin-Dugens, and occasionally outside speakers like the feminist journalist Marcelle Capy.[65] On one occasion, at a meeting on 23 June, three soldiers on *permission* were invited to speak. They were all members of the minority Socialist faction, and they spoke of the horrors of life at the front, the bad state of morale amongst soldiers and the talk of revolution to end the war by several soldiers in the *Chasseurs Alpins*. No mention seems to have been made of the mutinies at the front. They advocated close collaboration with local *syndicats* to co-ordinate strike activity in order to hasten the end of the war, and an all-out campaign of anti-war propaganda in the war factories of Grenoble and Vienne. They were, noted the *commissaire*, 'particularly well received' by the audience of some one hundred and fifty.[66]

It seems however that, although the number of Socialist meetings had multiplied, the speakers were really only preaching to the converted, for the attendances fluctuated rather than increased regularly with each meeting. 'I suggest we allow these meetings to continue', the *commissaire* advised the *préfet* in September 1917. 'They do not in themselves constitute a great threat since, despite being well advertised in *Le Droit du People*, the meetings do not seem to be growing in popularity.'[67] He added that to ban the meetings would be to provoke needless violence. He warned, however, that Socialist ideas should be kept as far as possible from the villages, and suggested that a determined effort be made to try to prevent a combined Socialist–Syndicalist activity which would seriously 'contaminate' the atmosphere in the larger factories in Grenoble and Vienne.

The *commissaire* was particularly busy during early September 1917, since he also produced for the *préfet* an eight-page, detailed report on the development of militant anti-war activity in Grenoble throughout 1917.[68] This concentrated mainly on the *Syndicat Confédéré des Ouvriers sur Métaux* which, despite its weak representation of the metallurgical workers of Grenoble (500 members out of

4000 workers), had become increasingly militant in its anti-war propaganda during the year. The *syndicat* had held eight meetings at the *Bourse du Travail* between March and August and attendance had fluctuated: 220 in March, nearly 500 in June, 350 in August. Significantly the main body of leaders had come from outside the *département*, being skilled workers from Belgium and the *départements* of the war zone in the North-East. These had been sent to work in the main factories of the Isère. Their activity and propaganda was particularly noted in the two major munitions factories of Grenoble, Bouchayer et Viallet and Fibrocol, where they constituted 11 per cent and 8 per cent, respectively, of the total workforce.

That potentially subversive elements were slipping through the net and finding work in munitions factories naturally caused the War and Interior Ministries some concern, and brought into focus the whole question of surveillance and security of establishments working for the National Defence. Entrance into State-owned munitions factories had always been rigidly controlled, so the problem centred on the recruitment of French and foreign labour by private establishments. No doubt because of the pressing need for labour of all kinds, adequate surveillance of munitions workers was slow to develop. From the beginning, applicants were supposed to produce an identity card showing name, age, profession, residence, military record and a signed photograph, but in the scramble for labour from 1915 onwards many industrialists simply hired workers willy-nilly, ignoring the prescriptions of the *Loi Dalbiez* and the constant exhortations by the *préfet* to keep a careful watch for spies and potential subversives. It was not until July 1915 that a *Service de Surveillance* was instituted in which the military governors of each region theoretically joined forces with civilian authorities in the *départements* and with industrialists. This was rather vague and haphazard, with ill-defined jurisdictions, and a further year elapsed before the two ministers concerned had properly authorised the *préfet*'s staff to employ military personnel for surveillance. However so few troops could be spared that even this measure proved inadequate, and in January 1918 the Minister of the Interior estimated that only 30 per cent of workers in war factories in the Isère were under proper surveillance.[69] Finally, by a law of 6 March 1918, any employer found guilty of hiring deserters, or any civilian guilty of exhorting soldiers to desert, was subject to imprisonment of from two months to one year and a fine of between three and five hundred *francs*.

These measures, combined with continued exhortations to workers to watch out for potential subversives, undoubtedly helped to minimise the dissemination of anti-war propaganda inside the factories. The authorities also had a useful sanction to employ against any *mobilisé* working on munitions production on *sursis d'appel*. If any of them were found to be causing trouble or engaging in strike activity they could be sent back to the front on active service. This measure was certainly used to good effect on 14 May 1918, when nearly all the war factories in Grenoble were subjected to a strike calling for increased wages, with Bouchayer et Viallet alone having more than two thousand strikers. A swift military response, the arrest of thirty-five striking *mobilisés*, gave the authorities a useful bargaining counter, and the strike leaders were obliged to call off the strike if the authorities agreed to reprieve the *rappelés*. The movement was therefore quickly defused and normal work resumed the following day.[70]

Female workers of course were not subject to this sanction and were freer to involve themselves in strike action or anti-war activity. Apart from Vienne, however, where a preponderance of the workforce were female textile workers, there is little evidence that females took a hand in directing subversive activities inside or outside factories. The exception was one incident at Fibrocol in Grenoble in May 1917, where an activist, Jean David, attempted to group eighty female munitions workers into a strike committee with the aim of developing branches in other major munitions factories and co-ordinating activities to turn strikes for wage increases into sabotage strikes against the war effort. The movement petered out within a few days and it seems that David had misjudged the mood of the female workers, many of whom had brothers, sons and husbands at the front, and almost all of whom were earning unprecedentedly high wages. As one of them put it: 'if it wasn't for the war, we wouldn't be employed here in the first place. We will support any action to improve our conditions, but we do not want to bring about a situation by which we might lose our jobs.'[71]

The basic tactics of all the anti-war activists in the *département* were, therefore, to create as many incidents as possible by encouraging *permissionnaires* to desert and, most importantly, to direct or prolong strike activity in the major factories and ultimately call a general strike to paralyse the war effort and hasten peace. The former tactic met with almost total failure during 1917 and

1918. Although the number of incidents between soldiers and civilians increased during these years, particularly in garrison towns, there is no evidence that these caused or resulted in a dramatically increased desertion rate. Undoubtedly there were isolated individual cases where soldiers were induced to desert by revolutionary activists, and certainly the incidences of violence, drunkenness and insubordination did increase on troop trains bringing soldiers to and from the front, but this tended to coincide with particularly low points in the general morale, such as the period immediately after the failure of the Nivelle Offensive in mid-1917. Of course cries of '*à bas la guerre*' could be heard in soldiers' talk at this time, together with complaints about incompetent and inhumane army officers, but, as in 1916, there were no incidences of successful concerted action to subvert military or civilian authority. As the *Commissaire de Police* of Grenoble stated, once the *permissionnaires* reached the railway stations they tended to split up and go their separate ways to their own destinations in villages and small towns. Moreover the police kept a well-mounted guard and constant watch over arrivals of troop trains at Grenoble. There is every indication that, in the main, revolutionary or antiwar propagandists continued to be treated with disdain, by soldiers, as *embusqués*. The few *permissionnaires* who did desert tended to do so for personal rather than political reasons. The case of Louis Péchard, tried for desertion by the *Conseil de Guerre* at Grenoble, was typical:

> I deserted because, like so many others, I have had enough of this war. I love my country as much as the next man, but I have seen so much killing, have lost so many good friends, seen too many brave men die. Most of all I just want to live in peace now. I am still young. I want time to recuperate, rest and think of the future. I want to marry and have children. No, I do not want to end the war by revolution or by violence. You will not find many soldiers who are willing to turn their guns on the Government. That way only leads to more bloodshed. We will have nothing to do with revolutionaries who try to thrust leaflets into our hands. What do they know of real violence? How do they know what it is like in battle? . . . I just couldn't face any more shooting.[72]

The implication here is that the often cited soldier–civilian dichotomy during the 1914–18 war was of more importance than any potential solidarity between discontented rank and file soldiers and civilian revolutionaries *vis-à-vis* the Government and Army High Command. Nor did the 'revolutionaries' meet with any more success in turning strike activity to their advantage during 1917, despite the considerable rise in the number of strikes in the Isère. Of course there is a sense in which any strike is a potential political threat to the Government, to social stability and the economic and political status quo; strikes in wartime doubly so. However in answer to the question 'did any of the strikes of 1917 have as a fundamental aim the overtly political and subversive motive of sabotaging production in order to shorten the war, to subvert civilian authority or to act as a prelude to revolutionary attacks on governmental authority?' the word must be 'no', not even during the crisis period of mid-1917. With one major exception, the same can be said of strikes in the Isère during 1918.

The police files record seventeen separate strikes involving fifty-eight establishments during 1917 and twenty-eight strikes involving two hundred and one different establishments in 1918, a total of forty-five separate strikes during the last two years of the war.[73] Eleven of the strikes occurred in Vienne, nine in Grenoble, three in Vizille and the rest in small towns in the *département*. Only four of these strikes were in munitions factories. By far the most affected industry was textiles (twenty-three strikes), followed by shoe making (five), building (four), metallurgical (three), glove making (three) and paper making and coal mining (one each).

The principal aims of the separate strikes were as follows: straightforward wage rises (thirty-one), against the introduction of piece-work (three), for the re-hiring of sacked workers (three), for the introduction of the 'English week' or *Semaine Anglaise* (two), for the establishment of wage differentials (one) and for the recognition of a *syndicat* (one). An interesting statistic is that three of the strikes had as a principle aim the sacking of foreign and colonial workers of the very types listed by the police as potentially subversive elements. The overwhelming majority, about 85 per cent, of the strikes were therefore economic in their aims, the remainder being concerned with questions of discipline and conditions of work. As to the success/failure rate, 40 per cent of the economic strikes were a total success and a further 25 per cent were partially successful. Only a minority therefore resulted in total failure for the strikers.

So much for the bare statistics of these strikes. What is noticeable about them is that in the police dossiers built up on each strike there is, with the one aforementioned exception, no hint of revolutionary Anarchist or pacifist activity of any kind. The only slogans recorded were economic ones. In nearly all cases, as soon as the employer or an independent arbitrator like the justice of the peace or *préfet* had given a decision, the strikes ended and work resumed, even in cases where the strikers lost their claims. There seems therefore to have been no attempt to prolong work stoppages unduly or with the intention of impairing the war effort. Indeed the longest single strike was one of weavers demanding increased wages in textile factories in the Vienne region, which lasted seventeen days during August and September 1918. Nor is there much evidence of a concerted strike movement between industries, of sympathy strikes, for example, between munitions and textile workers; there is no hint, in other words, of a guided revolutionary action.

The violent rhetoric of revolutionary or pacifist activists helps to explain the lack of co-ordination of anti-war activity, for this, as has been noted, tended to scare off rather than attract industrial workers. The average textile or metallurgical worker in the Isère was ready enough to strike for higher wages or for the introduction of the *Semaine Anglaise*, but was certainly not willing to convert the 'imperialist' war into a civil war, and appeared to be satisfied with the official propaganda that the war was being fought to rid France of the invader and recapture Alsace and Lorraine. Beyond this, exhortations to force the Government to declare an immediate armistice and make public the full and total details of French war aims (a major aim of minority pacifists of the CGT as outlined at their conference at St Etienne in May 1918) had little appeal. With a few exceptions, the war had not led to an impoverishment of the majority of textile or metallurgical workers in the *département*. There was virtually full employment for the first time within living memory, and opportunities for economic advancement particularly within industries working on defence contracts – those very industries where anti-war activity had to be concentrated in order to be fully effective – were unprecedented. Workers were more concerned to maintain existing living standards by demanding, and in the majority of cases receiving, increased cost-of-living indemnities, and to ensure that improved standards and opportunities would continue after the war had been won.

In this context the fate of a general strike at Vienne at the end of May 1918, the one incidence of an anti-war strike, is revealing. In the last week of February 1918 the *Sous-Préfet* of Vienne wrote to the *préfet* that a 'dangerous revolutionary situation' was developing in Vienne. There had recently been a big increase in the number of Anarchist songs and pacifist tracts distributed among the metallurgical and textile workers in the town, especially by young men in their late teens and non-mobilised Spaniards and Poles. The focus of this activity was the local *Bourse du Travail* and handwritten copies of revolutionary tracts calling for activity to force the Government to end the war at any price had been found on the walls of twelve of the leading textile enterprises.[74]

On 28 May Louis Cartalier, appearing before the *Conseil de Guerre* at Cherbourg for desertion, made the following statement:

> At the end of March, I entered into relations with the Anarchist nicknamed 'Ripa' at Vienne. From him I learned that revolutionary groups were preparing a big movement to provoke riots, stop *permissionnaires* from returning to the front and try to force an end to the war. The movement was to start simultaneously in various provincial cities, but Paris was not sufficiently prepared, so the movement was to be localised in the St Etienne, Lyon, Vienne region. A series of strikes was to start on 1 May. 'Ripa' told me that there were already stocks of arms and he asked me if I could provide two machine guns and grenades, for which he would pay me five *francs* each.[75]

The increased signs of subversive activity induced the authorities to take strong precautionary measures throughout March and April. On 5 March the Minister of the Interior issued a decree forbidding the singing of songs and distribution of tracts likely to disturb the peace. On 26 March the *préfet* forbade gatherings of more than six persons in the streets of the town, and the *sous-préfet* asked for, and received, a reinforcement of thirty *gendarmes* from Lyon and Grenoble.[76]

On 5 April the police seized a letter sent by Richetta, secretary of the *Syndicat du Textile*, to the Anarchist Charles Benoit in Paris outlining details for organising a general strike against the war. Active propaganda was being used in favour of a 'just and lasting peace' and a forty-eight-hour general strike to force the Government to make known all its war aims and its conditions for peace.

To this end the young textile workers of Vienne had, since February, been circulated with copies of the *'Internationale'* and several anti-war tracts exhorting the French Government to seek an immediate armistice with the Central Powers.[77]

This propaganda seems to have had little effect. Throughout April a number of private letters to the *sous-préfet* and *préfet* indicated that increasing numbers of unionised workers were anxious to distance themselves from revolutionary action. There were letters complaining of the appearance of Anarchist flags in the back streets of Vienne, and of the treacherous and offensive nature of the revolutionary appeal. One group of eighty unionised textile workers, styling themselves 'workers and patriotic citizens of Vienne, Isère', sent this petition to Clemenceau himself:

> We all have faith in you. We are all sad and disgusted to witness what is happening with our syndical leaders in Vienne. We want an increase in wages, yes, and we are loyal to our *syndicat*, but we do not want revolution. At each meeting at the *Bourse du Travail* our leaders tell us that we must create a general strike, make a revolution and send to you an ultimatum to end the war. If you do not agree, we are told that much blood will be spilt as it is in Russia. Every meeting is the same. We go to put forward our claims for better wages but all we are told is that we must use our position to put an end to the war first. We don't know why the authorities allow such talk, which excites the people at this hour of need. If Richetta's house was searched, many interesting things would be found.[78]

Many interesting things were indeed found when, on the night of 20 April, police raided the homes of Richetta, Miglioretti and Herclet, well-known Anarchists. The finds included thirty-five rifles, seven pistols, over two hundred rounds of ammunition, pamphlets, songs, letters, various Anarchist and Socialist writings and plans calling for demonstrations on 1 May as a prelude to revolution. As a result of this the three leaders were arrested and taken to appear before the *Conseil de Guerre* at Lyon on 22 April, where they were fined and bound over to keep the peace.[79] The apparent lenience of these sentences suggests that the authorities were frightened of provoking violent reactions among the anti-war activists in Vienne.

However, this contrasts with the official view of the textile workers' *syndicat* that the police and military authorities deliberately provoked a confrontation with revolutionary activists during May, hence the immediate release of the three leaders in the hope that they would resume their anti-war activities, scare off moderate syndical support and 'decapitate' the anti-war movement by giving a pretext to mount savage repressions of militants.[80] This is certainly borne out by the rapid increase in police strength. On 21 April a further detachment of fifty *gendarmes* arrived in Vienne from Lyon and on the following day sixty cavalrymen were seconded for policing duties. By the beginning of May the police strength at Vienne was one hundred *gendarmes* and one hundred and sixty cavalry, more than double the number at the end of 1917 and surpassing the entire police strength for Grenoble.[81]

In the event 1 May passed off peacefully enough, but during the following three weeks the militants and the police prepared for a possible confrontation. A curfew was placed on the town and from 6 May all cafés and places of entertainment were forced to close by eight o'clock in the evening. By 20 May ten members of the *Corporation du Tissage*, all of them Frenchmen in their late teens, had been arrested for illegally buying or carrying arms. Matters came to a head when Miglioretti and Richetta attended a conference of the pacifist minority of the *CGT* at St Etienne on 19 and 20 May. On their return to Vienne on the evening of 21 May the leaders addressed a meeting of three hundred textile and metallurgical workers at the *Bourse du Travail*. A general strike of all the workers of the major industrial enterprises in the town was called for the following day.

At six o'clock in the morning of 22 May pickets were posted outside the gates of all the factories concerned and the aims of the strike were made known to workers and management alike. There were few attempts to cross the picket lines; police reports mention incidents involving a mere twenty-seven workers outside two textile factories. By eight o'clock it was clear that there was a total stoppage of all industrial enterprises in the town: 4050 textile workers and 450 metallurgical workers were on strike. Forty-nine enterprises were affected. At ten o'clock the three leaders addressed a crowd of nearly two thousand strikers in a field on the outskirts of Vienne, repeating once again the reasons for the strike. According to police the majority of workers in the crowd were young and female, a number of them carrying placards calling for a cost-of-living indemnity or the introduction of an eight-hour day. Only one small group near the front of the crowd carried political or anti-war slogans and these, in the opinion of the *Commissaire de Police*, were stooges planted by the leaders. Certainly these were the most vociferous in the crowd, occasionally breaking into strains of the *'Internationale'*. There were, however, no violent incidents and after an hour the crowd dispersed peacefully, escorted into the centre of the town by squads of police.[82]

At midday the *sous-préfet* sent a telegram to the *préfet* claiming that the majority of the strikers and the local population disapproved of the anti-war speeches and that there seemed to be two strands of opinion, the majority wanting the strike used purely and simply as a threat, or lever, in order to gain increased cost-of-living indemnities. Those who genuinely seemed to support the extreme anti-war demands of the leaders were estimated at around fifty to sixty in number, nearly all of them textile workers and most of them young females of foreign origin. The small number of male French 'extremists' appeared to be very young, in their late teens, just approaching mobilisable age.[83]

On the following day, seeing that the total stoppage of textile workers was being maintained, but reassured by the relatively small number of hard-line militants in the strike and by the return to work of one-third of the metallurgical workers, the authorities decided to force the issue. All places of public entertainment were closed completely, an extra one hundred infantry were moved in from Lyon and all meetings at the *Bourse du Travail* were forbidden. A strike meeting had been scheduled for two o'clock, so the leaders led some three hundred strikers in small groups to the neighbouring village of Cote St Cyr just over the border in the *Département* of the Rhône. The *Préfet* of the Rhône immediately forbade any meetings or gatherings, but the demonstration went ahead none the less. Captain Henri Pierre, seconded by the military governor to police the strike, recorded what followed:

> At two o'clock in the afternoon I went into the village with twenty mounted soldiers and *gendarmes*. I ordered Richetta to disperse the crowd in groups of ten and send them back to Vienne. I gave him ten minutes to do this. He refused, saying that the meeting was being held to demonstrate against the 'capitalist' war and to make the workers realise that it was the textile and munitions bosses who were making money out of the war and who wanted to prolong it. I noticed, however, that most

of the crowd were beginning to disperse of their own accord, although when I arrested the three leaders there were hostile cries and scuffles between my troops and some of the women present. The three leaders were sent to jail at Lyon and fifty women and two male Spaniards were sent for trial in Vienne. The arrest of the leaders had been expected and awaited for a long time by the majority of the population, and produced a good impression. [84]

That evening the *sous-préfet* posted placards in all public places in Vienne reminding the workers mobilised on munitions work of the 'irregular situation' they were placing themselves in and threatening immediate recall to active service at the front of all those on *sursis d'appel* if they did not return to work the following day. On the morning of 24 May all the remaining metallurgical workers and nearly one thousand textile workers returned to work. The police reported no arrests for picket-line violence although there was some jostling outside the main armaments enterprises. The return to work of the munitions workers and the arrest of the leaders meant the end of the strike. With the situation well under control the *sous-préfet* allowed a meeting of the strike committee at the *Bourse du Travail* on the evening of 25 May. Recognising what was virtually a *fait accompli*, the committee voted unanimously for a return to work and an end of the strike on 29 May.

That same evening the *préfet* wrote to the Minister of the Interior that, after the arrest of the leaders, the strike movement lacked cohesion, direction or real aims, and that there was now an impatient desire to get back to work and resume normal conditions. [85] On 27 and 28 May there was almost total calm in the town and the return to work was effected without any incident or disorder. So confident of total victory had the authorities been that on the evening of 26 May thirty *gendarmes* left Vienne for Lyon and on 30 May Captain Pierre and his special cavalry troop left for Grenoble.

The strike had been a general one for two days and a partial one for a further four days. A total of twenty-seven thousand working days had been lost. [86] The three leaders, Miglioretti, Richetta and Herclet, were each sentenced to five years in jail by the *Conseil de Guerre* at Lyon. They were released in a post-war amnesty on 31 December 1918. On 26 June four textile workers, mobilised on *sursis d'appel*, were sent to rejoin their units on active service at the front.

From beginning to end the sole stated aim of the strike had been to force the Government to put an immediate end to the war.[87] No economic demands had been put forward. The strike had ended in a total victory for the police and military authorities. *Jusqu'au-boutisme* seems to have prevailed even in the town with the most highly political and potentially revolutionary industrial workforce in the Isère. Clearly the turning point was the arrest of the three extremist leaders after only two days and their replacement by a more moderate and conciliatory leadership. Can the strike be seen purely in terms of differences of opinion between 'élites' and 'masses'? The use of such concepts in the analysis of revolutionary and strike activity is not always helpful, yet it must be borne in mind that while there seems to have been very little dissent from metallurgical and textile workers in obeying the call for a general strike at the beginning, there was equally little dissent six days later from the call to the remaining textile workers to return to work under conditions of total defeat for the aims of the strike.

Richetta, Miglioretti and Herclet certainly held considerable influence over a large section of the textile and metallurgical workers in Vienne. They had been prominent in local syndical circles before the war and had provided firm, active and often successful leadership in strikes for higher wages prior to May 1918. Their continuing influence was to be demonstrated in 1919, when they led a long and bitter strike in the town. However police and military estimates of the number of workers who genuinely wanted an immediate end to the war, on whatever terms, never exceeded a hard core of seventy or eighty out of a combined industrial workforce of more than four and a half thousand, and only a fraction of these were willing to go all the way in preparing for civil war and revolution. The mass of workers were willing to follow their leaders up to a point by repeating political or anti-war slogans, but they were manifestly not prepared to sacrifice every-thing for 'revolution'. Although it is true that the majority of textile workers, as females and foreigners, did not face the threat of recall to the front, it has to be accepted that they too had much to lose. In the conditions of spring 1918 the average *tisseuse* in Vienne could not look with equanimity or certainty on a post-war future without potentially lucrative defence contracts providing full and regular employment and overtime bonuses. Similarly many of the Span-ish, Greek and Polish textile workers could not foresee the con-tinuing and increased demand for foreign labour after the war. For such people it was very much a case of 'better the devil you know' and its effect was to make the workers, even in 'Red Vienne', conservative-minded.

The prompt arrest of the extremist leaders, the early return to work of the metallurgical workers, the acknowledgement of helplessness in the face of the power of the authorities, the lack of co-ordination between workers in Vienne and those in Grenoble, and the lack of sympathy or interest in the 'resolute' rural population, doomed the Vienne strike from the start. Moreover its timing was not propitious. By the end of May 1918 it was just beginning to look as if the *jusqu'au-boutiste* ideal would materialise. The Americans were arriving in increasing numbers, Clemenceau and Foch were providing a firm, decisive leadership and, while a month earlier it had looked as if Paris faced the danger it had faced in September 1914, towards the end of May there was a growing public feeling that the German offensive might be spent and that, while the war might continue for some time yet, it was certainly going to be won. In the light of all this, why prejudice the war effort by mounting damaging and politically provocative strike action against the Government? As the correspondence from town and countryside to the front suggests, the extremists were out of touch with the morale of the public as a whole and with rank and file textile and metallurgical workers in particular.

Conclusions

The evidence of this study suggests that the workers of the farms and in the towns of the Isère had mentally resigned themselves to facing a continuation of the war through 1919 and, if need be, into 1920. In all the data from various sources on the question of public opinion and attitudes to the war of the local population, the word '*résignation*' appears most prominently, from the early days of the state of emergency and the mobilisation, through the dark days of Verdun, right up to the last days of the war. As has been seen, the bulk of opinion wavered somewhere in the middle, outside the extremes of outright *revanchisme* and overt opposition to the war. The vast majority of civilians put up with the war, even if they did not support it enthusiastically.

The disruptions to civilian life – to local industries and small businesses, agriculture, the Police and Education Services and religious life generally – were immense, yet this did not prevent a gradual hardening of the feeling that the war must be won, with no compromises. Whereas *jusqu'au-boutisme* could be associated with fanatics and political extremists before the war, throughout the war years this mentality permeated all layers of society. At no stage during the hostilities did moves to end the war short of total victory gain any currency in the population at large. Pacifism, aimed towards a negotiated peace of some kind, remained the ideal of an isolated minority. Equally, at no stage were the very institutions of the Third Republic seriously called into question or threatened. Bearing in mind the turbulent political history of France in the nineteenth century, the bitterness and divisions which had plagued the early Third Republic and the particular local revolutionary traditions of Vienne and Grenoble, this seems, on the face of it, remarkable.

It is less remarkable when one remembers the fact that, of all the belligerent countries in the First World War, France was the only one which had been invaded and occupied continuously. From the beginning the war for the French people had been a war of defence. It is far easier for governmental authorities and propagandists to evoke the need for sacrifice when one's own national survival is threatened. The common enemy must be defeated and, if this entails the shelving of political and religious differences, then so be it. It was a comparatively easy matter for propagandists to evoke the memory of 1792 or 1870, to hold forth the danger of French civilisation being corrupted and eventually destroyed by Prussian militarism.

This is not to say that the French home front held out during the war solely because of the *Union Sacrée*. Indeed the evidence from the Isère suggests that, as elsewhere in France, the concept of a *Union Sacrée* was virtually moribund by 1916. The point about the *Union Sacrée* is that it certainly functioned and succeeded during the first six months or so of the war. This in a sense was the crucial period. As has been seen, the propagandists of the *Union Sacrée* succeeded in implanting in the minds of the local population the need to rally together and be prepared to make sacrifices for the war effort. At the same time they achieved the remarkable feat of normalising the war in the minds of the population. Indeed the gradual return of political and religious differences in villages and towns from 1915, and the increased social tensions felt from 1917, contributed to this normalisation.

Thus right from the beginning the First World War was, for the French people, a total war, requiring total commitment. Once the awareness of the need for sacrifices had been established, it then became a question of 'how much of a sacrifice?' and 'for how long?' Here the immediate introduction of the *allocation militaire* was of paramount importance. Not only did it provide some practical assistance to those in need, it also established in the minds of the civilian population an awareness that the State was willing to play its part, was willing to give something back in return. The *allocation* helped to sustain many families during the crucial first nine months of the war when the local population was faced with large-scale unemployment.

As the war progressed and dragged on into 1915 and 1916, two dominant, inter-related themes emerged in public opinion: the need to condition and prepare oneself for one last effort, and the growing awareness, particularly after Verdun, that 'we have sacrificed too much to stop short of total victory'. The latter is really the key to understanding the *tenue* of the local population through the dark days of 1917 and 1918. Doubts about whether this total victory would ever be achieved were removed towards the end of 1917 by the entrance of the Americans into the war and by the appointment of Clemenceau. Thus by the winter of 1917–18 it became not a question of 'whether', more a question of 'when'.

The actual nature of the sacrifices to be made in the interests of the National Defence is also important. Of course Frenchmen were dying at a proportionately higher rate than their allies, and by the end of the war every *commune* had its share of dead or wounded. The ultimate sacrifice was therefore considerable. The point is that the financial and material sacrifices made by the population of the Isère were quite small. As has been pointed out, during 1916 and 1917 the predominant concern of most villagers and townspeople in their correspondence was with local financial and economic matters. From 1915 onwards few people in the Isère starved or went without work or some kind of income for very long. The period of greatest material and economic suffering in this sense was the first eight or nine months of war. The population at this time was sustained by the short-war illusion and by the belief that their sufferings were only temporary. As the war dragged on and total war became more of a reality, the sufferings could be ameliorated by the possibility of earning a higher wage, of drawing an *allocation*, of getting work on the farms and so on. By the crisis years of 1917 and early 1918 something of a vested interest in the continuation of the war had been created in the towns, the potential centres of serious anti-war activity. What price defeatism, pacifism and revolutionary talk in such circumstances? Those who were earning higher wages in war work would be scarcely likely to support drives for a negotiated peace, short of total victory.

In all of this, the work of the opinion-formers in the localities – the *instituteurs* and *institutrices*, the *curés* and *vicaires*, the *maires* and *adjoints* – was crucial. Faced with disruptions, depleted personnel and, in some cases, confusing and conflicting directives from above, they none the less contrived to sustain morale, carry out important administrative tasks, direct major aspects of the war effort and develop as far as possible the *jusqu'au-boutiste* mentality. The conclusions of this study stand, in the main, as testimony to their achievement.

TABLE 1 *Number of insoumis registered 20 August 1914, military sub-division of Grenoble (20 cantons, 80 communes), according to politics of municipality and population of commune*

Municipality	Population of commune											Total
	under 300	300– 500	500– 750	750– 1000	1000– 1500	1500– 2000	2000– 3000	3000– 4000	4000– 4500	Voiron 12 503	Grenoble	
Socialist			3	4	2			3				12
Radical Socialist	4	4	18	6	20	9	19	3		38		121
Progressive	1	1	4	2		2	2		20		210	242
Left Republican	2	6	6	2	2		11					29
Radical	4	12	1	9	4	3	6	4				43
Reactionary	1	3		1	7							12
Total	12	26	32	24	35	14	38	10	20	38	210	459

SOURCE AD 2R906, 16M273

TABLE 2 *Number of* insoumis *registered 20 August 1914, military sub-division of Grenoble, according to males of mobilisable age, by* canton

Canton	Number of males of mobilisable age	Number of insoumis
Allevard	1255	8
Bourg d'Oisans	2571	15
Clelles	520	4
Corps	734	16
Domène	2315	14
Goncelin	1829	13
Grenoble Est	5160	75
Grenoble Nord	5243	86
Grenoble Sud	8872	60
Mens	967	5
Monestier du Clermont	561	6
La Mure	2987	25
St Laurent du Pont	1732	11
Sassenage	1344	17
Le Touvet	1706	8
Valbonnais	837	2
Vif	1494	12
Villard de Lans	898	2
Vizille	2448	38
Voiron	4255	42

SOURCE AD 2R906, 16M273

TABLE 3 *Reactions to departure of* mobilisés *2–15 August 1914: expressions most commonly used in reports (49* communes*), according to politics of municipality*

Municipality	'resignation'	'resolution'	'patriotic demonstrations'	'enthusiasm'	'revanche'
Socialist			1		
Radical Socialist	3	11	1		1
Progressive		5	3	2	2
Left Republican	1	2	4	1	3
Radical		2	1		
Reactionary		4	1	1	

SOURCE AD 16M273, 13R54, 13R17, 53M19, 52M88

TABLE 4 *Reactions to departure of* mobilisés *2–15 August 1914: expressions most commonly used in reports (49 communes), according to villages and towns*

Location	'resig-nation'	'resolu-tion'	'patriotic demonstrations'	'enthusiasm'	'revanche'
Villages more than 15 km from *Chef-lieu*	3	11	2	1	2
Villages within 15 km radius of *Chef-lieu de canton*		8	4	1	1
Towns: population of more than 2000	1	5	5	2	3
Total	4	24	11	4	6

SOURCE AD 16M273, 13R54, 13R17, 53M19, 52M88

TABLE 5 *Average daily wage of selected industrial occupations, based on 8-hour working day, in munitions factories in Grenoble*

Occupation	January 1917	December 1917	June 1918
Male:			
Foreman	8fr.50	11fr.50	14fr.00
Blast furnace operator	7fr.50	10fr.00	12fr.00
Lathe operator	7fr.50	10fr.00	12fr.20
Shell case packer	6fr.50	9fr.00	11fr.00
Manual labourer	5fr.00	7fr.30	9fr.00
Female:			
Forewoman	6fr.00	7fr.90	9fr.00
Lathe operator	5fr.50	7fr.50	8fr.50
Cartridge packer	4fr.70	6fr.40	7fr.50
Cleaner	4fr.00	5fr.20	6fr.00

SOURCE AD 163M2

TABLE 6 Average daily wage of selected industrial occupations, based on 8-hour day, according to arrondissements of the Isère (excluding munitions work)

Occupation	1914				January 1917				October 1919			
	Grenoble	St Marcellin	La Tour du Pin	Vienne	Grenoble	St Marcellin	La Tour du Pin	Vienne	Grenoble	St Marcellin	La Tour du Pin	Vienne
Unskilled labourer	3fr.20	2fr.80	2fr.80	3fr.10	4fr.90	4fr.50	4fr.50	4fr.80	8fr.30	7fr.50	7fr.50	8fr.10
Railway worker	3fr.20	2fr.80	2fr.80	3fr.10	4fr.90	4fr.50	4fr.50	4fr.80	8fr.30	7fr.50	7fr.50	8fr.10
Stone mason	4fr.80	4fr.30	4fr.30	4fr.60	6fr.00	5fr.60	5fr.60	6fr.00	12fr.50	11fr.20	11fr.20	12fr.20
Plasterer	4fr.00	3fr.60	3fr.60	4fr.00	5fr.50	5fr.10	5fr.10	5fr.50	10fr.40	9fr.30	9fr.30	10fr.30
Carpenter	4fr.40	4fr.00	4fr.00	4fr.30	6fr.30	5fr.90	5fr.90	6fr.10	10fr.45	9fr.40	9fr.40	10fr.30
Blacksmith	4fr.80	4fr.30	4fr.30	4fr.80	6fr.50	6fr.00	6fr.00	6fr.50	12fr.50	11fr.40	11fr.40	12fr.20
Locksmith	4fr.40	4fr.00	4fr.00	4fr.30	6fr.00	5fr.60	5fr.60	5fr.90	10fr.40	9fr.20	9fr.20	10fr.20
Mechanic	4fr.80	4fr.30	4fr.30	4fr.70	6fr.50	6fr.10	6fr.10	6fr.50	12fr.50	11fr.50	11fr.50	12fr.50
Plumber	4fr.80	4fr.30	4fr.30	4fr.80	6fr.00	5fr.60	5fr.60	6fr.00	12fr.50	11fr.50	11fr.50	12fr.20
Electrician	4fr.50	4fr.00	4fr.00	4fr.50	6fr.00	5fr.60	5fr.60	6fr.00	12fr.20	11fr.30	11fr.30	12fr.00
Weaver	4fr.30	3fr.90	3fr.90	4fr.20	6fr.00	5fr.60	5fr.60	6fr.00	11fr.80	11fr.00	11fr.00	11fr.50

SOURCE AD 163M2

TABLE 7   *Basic daily food requirement for the average male industrial worker weighing 70 kgs, based on a minimum of 3300 calories per 8-hour working day (calculated by the* Commission Scientifique Interalliée du Ravitaillement, *27 March 1918)*

Food	Quantity (grammes)	Calories	Total price
Bread	500	1510	
Refrigerated meat	100	269	
Fresh meat	50	150	
Lard	40	352	
Pork fat	20	120	
Oil	20	186	
Potatoes	500	350	
Rice	75	265	
Dry vegetables	75	270	
Sugar	25	105	
Milk	25	42	
Total		3616	1fr.75

SOURCE   AN F^{23} 188

TABLE 8   *Average weekly budget of a childless working-class couple, Grenoble, March 1917: both husband and wife working in munitions factories*

Income, based on 60-hour working week:		
Husband	55fr.00	
Wife	32fr.00	87fr.00
Expenditure		
Food	22fr.75	
Rent	10fr.00	
Fuel	6fr.00	
Transport	6fr.50	
Newspapers, clothing and		
other items	15fr.00	62fr.25
Surplus		24fr.75

SOURCE   Report undertaken by a representative of the *Ministre du Travail et Prévoyance Social*, AD 13R790

TABLE 9   *Average weekly budget of a working-class family with 2 children, Grenoble, March 1917: husband only working in munitions factory*

Income, based on 60-hour working week:		
Husband	55fr.00	55fr.00
Expenditure		
Food	25fr.00	
Rent	10fr.00	
Fuel	5fr.00	
Transport	3fr.00	
Clothing and other items	10fr.00	53fr.00
Surplus		2fr.00

SOURCE   Report undertaken by a representative of the *Ministre du Travail et Prévoyance Social*, AD 13R790

TABLE 10   *Composition of female workforce recruited between December 1916 and August 1918 at the Atelier de Chargement des Grenades, Dépôt du 140me Régiment d'Artillerie Lourde, Grenoble (522 females)*

Age group	Age and situation			Previous occupation								Daily distance travelled to work (km)					
	Total number	Married no children	Married with children	Textiles	Metall-urgical	Paper making	Other industries	Office work	Shop work	Farm work	None	0–2	3–5	6–8	9–10	11–15	Over 15
15–24	120	41	26	51	11	21	11	9	7	4	6	46	38	13	10	8	5
25–34	230	57	135	109	22	53	21	10	6	2	7	72	87	31	15	13	12
35–44	96	19	65	50	3	6	13	4	5	4	11	49	30	9	3	3	2
45–60	69	9	52	43	2	3	1	3	1	3	13	27	30	8	1	2	1
Over 60	7	1	4	3	–	–	–	–	–	2	2	1	2	2	–	1	1
Totals	522	127	282	256	38	83	46	26	19	15	39	195	187	63	29	27	21

SOURCE   AD 13R34

TABLE 11 *Workforce in munitions and allied production in the Isère, 1915–18: large enterprises working directly on munitions and small enterprises executing sub-contracts (percentages in brackets)*

	Oct. 1915		Sept. 1916		July 1917		May 1918	
Number of establishments	114		171		202		236	
French males	6 010	(66.5)	7 496	(64)	6 174	(44)	5 508	(33)
POWs	440	(4.5)	517	(4)	821	(6)	857	(5)
Colonials	211	(2)	319	(3)	916	(6)	1 121	(7)
Foreigners, other than colonials	960	(11)	1 097	(9)	2 113	(15)	2 923	(17)
Females	1 150	(16)	2 331	(20)	4 096	(29)	5 821	(38)
Total workforce	9 131		11 760		14 120		16 230	

SOURCE   AD 120M113, AN F^{22} 530

TABLE 12 *Civilian–military correspondence 1917–18: Percentages of references to the eventual outcome of the war and the desire for peace in letters opened by* Contrôle Postal, *14th Military Region*

	Outcome of war			Desire for peace		
Date	Belief in total victory	Fear of defeat	Uncertain	Victorious for France	Negotiated	At any price
Jan. 1917	15	–	2	12	2	–
April 1917	21	1	5	11	1	1
July 1917	28	8	15	25	9	1
Oct. 1917	17	3	5	17	3	–
Jan. 1918	14	1	1	19	2	–
April 1918	13	2	2	17	1	–
July 1918	32	8	2	19	5	1
Oct. 1918	67	1	1	37	1	–

SOURCE   SHA 7N955, 7N992, 16N1536

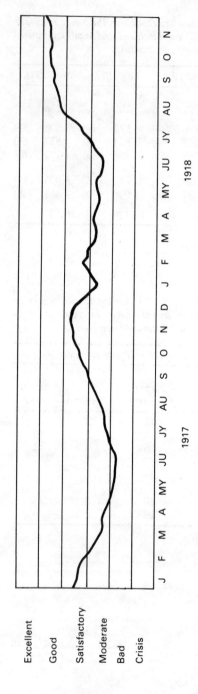

Key

'*Crisis*' More than 25% references to peace at any price, revolution, attacks on the Government or the régime. Repetition of Anarchist or pacifist slogans.

'*Bad*' More than 50% references to a negotiated peace. 25% attacks on Government's conduct of the war. More than 25% references to or expressions of defeatism.

'*Moderate*' Less than 50% references to excessive length of war. Less than 25% references to negotiated peace. Less than 10% references to or criticisms of the Government. More than 50% references to economic crisis.

'*Satisfactory*' Less than 10% references to length of war. Less than 10% references to negotiated peace. Less than 5% references to defeatism. More than 75% references exclusively to economic problems.

'*Good*' More than 95% favourable references to total victory. Less than 1% references to defeatism or anti-war slogans. Main concentration on economic or purely local affairs.

'*Excellent*' Almost unanimous belief in total victory. Total absence of defeatist talk.

FIGURE 1 *Fluctuations in morale 1917–18, according to references and sentiments expressed in civilians' and soldiers' letters, police, préfet's and military governor's reports, Département of the Isère (villages only)*

Notes

INTRODUCTION

1. P. Barral, *Le Département de l'Isère sous la Troisième République* (Paris, 1962) p. 534.
2. J. Mollin, 'La Voie Ferrée de l'Oisans', *Revue de Géographie Alpine*, 1945, pp. 672–92.
3. Barral, op. cit., p. 87.
4. A. Allix, *l'Oisans, Etude Géographique* (Grenoble, 1929).
5. Barral, op. cit., p. 59.
6. AN F162, Isère, Letter from *préfet* to Minister of the Interior, 1 June 1882.
7. AD 8M42, *Elections Municipales* 1912.
8. Ibid.
9. Barral, op. cit., p. 544.
10. AD 52M76, *Journée du 1er Mai: Rapports de Police 1901–19*.

CHAPTER 1

1. *Le Petit Dauphinois*, 27 July 1914.
2. *La Croix de l'Isère*, 28 July 1914.
3. Ibid., 30 July 1914.
4. *Le Petit Dauphinois*, 30 July 1914, 1 August 1914.
5. AD 52M66, *Journaux 1880–1914*.
6. C. H. Petit-Dutaillis, 'L'Appel de Guerre en Dauphiné', *Publication du Comité des Annales de l'Université de Grenoble*, 1915, p. 3.
7. Ibid.
8. AD 13R54, *instituteur*, Vatilieu.
9. Ibid., *instituteur*, Malleval.
10. Ibid., *instituteur*, Izeau.
11. Ibid., *instituteur*, Cognin.
12. Petit-Dutaillis, op. cit., p. 5.
13. AD 13R54, *instituteur*, St Cassien.
14. Ibid., *instituteur*, Chatte.
15. Ibid., *instituteur*, Sardieu.
16. Ibid., *instituteur*, St Cassien.
17. Ibid., *instituteur*, Sillans.
18. Ibid., *instituteur*, St Etienne-de-St-Geoirs.
19. Ibid., *instituteur*, St Paul d'Izeau.
20. *Le Petit Dauphinois*, 2 August 1914.
21. AD 13R54, *instituteur*, Rives.
22. Ibid., *instituteur*, Tullins.
23. *Le Petit Dauphinois*, 2 August 1914.
24. *La Croix de l'Isère*, 3 August 1914.
25. 'Extrait du journal de guerre du Sergeant Paul Gourdant', *Bulletin de la Société des amis de Vienne*, 74, p. 15.

26. AD 53M19, report of *Commissaire de Police*, Vienne, 1 August 1914.
27. Paul Gourdant, op. cit., p. 15.
28. *Le Petit Dauphinois, La Croix de l'Isère, La Dépêche Dauphinoise, Le Droit du Peuple*, 1 and 2 August 1914.
29. AD 53M19, report of *Commissaire de Police*, Grenoble, 2 August 1914.
30. Ibid.
31. Paul Gourdant, op. cit., p. 17.
32. Private diary and correspondence of Henri and Louise Perrin (hereafter cited as 'Perrin Correspondence').
33. J. L. Fenix, *Histoire passionante de la vie d'un petit ramoneur Savoyard* (Grenoble, 1978).
34. AD 13R54, *instituteur*, Palenfry-en-Gua.
35. A law of 5 August 1914 gave *mobilisés* four days' grace in which to present themselves to the military authorities, after which they would be classified as *insoumis*.
36. AD 13R54, *instituteur*, Monestier du Percy.
37. Ibid., *instituteur*, Notre Dame-du-Commiers.
38. Ibid., *instituteur*, Sechilienne.
39. AD 52M89, report of *préfet* to Minister of the Interior, 18 August 1914.
40. In the event the national average was around 1.5 per cent.
41. AD 2R906, *Déserteurs et insoumis*, An VIII–1920.
42. Ibid.
43. AD 13R17, report of Rector of the Academy of Grenoble to *préfet*, 8 August 1914.
44. S. Bernstein, 'Le Parti Radical–Socialiste durant la Première Guerre Mondiale' in P. Fridenson (ed.), *1914–18: L'Autre Front, Cahiers du Mouvement Social*, No. 2, 1977, p. 71.
45. J. J. Becker, 'Union Sacrée et idéologie bourgeoise', *Revue Historique*, 535, 1980.
46. *La Croix de l'Isère*, 2 August 1914.
47. *La République de l'Isère*, 1 August 1914.
48. *Le Droit du Peuple*, 5 August 1914.
49. *La Semaine Religieuse de Grenoble*, 13 August 1914.
50. AD 13R17, report of Rector of the Academy of Grenoble to *préfet*, 9 August 1914.
51. AD 13R54, *instituteur*, Rives.
52. *Vienne et la Guerre*, 22 August 1914.
53. AD 13R17, report from *Sous-Préfet* of Vienne to *préfet*, 13 October 1914.
54. Perrin Correspondence, 28 September 1914.
55. AD 13R54, *instituteur*, Renage.
56. Ibid., *instituteur*, Sillans.
57. Ibid., *instituteur*, St Cassien.
58. Ibid., *instituteur*, Sechilienne.
59. Ibid., *instituteur*, Viriville.
60. Ibid., *instituteur*, St Etienne-de-St-Geoirs.
61. Ibid., *institutrice*, Les Thébauds de Sechilienne.
62. *La Semaine Religieuse de Grenoble*, 15 October 1914.
63. AD 14M11, *préfet*'s circular, 5 August 1914.

64. *La Semaine Religieuse de Grenoble*, 6 August 1914.
65. *Bulletin de l'Enseignement Primaire de l'Isère*, September 1914.
66. AD 13R54, *instituteur*, Sardieu.
67. The others were: Paris, Nord, Rouen, Le Mans, Orléans, Châlons-sur-Marne, Besançon, Bourges, Tours, Rennes, Nantes, Limoges, Clermont-Ferrand, Marseille, Montpellier, Toulouse, Bordeaux, Troyes, Chaumont.
68. SHA 7N977.
69. Ibid.
70. AD 13R20, confidential report from Minister of War to *préfets*, 22 March 1915.
71. Ibid., circular from Minister of War to military governors, 20 August 1914.
72. *Le Petit Dauphinois*, 21 September 1914, 17 October 1914.
73. *La Croix de l'Isère*, 30 October 1914.
74. *Le Droit du Peuple*, 5 August 1914.
75. Ibid., 2 October 1914.
76. The official readership figures for the two combined never exceeded 15000.
77. AN F^7 12841.
78. AD 13R54, *instituteur*, St Paul d'Iseaux, 6 August 1914.
79. Ibid., *instituteur*, La Fortresse, 15 August 1914.
80. Ibid., *instituteur*, St Cassien.

CHAPTER 2

1. *La Croix de l'Isère*, 28 August 1914.
2. AD 13R17, report from Rector of the Academy of Grenoble to *préfet*, 3 October 1914.
3. AD 13R54, *institutrice*, Livet et Gavet.
4. AD 123M10–11.
5. M. Auge-Laribé and P. Pinot, *Agriculture and Food Supply During the War* (New York, 1926) p. 4.
6. *Le Droit du Peuple*; 5 July 1914; *La Croix de l'Isère*, 4 July 1914.
7. *Le Petit Dauphinois*, 7 August 1914.
8. AD 13R17, letter from *Maire* of Corrençon-en-Vercors to *préfet*, 13 September 1914.
9. Ibid., notes of Rector of the Academy of Grenoble, survey of 10 *communes*, 9 August 1914.
10. J. Miège, 'La Mécanisation de l'Agriculture Alpestre', *Comité des travaux historiques et scientifiques: bulletin de la section de géographie*, 1952, 107–17.
11. AD 13R17, letter from *Préfet* of Isère to *Préfet* of Haute-Savoie, 28 September 1914.
12. AD 13R54, *instituteur*, Renage.
13. AD 13R17, notes of the Rector of the Academy of Grenoble, 10 August 1914, 3 September 1914.
14. AD 13R54, *instituteur*, Malleval.

15. AD 13R39, report of *Sous-Préfet* of Vienne to *préfet*, 14 August 1914.
16. AD 35J13, *Archives des Syndicats Libres, Correspondance Mottard*.
17. AD 13R789, *Maire* of Grenoble to *préfet*.
18. AD 165M1, *préfet* to Minister of the Interior, 28 August 1914.
19. AD SC 3037, *Archives des Bénéfices de Guerre*, Vizille.
20. AD 13R17, letter from *préfet* to Minister of the Interior, 15 September 1914.
21. AD 35J42, *Archives des Syndicats Libres, conditions du travail*.
22. P. Masson, *Marseille pendant la Guerre* (Paris, 1927) p. 7.
23. AD 13R54, *instituteur*, Roybon.
24. AD 13R789, letter of military governor to *préfet*, 4 October 1914.
25. P. Masson, op. cit., p. 27; R. Courteault, *Bordeaux pendant la Guerre* (Paris, 1927) p. 40.
26. AD 13R17, 18, 19, *Correspondance générale de la Préfecture*, August 1914–February 1915.
27. The majority of *instituteurs*' notes for villages and small towns indicate this.
28. AD 123M140, SC 3037, *Archives des bénéfices de guerre*, Venosc.
29. Perrin Correspondence, letter from Louise to Henri, 9 August 1914.
30. Ibid., letter from Louise to Henri, 20 November 1914.
31. AD SC 3037, *Archives des bénéfices de guerre*, Vienne.
32. Ibid.
33. AD 13R54, noted by eight *instituteurs* during August and September 1914.
34. AD SC 3037, *Archives des bénéfices de guerre*.
35. Reported daily in *Le Petit Dauphinois* 20 July 1914–10 August 1914 but rarely thereafter.
36. AD *Tribunal Correctionnel, jugements*, Grenoble 1914.
37. AD 13R17, Inspector of the Academy of Grenoble to *préfet*, 10 August 1914.
38. AD 13R150, *Allocations militaires: statistiques*.
39. AN F^{12} 8020.
40. Oral testimony: Mme M. Rodet, Grenoble.
41. AD 13R17, letter from *Maire* of Bourg d'Oisans to *préfet*, 10 September 1914.
42. *Le Petit Dauphinois*, 23 August 1914.
43. *Le Droit du Peuple*, 5 September 1914.
44. E. Herriot, *Lyon* (Paris, 1926) p. 24.
45. AD 13R17, telegram from *préfet* to Minister of the Interior, 20 December 1914.
46. *La Croix de l'Isère, Le Petit Dauphinois, Le Droit du Peuple*, 24–26 August 1914.
47. AD 13R54, *instituteur*, Viriville.
48. Oral testimony: M. Druet, Grenoble.
49. Ibid., M. André, Grenoble.
50. AD 13R54, *institutrice*, Sechilienne; *instituteur*, Malleval.
51. M. Huber, *La Population de la France pendant la Guerre* (Paris, 1927) pp. 176–7. Neighbouring *départements* (Haute-Savoie, Rhône and Drôme) received 2741, 4908 and 4646 respectively.

52. AD 13R210, *préfet*'s circular 31 October 1914.
53. AD 13R211, *préfet*'s circular to *maires* 11 June 1915.
54. AD 13R17, letter from *préfet* to Minister of the Interior, 3 January 1915.
55. AD 13R210, telegrams from *Maires* of La Terrasse and Varces to *préfet*, November 1914.
56. AD 14M11.
57. AD 15M20.
58. Ibid.

CHAPTER 3

1. AD 13R54, *instituteur*, Renage.
2. R. Blanchard, *Grenoble et sa région pendant la Guerre*, p. 21.
3. AD 13R79.
4. Blanchard, op. cit., pp. 40–2.
5. Ibid.
6. AD SC 3037, *Archives des bénéfices de guerre*, Vizille.
7. Ibid., Grenoble.
8. Ibid., Voiron.
9. Blanchard, op. cit., p. 33.
10. AD 165M1, report from *sous-préfet* to *préfet*, 13 December 1914.
11. AD 13R179, *Inspection du travail*.
12. Ibid.
13. AN F^{12} 8018.
14. AN 94AP72, *Fonds Albert Thomas*.
15. AN ADXIX W54.
16. Ibid.
17. AD 13R790, *Enquête sur le développement économique 1915–19*.
18. R. Blanchard, op. cit., p. 31.
19. Ibid., p. 33.
20. Ibid.
21. *Le Droit du Peuple*, 20 December 1914.
22. AD 13R39, *Loi Dalbiez: application communal de la Loi de 17 Août 1915*.
23. AD 13R129, *Sous-Préfet* of Vienne to *préfet*, 23 March 1915. Only seven *communes* in the *Arrondissement* of Vienne benefited from having *permissionnaires* during 1915.
24. AD 13R790, *SCAE*, 3 March 1916.
25. AD 13R129, letter from a farmer at La Côte St André to *Sous-Préfet* of Vienne.
26. *Le Droit du Peuple*, 13 June 1915.
27. AD 13R790, minutes of the *SCAE*, 13 July 1916.
28. AD 13R179, Minister of Agriculture to *préfet*, 7 April 1915.
29. Ibid., *préfet* to Minister of Agriculture, 1 May 1915.
30. AD 13R129, circular from *préfet* to *maires*, 28 April 1915; response from *maires* during first week of May.
31. Ibid.
32. AD 25J55, *Archives de la Compagnie des Mines de La Mure*.

33. Ibid.
34. Ibid.
35. Ibid.
36. AD 13R17, letter from *Commissaire de Police* of La Mure to *préfet*, 3 January 1916.
37. AD 25J55.
38. AD 13R54, *institutrice*, Livet et Gavet.
39. AD 13R790, reports of the *SCAE*, 13 July 1916, 21 August 1916.
40. AN 94AP 348, circular from Albert Thomas to the provincial press, 21 January 1916.
41. Ibid.
42. *Le Droit du Peuple*, 17 April 1916.
43. *La Croix de l'Isère*, 21 May 1916.
44. Chambre de Commerce de Grenoble, *Guide Industriel du Dauphiné* (Grenoble, 1916).
45. AD 122M113.
46. Ibid.
47. Ibid.
48. AD 13R790, report to the *SCAE*, 3 March 1916.
49. *Le Droit du Peuple*, 4 May 1916.
50. Ibid., 21 May 1916.
51. AD 13R21, report from *Commissaire de Police* of Grenoble to *préfet*, 21 June 1916.
52. Ibid., *Correspondance générale de la Préfecture*, 19 October 1916.

CHAPTER 4

1. *Le Petit Dauphinois*, 17 April 1916, 21 April 1916; *Le Droit du Peuple*, 8 March 1916, 12 March 1916.
2. *Le Droit du Peuple*, 23 July 1916; *Le Petit Dauphinois*, 25 July 1916.
3. AD 35J157, *Collection St Olive: Instructions sur la censure*, 1914–18.
4. AD 13T3/16.
5. *Le Réveil du Dauphiné*, 2 November 1888.
6. AD 4T3/12.
7. AD 4T1/20.
8. AD 52M88, report from *préfet* to Minister of the Interior, 22 June 1911.
9. AD 13R17, letter from *préfet* to Rector of the Academy of Grenoble, 7 November 1914.
10. *Bulletin de l'Enseignement Primaire, Département de l'Isère*, June 1915.
11. Ibid., November 1914, ministerial circular.
12. AD 1J1140, *Collection St Olive, Carnets de l'école pendant la Guerre*.
13. AD 4T1/20, report by Inspector of the Academy of Grenoble, May 1915.
14. *Le Droit du Peuple*, 6 October 1915.
15. AD 4T1/20.
16. AD T79.
17. Ibid.

18. Oral testimony: Mme Plissonier, Grenoble.
19. Ibid. Lavaldens had a population of 421 in 1911.
20. AD 13R54, *instituteur*, Monestier du Percy.
21. AD 4T2/242.
22. AD 13R54, *institutrices*, Sechilienne, Livet.
23. Oral testimony: M. Druet, Grenoble.
24. AD 13R54, *instituteur*, Rives.
25. AD 1T251.
26. Ibid.
27. AD 1T235.
28. AD 4T3/3.
29. AD 4T1/20.
30. G. Le Bras, 'Notes de statistiques et d'histoire religieuse, diocèse de Grenoble', *Revue d'histoire de l'Eglise de France*, 1936, pp. 474–5.
31. AD 13R16, letter from *préfet* to the Minister of the Interior, 14 March 1914.
32. P. Barral, *Le Département de l'Isère sous la Troisième République*, p. 259.
33. C. Emerique, 'Essai sur la vie ouvrière dans le Département de l'Isère de 1871 à 1914', *Diplôme d'Etudes de Grenoble*, 1953.
34. *La Semaine Religieuse de Grenoble*, 3 December 1914.
35. Ibid., 11 February 1915.
36. Ibid., 4 August 1915.
37. Ibid., 13 August 1914, 20 August 1914, 27 August 1914.
38. Perrin Correspondence, letter from Louise to Henri, 19 September 1914.
39. Ibid., letter from Henri to Louise, 13 November 1914.
40. Ibid., letter from Henri to Louise, 23 February 1915.
41. *Le Droit du Peuple*, 24 December 1914.
42. *La Semaine Religieuse de Grenoble*, 26 August 1915.
43. Perrin Correspondence, letter from Louise to Henri, 3 July 1915.
44. AD 13R19, report from *préfet* to Minister of the Interior, 4 January 1916.
45. AD 2/J42.
46. AD 27J14/2.
47. *Livre d'or du Diocèse de Grenoble pendant la Guerre*, 1914–18, p. 24.
48. AD 27J3/28.
49. AD 27J3/30.
50. *La Semaine Religieuse de Grenoble*, 21 October 1915.
51. AD 2J13.
52. AD 2J43.
53. *La Croix de l'Isère*, 27 September 1914.
54. *La Semaine Religieuse de Grenoble*, 3 December 1914; *La Croix de l'Isère*, 14 March 1915.
55. AD 13R18, letter from *institutrice*, St Bardille et Pipet, to *préfet*, 3 January 1915.
56. AD 13R21, reports from *Sous-Préfets* of Vienne, St Marcellin and La Tour du Pin to *préfet*, February 1916.
57. AD 13R22, report from *préfet* to Minister of the Interior, 21 December 1916.

58. See J. N. Jeanneney, 'Les Archives des Commissions de Contrôle Postal aux armées 1916–18', *Revue d'Histoire Moderne et Contemporaine*, 15, 1968.
59. SHA 7N955, *Contrôle Postal 14 Région Militaire*, 1915–16.
60. AD 52M63, police report, 8 June 1915.
61. AD 52M64, police report, 13 August 1915.
62. AD 13R54, *institutrice*, Sechilienne.
63. Ibid., *institutrice*, Livet et Gavet.
64. AD 13R21, letter from *Commissaire de Police* of Grenoble to *préfet*, 4 December 1916.
65. AD 13R21, letter from a war widow at Pontcharra to *préfet*, 14 October 1916.
66. SHA 5N389.
67. *Journal Officiel: Chambre de Deputés*, 3 June 1915, 30 November 1915, 22 April 1916.
68. Ibid., 21 September 1916.
69. AN F[7] 13604, *Union des Syndicats de l'Isère*, 1908–19.
70. Ibid., police report, 29 May 1916.
71. AD 13R21, *Correspondance générale de la Préfecture*.
72. Ibid., police report, 28 September 1916.
73. Ibid., police report, 26 October 1916.
74. Ibid., police report, 28 October 1916.
75. AN ADXIX W3, *Statistiques des grèves, Isère*; AD 166M10, *Grèves* 1914–16.
76. AD 2R906, 7, 8.

CHAPTER 5

1. *Le Droit du Peuple*, 2 February 1917.
2. AN F[7] 13356. At that time 77 *départements* were listed as having munitions establishments working directly for the *Intendance*. In terms of numbers, the Isère ranked fourteenth.
3. R. Blanchard, *Grenoble et sa région pendant la Guerre*, p. 42.
4. Ibid.
5. Ibid., p. 47.
6. AD 13R53.
7. Blanchard, op. cit., p. 16.
8. AD 13R53.
9. Ibid.
10. Ibid.
11. AD 13R24, *Correspondance générale de la Préfecture*, 1914–18.
12. AD 13R53.
13. AD 13R598.
14. Ibid.
15. AD 13R84.
16. AD 13R88.
17. Ibid.
18. Ibid.

19. AD 13R53.
20. See, for example, C. Vallée, 'La vie chère – ses causes', *Nouvelle Revue*, 1 November 1918.
21. M. Noël, 'La vie chère et les allocations d'assistance', *Revue Philanthropique*, June 1916, p. 252; C. Gide, 'La Guerre et l'organisation Nationale d'alimentation', *Revue de l'Economie Politique*, 30, 1916, pp. 1–17; 'L'Influence de la Guerre sur les prix', *Revue de l'Economie Politique*, May 1915, pp. 197–217.
22. *Le Droit du Peuple*, 12 March 1916.
23. AD 13R605.
24. Ibid.
25. *Le Droit du Peuple*, 17 March 1918.
26. AD 13R53.
27. AD 25J35, *Archives de la Compagnie des Mines de La Mure*.
28. *Le Droit du Peuple*, 13 January 1917.
29. AD 13R24.
30. AD 9U 3105, 2652, 2108, *Jugements simple police*, Vizille, Valbonnais, St Jean du Bournay, 1917.
31. *La Croix de l'Isère*, 12 January 1918.
32. Ibid.
33. Ibid., 27 May 1918.
34. *Le Droit du Peuple*, 24 August 1917.
35. AD 13R53.
36. See J. McMillan, *Housewife or harlot? The place of women in French society 1870–1940* (Brighton, 1981).
37. AD 166M10, report commissioned by the *préfet*.
38. AD 35J26, *Archives des Syndicats Libres Féminins*.
39. AD 13R153.
40. Ibid.
41. AD 13R150, *Allocations Militaires, statistiques*.
42. Ibid.
43. AD 13R160, *Allocations: Commissions Cantonales*, Bourg d'Oisans, AC Venosc, *Bureau de Bienfaisance; registre*, 1900–30.
44. AD SC 3037/1, *Archives des Bénéfices de Guerre*.
45. AD SC 3037/18.
46. AD SC 3037/20, 16M300. By 1921 the population of the town was 2035.
47. AD SC 3037/31.
48. Ibid.

CHAPTER 6

1. AD 52M66.
2. *Le Petit Dauphinois*, 2 January 1917.
3. *Le Droit du Peuple*, 13 January 1917.
4. *Le Petit Dauphinois*, 3 April 1917.
5. *Le Droit du Peuple*, 18 March 1917, 19 March 1917.
6. Ibid., 15 May 1917.

7. Ibid., 10 November 1917, 19 November 1917.
8. Ibid., 24 December 1917.
9. *La Croix de l'Isère*, 27 April 1917; *Le Droit du Peuple*, 25 April 1917.
10. *Le Droit du Peuple*, 23 September 1917.
11. *La Croix de l'Isère*, 3 February 1918.
12. *Le Petit Dauphinois*, 19 April 1917, 20 April 1917, 25 April 1917, 8 May 1917.
13. A perusal of censored articles confirms that journalists knew little or nothing about the mutinies and the reprisals taken by the High Command. The standard work on the mutinies is G. Pedroncini, *Les Mutineries de 1917* (Paris, 1967), which corroborates the view that the general crisis at the front was a well-kept secret.
14. *Le Petit Dauphinois*, 22 November 1917.
15. *Le Droit du Peuple*, 18 November 1917.
16. *La Croix de l'Isère*, 2 January 1918.
17. *Le Petit Dauphinois*, 1 January 1918.
18. Ibid., 15 February 1918.
19. *La Croix de l'Isère*, 14 November 1918.
20. *Le Droit du Peuple*, 12 November 1918.
21. *Le Petit Dauphinois*, 12 November 1918.
22. SHA 7N955, *Rapports Divers sur le contrôle de la correspondance à l'Intérieur; l'état de l'opinion en France 1915–21.*
23. SHA 5N268, *Bulletins mensuels résumant la situation morale à l'intérieur provenant du 2me Bureau de l'E.M.A.*, October 1917–August 1919.
24. SHA 7N955.
25. Ibid.
26. Ibid.
27. Ibid.
28. SHA 16N1538, report from *préfet* to Minister of the Interior, 17 June 1917.
29. SHA 7N955.
30. Ibid.
31. AD 13R22, letter from *Maire* of Bourg d'Oisans to *préfet*, 22 September 1917.
32. SHA 7N955.
33. Ibid.
34. Ibid.
35. Ibid.
36. Ibid.
37. SHA 5N268.
38. SHA 7N955.
39. SHA 5N268.
40. SHA 7N955.
41. AD 13R23, report from *préfet* to Minister of the Interior, 14 November 1918.
42. Ibid., report from *Sous-Préfet* of Vienne to *préfet*, 13 November 1918.
43. Ibid., letter from *institutrice*, Allevard, to *préfet*, 15 November 1918.
44. Ibid., telegram from *Maire* of Rives to *préfet*, 13 November 1918.
45. Ibid., letter from *Maire* of Bourg d'Oisans to *préfet* 16 November 1918.

46. Ibid., letter from *institutrice*, Lalley, to *préfet*, 14 November 1918.
47. Ibid., letter from *Maire* of La Motte d'Aveillans to *préfet*, 14 November 1918.
48. Oral testimony: Marie Plissonier.
49. AD 2R906.
50. Ibid.
51. Ibid.
52. AD 13R237.
53. Ibid.
54. AN F30 2140.
55. *La Semaine Religieuse de Grenoble*, 3 January 1918.
56. Ibid.
57. Ibid.
58. AD T79, report by *institutrice*, Valbonnais, 9 December 1917.
59. Ibid., report by *instituteur*, Roche, 9 August 1918.
60. Ibid., *instituteur*, Ternay.
61. Ibid., *instituteur*, Feyzin.
62. Ibid., *institutrice*, Saint-Priest.
63. AD T79, *Fonds du Rectorat*.
64. SHA 16N1538.
65. AD 13R23, reports from *Commissaire de Police* of Grenoble to *préfet*, 1917.
66. Ibid.
67. Ibid., letter from *Commissaire de Police* to *préfet*, 3 September 1917.
68. AN F[7] 12992.
69. AN F[7] 13356.
70. AD 166M11, police report, 19 May 1918.
71. AN F[7] 13356.
72. AD 82M3, *Sûreté Genérale*.
73. AD 166M11–13.
74. AD 166M11, reports dated 23, 25, 27 February.
75. AD 166M11.
76. Ibid.
77. AD 75M10, letter addressed to Charles Benoit, 10 November 1917.
78. AN F[7] 12992.
79. AD 166M11.
80. AN F[12] 12992.
81. AD 166M11.
82. AN F[7] 13356.
83. AD 166M11, telegram, 22 May 1918.
84. Ibid., report, 23 May 1918.
85. Ibid., letter from *préfet* to Minister of the Interior, 26 May 1918.
86. AN AD XIX W3, *Statistiques des grèves*, 1918.
87. The general strike at Vienne was one of only six strikes in the whole of France directly aimed at putting an end to the war. Four of the others took place in May 1918 following on from the St Etienne Conference.

Sources

ARCHIVE SOURCES

Archives Départementales de l'Isère, Grenoble

1   Police et Administration Générale

8M42	Eléctions Législatives 1914
14M11	Composition des municipalités après la mobilisation
15M20	Administration des Communes pendant la Guerre 1914–18
16M300	Municipalités 1908–27
52M62–6	Police Générale: rapports de police
52M76	Rapports de police 1901–19
52M88–9	Rapports mensuels du Préfet 1911–24
53M19	Rapports de police 1900–15
75M10	Anarchistes: rapports de police
82M1–3	Sûreté Générale: rapports de police 1915–21
120M111–13	Etablissements travaillant pour la Défence Nationale
123M10–11	Population par commune 1911–21
165M1	Chômage: rapports de police 1914–22

2   Guerre et Affaires Militaires

2R906	Déserteurs et insoumis
2R907	Déserteurs 1918–21
13R16–25	Correspondance Générale de la Préfecture concernant la Guerre 1914–18
13R39	Loi Dalbiez: application
13R53	Comité et Sous-Comité départemental d'Action Economique: la vie économique 1914–18
13R54	Rapports des instituteurs divers 1914–21
13R84	Réquisitions divers 1914–18
13R87–9	Correspondance divers au sujet des réquisitions 1914–18
13R129	Prisonniers de guerre, étrangers et main d'œuvre agricole
13R149–86	Allocations Militaires, renseignements, correspondance, statistiques cantonales
13R237–8	Logement des réfugiés
13R204	Réfugiés: statistiques, renseignements par commune
13R597–8	Réfugiés: renseignements divers
13R605	Ravitaillement: renseignements 1914–18
13R789–90	Travail et Prévoyance social 1914–15

3   Enseignement, Affaires Culturelles

1T235	Renseignements 1914–24
1T251	Instruction publique 1913–23
4T1/20	Rapports des Inspecteurs d'Académie 1907–38

4T3/3   *Promotions et mutations d'instituteurs et institutrices* 1912–20
4T3/12   *Syndicat des Instituteurs* 1912–35
13T3/16   *Monuments aux morts*
T79   *Fonds du Rectorat* 1914–23

4 Syndicats Libres Féminins
35J13   *Correspondance Mottard*
35J26   *La Voix Professionnelle* 1912–35
35J42   *Conditions du travail*

5 Compagnie des Mines de La Mure
25J35   *Gestion* 1914–22
25J55   *Personnel* 1914–22

6 Archives Ecclésiastiques
27J3/30   *Bourg d'Oisans: correspondance des curés*
27J3/28   *Registres*
27J14/2   *Saint-Pancrasse: listes des confirmés*

7 Juges de Paix
9U 3105   *Tribunal de Paix et de Simple Police: Canton Vizille* 1913–21
9U 2652   *Tribunal de Paix et de Simple Police: Canton Valbonnais* 1913–21

8 Archives des Bénéfices de Guerre
SC 3037

Archives Nationales, Paris

F^7 *Socialistes* 12495–12502, 12525, 13609
              CGT 13571–4
              Anarchistes 135053–8
              Anti-militarisme 13333–49, 13370
              Eléctions Legislatives 1914 12282
              Opinion Publique 1914 12934–9
              Rapport sur la situation dans les départements: Isère 1916–21 12992
              Usines de Guerre 1915–19 13356–61
              Bulletins confidentiels résumant la situation morale à l'Intérieur
              1916–18 13371–6
F^{12} *Papiers de Service d'Action Economique* 1915–18, Isère 8009
              Mobilisation Civile 1917–18 8018
              Réquisitions 1914–18 8019
              Agitation Ouvrière 1915–18 8023–4
              Problème Agricole 1916–17 8025–6
F^{22} *Travail et Prévoyance Sociale, usines de guerre* 530–9
              Inspection du travail 1914–17 575–6
94AP   *Fonds Albert Thomas: Usines de Guerre* 348/3
                 Main d'œuvre étrangère 348/4
                    La crise de main d'œuvre agricole 360/2
                    Lettres adressées à Albert Thomas pendant la Guerre 361

Archives Militaires, Service Historique de l'Armée, Vincennes, Paris

5N85   *Opinion morale, indiscipline, mutineries, grèves, déserteurs,*
                1914–18
5N159–63   *Documents de GQG des ministres, préfets, gouverneurs et com-*
                mandants des Régions Militaires 1914–18
5N267–8   *Bulletins confidentiels résumant la situation morale à l'Intérieur*
7N955   *Rapports sur le Contrôle de la correspondance a l'Intérieur: état de*
                l'opinion en France 1915–21
7N977   *Section de centralisation des renseignements 1914–17*

NON-ARCHIVE SOURCES

Unprinted

Perrin Correspondence: Correspondence of Henri and Louise Perrin 1914–18. Four hundred and forty letters and diary currently in the possession of Michel Perrin, Vienne, Isère.

Oral testimony: Twenty-five interviews conducted in the Isère with military and civilian veterans of the 1914–18 war. Arranged through the services of the *Association des Veuves et Orphelins de Guerre*, Grenoble.

Press: Newspapers and Magazines

Le Petit Dauphinois, January 1914–December 1919
La Dépêche Dauphinoise, January 1914–December 1919
La République de l'Isère, January 1914–December 1919
Le Droit du Peuple, January 1914–December 1919
La Croix de l'Isère, January 1914–December 1919
La Guerre et l'Image, September 1914–November 1918
Vienne et la Guerre, September 1914–November 1918
La Semaine Religieuse de Grenoble, August 1914–November 1918

Select Bibliography

The historical literature on the 1914–18 war, for France alone, is vast. This list is therefore confined to those works which have been most relevant to my own researches.

Alegré, J., 'Les Instituteurs', *Europe*, May–June 1964.

Allix, A., *Les Colporteurs de l'Oisans* (Grenoble, 1925).

Allix, A., *L'Oisans, étude géographique* (Grenoble, 1929).

Amalvi, C., 'Les guerres des manuels autour de l'Ecole Primaire en France 1899–1914', *Revue Historique*, 532 (1979).

Auge-Laribé, M., and P. Pinot, *Agriculture and Food Supply in France during the War* (Yale, 1926).

Barral, P., *Le Département de l'Isère sous la Troisième République* (Paris, 1962).

Barthas, L., *Les Carnets de Guerre de Louis Barthas, Tonnelier, 1914–18* (Paris, 1980).

Becker, J. J., 'L'Appel de guerre en Dauphiné', *Le Mouvement Social* (1964).

———, 'A Lille au début de la Guerre de 1914', *Revue Historique*, 216 (1976).

———, *1914: Comment les Français sont entrés dans la guerre* (Paris, 1977).

———, *Les Français dans la Grande Guerre* (Paris, 1980).

———, 'Union Sacrée et idéologie bourgeoise', *Revue Historique*, 535 (1980).

Becker, J. J., and A. Kriegel, *1914: La Guerre et le Mouvement Ouvrier Français* (Paris, 1964).

Beneton, P., 'La génération de 1912–14, image, mythe et réalité', *Revue Française de Science Politique*, 21 (1971).

Bertrand, L., 'Marseille pendant la Guerre', *Revue des Deux Mondes*, 17 (1917).

Blanchard, R., *Grenoble et sa région pendant la Guerre* (Grenoble, 1918).

Bouyoux, P., *L'Opinion publique à Toulouse pendant la Guerre 1914–18* (Paris, 1970).

Caron, P., *The Refugees and Interned Civilians* (Yale, 1926).

Cassin, C., *The Wounded Soldiers* (Yale, 1926).

Chatelle, A., and G. Tison, *Calais pendant la Guerre 1914–18* (Paris, 1927).

Courteault, R., *Bordeaux pendant la Guerre* (Paris, 1927).

Coyne, E., *Le Tour de France d'un Préfet de 1914* (Montauban, 1915).

Crehange, M., *Placement et Chômage pendant la Guerre* (Paris, 1927).

Ducasse, A., J. Meyer and G. Perreux, *Vie et mort des Français 1914–18* (Paris, 1965).

Duroselle, J. B., *La France et les Français 1914–20* (Paris, 1972).

Dutton, D., 'The *Union Sacrée* and the French Cabinet crisis of October 1915', *European Studies Review*, Vol. 8 (1978).

Facon, P., and J. Nicot, 'La crise du moral en 1917 dans l'armée et la Nation d'après la Commission de Contrôle Postal de Belfont', *Actes du Congrès National des Sociétés Savants*, 1978.

Fenix, J. L., *Histoire passionnante de la vie d'un petit ramoneur Savoyard* (Grenoble, 1978).

Fontaine, A., *L'Industrie Française pendant la Guerre* (Paris, 1925).
Fridenson, P., (ed.) *1914–18: L'Autre Front, Cahiers du Mouvement Social,* No. 2 (Paris, 1977).
Gallo, M., 'Quelques aspects de la mentalité et du comportement ouvriers dans les usines de guerre 1914–18', *Le Mouvement Social,* 1966.
Gide, C., 'De l'influence de la Guerre sur les prix', *Revue de l'Economie Politique,* 1915.
Gide, C., 'La Guerre et l'organisation nationale d'alimentation', *Revue de l'Economie Politique,* 1916.
Gignoux, M. J. C., *Bourges pendant la Guerre* (Paris, 1926).
Herriot, E., *Lyon pendant la Guerre* (Paris, 1926).
Huber, M., *La population de la France pendant la Guerre* (Paris, 1931).
Hunter, J., 'The problems of the French birth rate on the eve of World War I', *French Historical Studies,* 1962.
Jeanneney, J. N., 'Les archives de contrôle postal aux armées 1916–18', *Revue d'Histoire Moderne et Contemporaine,* 15, 1968.
Julliard, J., 'La CGT devant la Guerre 1900–14', *Le Mouvement Social,* 49, 1964.
Kriegel, A., 'Patrie ou révolution: le Mouvement Ouvrier Français devant la guerre', *Revue Economique et Sociale,* 43, 1965.
Kriegel, A., 'L'opinion publique française et la Révolution Russe', in *La Révolution d'Octobre et le Mouvement Ouvrier Européen* (Paris, 1967).
Levainville, J., *Rouen pendant la Guerre* (Paris, 1926).
Liens, G., 'L'opinion à Marseille en 1917', *Revue d'Histoire Moderne et Contemporaine,* 1968.
McMillan, J., *Housewife or Harlot? The place of women in French society 1870–1940,* (Brighton, 1981).
Masson, P., *Marseille pendant la Guerre* (Paris, 1927).
Noël, M., 'La vie chère et les allocations d'assistance', *Revue Philanthropique,* June 1916.
Ozouf, J., 'L'Instituteur 1900–1914', *Le Mouvement Social,* 1963.
Ozouf, J. & M., 'Le thème du patriotisme dans les manuels scolaires', *Le Mouvement Social,* 49, 1964.
Ozouf, M., *L'Ecole, l'Eglise et la République 1871–1914* (Paris, 1963).
Pascal, J., *Mémoires d'un instituteur* (Paris, 1974).
Pedroncini, G., *Les Mutineries de 1917* (Paris, 1967).
Peiter, H. D., *Men of good will: French businessmen and the First World War* (PhD thesis, University of Michigan, 1973).
Perroux, G., *La vie quotidienne des civils pendant la Grande Guerre* (Paris, 1966).
Petit-Dutaillis, C. H., 'L'Appel de Guerre en Dauphiné', *Publication du Comité des Annales de L'Université de Grenoble,* 1915.
Picard, R., *Le Mouvement Syndical pendant la Guerre* (Paris, 1927).
Prost, A., *L'Enseignement en France 1800–1967* (Paris, 1968).
Prost, A., *Les Anciens Combattants et la société française 1914–39* (Paris, 1977).
Reboul, R., *Mobilisation industrielle: les fabrications de Guerre en France 1914–18* (Paris, 1925).
Renouvin, P., 'The role of public opinion', in G. Panichas (ed.), *Promise of greatness: the War of 1914–18* (London, 1968).

Renouvin, P., 'L'Opinion publique en France pendant la Guerre 1914–18', *Revue d'Histoire Diplomatique*, 4, 1970.

Robert, J. L., 'Les luttes ouvrières pendant la Première Guerre Mondiale', *Cahiers d'Histoire de L'Institut Maurice Thorez*, 1977.

Rosmer, A., *Le Mouvement ouvrier pendant la Guerre de l'Union Sacrée à Zimmervald* (Paris, 1936).

Ruffin, G., 'L'Opinion publique en 1917 dans l'arrondissement de Tournon', *Revue d'Histoire Moderne et Contemporaine*, 1968.

Sellier, H., *Paris pendant la Guerre* (Paris, 1926).

Taissey, C., *La CGT dans l'Isère de 1911 à 1918* (Mémoire, Grenoble, 1972).

Talmard, J. L., *Pages de guerre d'un paysan 1914–18* (Lyon, 1971).

Tersen, E., 'Panorame de la France en 1914', *Europe*, May–June 1964.

Thomas, A., *Organisation of the war industries* (Yale, 1926).

Vallée, C., 'La vie chère – ses causes', *Nouvelle Revue*, November 1918.

Vatin, P., 'Politique et publicité – la propagande pour l'emprunt en France 1915–20', *Revue d'Histoire Moderne et Contemporaine*, 27, 1980.

Weber, E., 'Some comments on the nature of the Nationalist revival in France before 1914', *International Review of Social History*, 3, 1958.

Weber, E., *The Nationalist revival in France 1905–1914* (University of California, 1959).

Wohl, R., *The generation of 1914* (London, 1980).

Index